CORPORATION ON A TIGHTROPE

CORPORATION ON A TIGHTROPE

BALANCING LEADERSHIP, GOVERNANCE, AND TECHNOLOGY IN AN AGE OF COMPLEXITY

JOHN G. SIFONIS AND BEVERLY GOLDBERG

New York   Oxford
Oxford University Press
1996

Oxford University Press

Oxford   New York
Athens Auckland Bangkok Bombay
Calcutta Cape Town Dar es Salaam Delhi
Florence Hong Kong Istanbul Karachi
Kuala Lumpur Madras Madrid Melbourne
Mexico City Nairobi Paris Singapore
Taipei Tokyo Toronto

and associated companies in
Berlin Ibadan

Library of Congress Cataloguing-in-Publication Data
Sifonis, John G.
Corporation on a tightrope: balancing leadership, governance,
and technology in an age of complexity /
John G. Sifonis and Beverly Goldberg
p. cm.   Includes bibliographical references and index.
ISBN 0-19-509325-9
1. Leadership. 2. Corporate governance.
3. Competition. 4. Information technology—Management.
I. Goldberg, Beverly. II. Title
HD57.7.G66 1996   658.4'092—dc20   96-1462

1 3 5 7 9 8 6 4 2

Printed in the United States of America
on acid-free paper

To Leslie Reed

‖ PREFACE

Corporation on a Tightrope is about developing an organization that can survive beyond tomorrow. It is meant to serve as a guide to building a new kind of organization, one that is flexible enough both to grow quickly in the face of opportunity and to retrench smoothly in the face of adverse conditions. It shows how a corporation can expand rapidly into new areas in order to preempt competitors and how it can reduce the pain of contracting when markets shift or the economy falters. Throughout, it emphasizes the need to challenge assumptions, to think about the three major forces in the organization (governance, technology, and leadership) concurrently, and to adapt rationally to a business environment that seems to change constantly.

Developing this new organization is not easy. It requires understanding how all the components of the organization fit together in order to be able to shape and reshape it so that it always functions as a highly adaptive whole. It requires learning to deal with uncertainty and nonlinearity. It requires putting in place principles that demand constant attention. It requires learning to think differently about what constitutes success. It requires believing that an organization that never knows what the future holds but is always poised to change to meet it is an organization that will achieve long-term survival and profitability.

THE MARCH OF CHANGE

Over the past few years of working together on our first book, *Dynamic Planning,* and on consulting assignments, we observed a sea change in the corporate world that reflected changes in the world in general. In the global environment, integration and dis-integration became bywords: nations were coming together (Germany) and falling apart (Yugoslavia); the patterns of trade were changing (NAFTA, GATT, WTO, emerging trading blocks, reopening of closed doors); politics were no longer as usual (the fall of incumbency and the emergence of a Ross Perot, the fall of communism, the rise of terrorism); methods of communication were undergoing profound changes, bringing the world ever closer to the true "global village" (CNN, communications satellites, the emergence of the information highway, and the alliances of the Baby Bells with media giants). In the business world, multiparty alliances, partnerships, global financial services, and flattened, empowered, and virtual organizations seemed to offer substitutes for the massive, vertically integrated, tightly knit organizations that no longer seemed viable.

One painfully clear change was that while technology was making it easier to know what was happening on the surface, it was making it much harder to get one's hands around why these things were happening. For one thing, the changes kept happening faster and faster. For another, as accessing information became easier, research became paradoxically more and more difficult. An abundance of information and instant analysis on any and every subject—through Internet, CompuServe, on-line magazines and journals—threatened to overwhelm the time available to learn and to obviate the need for abstract thinking and analysis (now there are pundits everywhere telling you what your conclusion should be). We were particularly sensitive to this dilemma created by technology because the book we were completing as we watched all this happen was going to tell senior executives that their organizations needed to keep track of developments in the world outside—which seems like an overwhelming task—and then use that information in the context of their own organizations—which requires well-honed analytical skills.

THE EFFECTS ON ORGANIZATIONS

We realized that the changes swirling around and within organizations were often forced by advances in technology. Technology is behind the expansion of information; technology is speeding up product development; and, depending on who you listen to, technology either is improving productivity or not bringing the productivity gains it promised. However, leadership was changing at the same time, particularly as organizations began to consider knowledge a major resource. The shape of organizations was changing in response to changes in leadership and technology—and as organizations were reaching out more and more to the global arena.

We were then, and we are still, trying to help organizations find ways to move ahead—and avoid being paralyzed by these changes swirling around them. To ensure their success, we push our clients to think and plan with the aid of the Dynamic Planning Framework presented in *Dynamic Planning*. We know that much of this planning requires changes in the work that our clients do and the way they do it, which itself has implications for leadership and for the shape of organizations, and that both these changes in the kind of work an organization does and the way in which it is done are dependent on technology, but they also drive technology in often unpredictable ways.

As we were working with organizations and discussing the issues they were facing with our colleagues as well as reading about them, it became clear that new kinds of leaders—and leaders at many levels—with many different skills were needed; that changes in the architecture or internal governance of the organization would have to take place; and that these changes would impact technology as well as be impacted by it. We also began to see very clearly that the Dynamic Planning Framework served two purposes: it was helping organizations plan how to remain competitive while helping them change as the long-term future seemed to change. The latter was clearly the more difficult process, requiring something more than the practical steps in the Framework.

The leaders of the organizations we work with have been asking, over and over in various ways, the same set of questions: "Where is the organization going? You're telling us how to plan, but in light of all the uncertainty, how do we sell that kind of complex planning? Just what is the point of long-term planning for a future that might not be there when we get there?"

It seemed that what we had to do was develop a better way of explaining the deep cultural and physical changes needed to reshape organizations so they would be ready for that unknown future. At that time, we were hearing a great deal about complexity theory and the possibilities for its practical applications. As a result, we began to explore the work of Dr. Stuart Kauffman and his colleagues at the Santa Fe Institute. Once we had developed some concrete ideas about practical applications of complexity theory to business, we visited with them to discuss those ideas. The discussions that we had there helped us to crystallize the ideas that appear in the book you are holding in your hands. It is our view of the future of the enterprise, of the flexible organization that will be able to maintain its balance between the chaos that pulls it into uncharted depths and the order that could cause it to collapse under its own weight. The book also presents a set of practical tools in the form of principles that allow the organization of the future to adapt to rapid change, bending but never breaking in the face of events that will leave less highly evolved competitors in the dust.

John G. Sifonis
Beverly Goldberg
New York

‖ ACKNOWLEDGMENTS

*F*irst, we must thank all those very busy people in leadership positions both in organizations that are moving to the new form or are close to it and in organizations that are in trouble and have been trying numerous quick fixes: they have spent their valuable time discussing the problems facing business today with us. Many asked not to be mentioned because much of what we learned from them was what they knew was being done wrong; others, as you will see in the pages that follow, were happy to be quoted.

Second, we would like to express our thanks to a number of people who have helped us shape the ideas behind the book:

The members of the Siberg Advisory Board, especially John C. Henderson, director of the Systems Research Center of Boston University; Luis Rubio, director general of Centros de Investigacion Para el Desarrollo (CIDAC) of Mexico; and, for long discussions on the concept of business networks and portfolios of competencies, N. Venkatraman, associate professor of management, Boston University School of Management.

Frank Sonnenberg, president of Sonnenberg Haviland & Partners, has not only been a friend to us both, but as coauthor of an article on business ethics with Beverly Goldberg has contributed directly to our thoughts in this critical area.

Martha Peak of *Management Review*, Ken Shelton of *Executive Excellence*, and James Kristie of *Directors & Boards* have worked with us to shape articles for their magazines, portions of which appear in the pages that follow.

Third, we have had the luxury of having three fine editors work with us throughout the course of writing this book, and we are grateful to them:

Carol Kahn Strauss has once again applied her deft hand to our prose, improving it immeasurably. Perhaps more important, she has questioned and challenged us, forcing us to think through our logic.

Herbert Addison, our editor at Oxford, has guided and shaped this book from the start; he also showed remarkable restraint when we submitted the outline for it before we had turned in our first book.

Jason Renker has helped us in numerous ways, reviewing chapters, helping us think through the scientific concepts, and copy-editing the final manuscript.

In addition, Trina King provided the kind of research assistance that only a skilled librarian can, and indexed the book as well. Brenda Melissaratos has gone over the manuscript, especially the bibliographic materials, helping us find errors. We were also fortunate to have Carol Starmack design and typeset the book and Claude Goodwin prepare the illustrative material.

Fourth, we are grateful to many at the Twentieth Century Fund: the members of the board and Richard C. Leone, president, for guidance and enthusiastic encouragement; the staff, especially Rashida Valvassori, Sarah Wright, and Kathie Young, for help of all sorts on their own time.

Of course, to our children—thank you for everything.

Finally, to those who have been exploring the world of chaos and complexity, especially Dr. Stuart Kauffman, we are particularly grateful; they provided us with an opportunity to practice what we preach—continual learning.

‖ Contents

CORPORATION ON A TIGHTROPE

1

No Silver Bullet, No Quick Fix

Business success does not rest upon infallible judgment. It rests rather upon the courage to experiment and the ability to learn from mistakes. . . . Experimentation, even taking into account the experiments that do not succeed, is, in the long run, safer than too great caution. The moment a business man ceases to be an experimenter and comes to regard himself as an expert in business theory and practice, he may be sure that dry rot has set in.

Edward A. Filene[1]

*T*hose words, written five years before the Great Depression by Edward A. Filene, successful Boston businessman and philanthropist, present a sound idea. After all, the retail empire Filene founded survived the depression intact and continues today in the form of Federated Department Stores. Does that mean that those seeking solutions to the problems affecting their businesses will solve all their problems by focusing on "experimentation"?

We do not believe that it does. Should experimentation be a part of their arsenal? The answer to that question is, Yes—especially if they pay close attention to the words that follow: "Experimentation, *even taking into account the experiments that do not succeed, is, in the long run, safer than too great caution.*"

3

We chose a quote that highlighted one of the many things we believe necessary to create a dynamic, flexible enterprise in order to make the point that there is a tendency today to seize any good idea and decide that it is *the* answer. Responding to the speed with which everything is changing by deciding that a single action can provide a magic solution to the problem of the moment just does not work. If a quick fix is what you are looking for, this book will not help you. Problems as deep and complex as those facing business today do not have simple solutions. In fact, the very complexity of business requires looking for both new ways of thinking about organizations and powerful tools for managing them in order to compete successfully in the future.

Our analysis of and work with organizations of many sizes and kinds over the past two decades, along with an exploration of the new field of complexity, have lead us to conclude that tomorrow's successful organizations will be highly complex, adaptive systems that can grow rapidly to seize opportunities. They will control their growth carefully, avoiding the formation of large bureaucracies that inhibit creativity and innovation as well as avoiding the addition of employees and plant that will be useless when markets again change. They will not be traditional hierarchical organizations. In fact, Dee W. Hock, founder and former president of Visa International, says that the traditional hierarchical organization is an "aberration of the Industrial Age, antithetical to the human spirit, destructive of the biosphere, and structurally contrary to the whole history and methods of physical and biological evolution." Based on this belief, Hock has spent "much of his life patiently building an organization [Visa] . . . capable of evolution and self-determination."[2]

The new flexible, dynamic organization that we believe will be the organizational form of the future is already being built in a number of nations. Organizations such as Transnet of the Republic of South Africa, especially PX (its business unit that is an equivalent of Federal Express); Boeing, particularly its operational model for the design and building of the 777; Shell Oil Company; Motorola; ABB Asea Brown Boveri (a merger of two well-established companies—ASEA of Sweden and Brown-Boveri of Switzerland); and Unilever (an Anglo-Dutch company) have moved toward the fully evolved form. Some newer organizations, such as Destec Energy, Lyondell Petrochemical, and many of the new technology companies that inhabit Silicon Valley (most notably, Hewlett-Packard, Sun Microsystems, and Intel

Corporation) are close to the new model. Organizations set up to disappear—"virtual" organizations—are thriving and may live on as new, flexible organizations, the most notable example being NUMMI (New United Motor Manufacturing, Inc.), a joint venture by General Motors and Toyota that was created to exist for twelve years but with built-in worker protection. In addition, such organizations as the Audubon Society and other environmental groups set up to address specific issues are close to this new model.

Moreover, many utilities, such as Central and South West and UtiliCorp, which are rushing to change to survive deregulation, are moving toward a more flexible form, seeking new businesses to enter and new ways to work. At the same time, numerous companies have turned to outsourcing or alliances to take advantage of their core competencies—a clear move toward a new form. British Petroleum has outsourced both its financial and its information technology functions. Nike does not manufacture the shoes it sells, and more than three-quarters of the components used in Canon's copiers are manufactured elsewhere. Apple created a cluster of alliances (with Pacific Bell, Random House, SkyTel, Sharp, Motorola, and Bellcore) for its Newton hand-held personal computer. Furthermore, there is the recent development of constellations of organizations in two sectors in particular—multimedia entertainment and health care—that are so new that the relationships being built are in a state of flux. There are indications that these new organizations will adopt a very flexible form.

Another form of the new organization has developed in Italy, Germany, and some northern European countries and is spreading to Canada—the joining together of small- and mid-sized manufacturing companies in associations or networks that provide guidance and assistance for exporting, arranging the sharing of technology experience, and the training of workers through apprenticeship systems. The exchanges of information about technology and processes allow new products to be brought to market very rapidly: these "companies often take their ideas to market so fast that they don't bother to patent them. . . . Dortmund-based Geers moved the world's smallest hearing aid, which uses a microchip, from drawing board to retail shops in just nine months. . . . By contrast, rival Siemens took nearly three years to get its micro hearing aid to market."[3] These associations or networks become, in effect, the nerve centers of huge, multinational organizations such as ABB, with the individual companies filling the role of the smaller local units.

Finally, some leaders whose companies are not yet on this list are devoting a great deal of time and attention to finding the right mix of qualities to ensure that their companies can not only survive but grow. As will be seen throughout this book (but most notably in Chapter 11) through examples and quotes from thought leaders in senior management positions, organizations that have begun moving toward this form stress long-term, holistic thinking; they tend to accept change as a good; and they have persevered through periods of initial discomfort to move in this new direction.

Organizations that decide to take this path to long-term competitiveness will find it requires making a number of changes in the way leaders lead, in the way organizations are governed, and in the use of technology and the kinds of technology used. All of this requires learning a great deal about the management of complex adaptive systems—such as the human body, weather, and organizations—and the ways in which they continually evolve. That knowledge, in turn, will make clear the need for a set of tools— seven principles—that can keep organizations lean, strong, flexible, and poised for growth.

The first step in understanding this new organizational form and its practical value is to look for the reasons why so many organizations got into trouble in the late 1980s and early 1990s—to see what went wrong. The next is to turn to comparisons—to examine some approaches to similar problems in the past (to see if solutions were found that worked or that were not heeded yet may have had merit) and then to examine developments in disciplines other than business management and organizational development to see if they have dealt with similar problems and if they have found clues to a solution. The third and most difficult step is to analyze carefully the information collected from the first two steps and apply what has been learned to future actions.

What Went Wrong?

In 1992, Ralph S. Larsen, chairman and chief executive officer of Johnson & Johnson, pointed out that, "in the five years just past 143 companies have disappeared from the *Fortune* 500."[4] Companies that had focused on simply doing more of whatever it was they traditionally did eventually found themselves overtaken by events. A number of America's most celebrated firms found themselves in deep trouble for this reason. General Motors focused on making ever-larger cars that guzzled gas in the midst of a series of energy crises; IBM focused on its mainframe technology as the world began to link together ever-more-powerful personal computers; and Sears focused on supplying products to the middle class in malls as buyers turned to discounters, boutiques, and up-scale stores, depending on the specific purchase they wanted to make and could afford.

As the world approached the last decade of the twentieth century—a decade already marked by enormous changes—these businesses were still being run by their managers the way they had been when business was not global, technology was not an issue, large businesses tended to center on manufacturing a single product, and owners tended to lead by telling their subordinates exactly what to do.

Many still believed, as Alfred Chandler summed up in 1962, that the management of business involved planning and directing the "use of resources to meet the short-term and long-term fluctuations and developments in the market."[5] This belief was based on a number of assumptions: that products would not change dramatically, that the processes used to produce them would remain basically the same, that new competitors would occasionally appear but the playing field would be level.

These theories had worked admirably for decades, and continued to even as business became more global in the post–World War II period. Indeed, then it seemed impossible for America to do anything wrong when it came to industrial development and growth. Our products were needed here and abroad after years of painful rationing and shortages and the destruction of much of the industrial capability of Europe during the war. It was also during this period that nations on other continents began to enter the modern age, spurred in part by the increased knowledge of the world around them brought to their shores by the war, and in part by our search for new markets.

The result of all these changes was that the demand for America's goods—and services—increased dramatically. We became the world's largest store. We had the capacity to produce what the world wanted, in whatever quantities it needed. We alone had the ability to respond to the demands of the marketplace. We were the economic "Masters of the Universe."

Enjoying our successes, we as a nation failed to notice two developments that would have a dramatic effect on us. First, by the late 1960s, those nations that had suffered the greatest economic devastation from the war were experiencing a solid recovery, and some, particularly Germany and Japan, were moving ahead rapidly. Second, the technological innovations that resulted, in large part, from enormous government-funded research and development programs of the cold war were beginning to bear fruit. We applied these advances to our businesses when they seemed useful—at first, only to supplement what we had in place.

Before long, these advances in technology, especially in information and communications technology, were affecting every aspect of business and finance. Technology not only brought us advantages, but it facilitated the spread of new techniques and ideas, providing others with the ability to reverse-engineer products to the point where, according to *Business Week*, "a U.S. company can easily spend, say, $1 million developing a new product only to watch helplessly as lower-cost imitations flood the market before the product reached breakeven."[6] As if these changes were not causing enough turmoil, a massive global economic downturn in the late 1980s reduced demand for all products. The search for solutions to these new challenges grew intense.

Some companies, finally awakening to what had happened in other parts of the world, turned to Japanese businesses for ideas, quickly adopting quality and teams as a solution. Then along came a parade of management gurus whose words were seized upon and adopted by many in one way or another. American business tried reengineering; it turned to downsizing; it embraced empowerment; it rightsized. To some extent, all of these approaches worked; there were profits at the end of the year, and productivity seemed to be rising.

At the same time, the economy picked up. Suddenly, corporations that had managed to become fashionably lean and mean realized that their competitors had done the same. Today, the marketplace is once again level; no more cuts can be made without losing core competencies. Now, the only road to success is growth. Corporations, however, are not willing to expand the way they did in the past. Everyone is far too conscious of the dangers inherent in growing carelessly, in constructing costly redundancies and bloated bureaucracies. Organizations seeking long-term success are looking beyond immediate growth to determine what must be done to ensure that when the next shift comes along—whether as a result of economic, political, technological, or social upheavals—they can react quickly and effectively.

COMPARISONS

Of course, the period from the beginning of the Industrial Age to the dawning of the Information Age has not been all smooth sailing. Problems arose before the Great Depression, for example, that created concerns about labor and management relations that were not addressed by business, resulting in the strengthening of the union movement and a great deal of government intervention to ease social ills. We have chosen to discuss Edward Filene, the retailer who founded the department store chain carrying his name and who implemented many modern principles of management in the 1920s, as a representative of those who examined the problems of the workforce in that era because so much of what he saw then still applies today. We will then return to the present, to look at some explorations into the science of complexity and chaos over the past few years that are providing practical applications for use in other fields to see if they also have practical applications to the world of business.

LOOKING BACK

Today is certainly not the first time business has faced a turning point. In 1924, Filene wrote a book called *The Way Out.*[7] One of his goals in writing the book, he said, was "to help a little toward putting American business and industry upon a sounder and more rational basis." Many of the reasons presented in the book as a rationale for businessmen to take a long-term view of their behavior toward employees also apply to the solutions we will offer to today's problems. He believed so strongly in the need for reform of the difficult situation of workers as a condition for economic, and hence business, success that he set up and endowed a research foundation— the Twentieth Century Fund—in order to be certain that these problems would continue to be addressed after his death.

In addition, we are examining his ideas because they presage many of the theories currently being applied to business problems.

Unfortunately, these ideas are usually adopted on a piecemeal rather than holistic basis. For example, Filene suggested that "the successful businesses of the future will be the businesses that improve the processes and reduce the costs of production, rid distribution of its present indefensible wastes, bring the price of the necessities of life lower and lower." (Almost seventy years elapsed between those words and the focus on business process reengineering, supply chain improvements, and competitive pricing—which rarely are put in place at the same time in any company.)

Filene offered his readers guidelines aimed at improving business in the long term, but he warned that "no policy can be permanently adopted until the managers, the directors, and, in some cases, until the mass of the employees, find it acceptable and agree to adopt it." A leader can "go only as fast as he can carry his associates with him. . . . [He] must be a patient leader and a good lobbyist." (Change management was not in the business vocabulary of the time, but Filene knew it was necessary for the implementation of new ideas.)

Filene also called for the development of an industrial democracy in which employees would have a say in the conditions of work; for raising wages, lowering prices, and shortening the workday to provide people with the time and means to acquire an adequate education. He believed that "good business rests on prosperous customers," and warned that if there weren't ample markets for our goods, what he called "super-competition" would develop, which would mean a "battle of price-cutting which will quickly lead to a campaign of wage-cutting." That in turn, he warned, "will let us in for all sorts of political, social, and industrial conflict." The result: employees will band together—unions and strikes; they will try to control the government; and the class struggle will intensify. (The increasing gap in wages and wealth in this country today indicates a loss of the middle class. This is reflected in growing civic disengagement, a setting in which it becomes easier for extremism to flourish.)

In addition, Filene predicted that the "big business successes during the next ten or twenty years will be made by the men who are now best able to anticipate the changes that are coming in business and industry and who most wisely adjust their policies to them." (The need for long-term thinking and scenario planning is just as important today.)

Filene called for ensuring the future of any individual business by training a cadre of senior executives who could carry it forward. (Today, boards, concerned with the speed with which everything moves, are insisting on succession planning to avoid any delay in replacing their organizations' leaders.)

Almost all of Filene's advice seems as applicable today as it was in the 1920s. Indeed, as noted, many of his ideas are, when adopted piecemeal, the "quick fixes" we argue against. The problem, of course, is not with his ideas, but rather with the tendency to take a suggestion and apply it without first tailoring it to the culture of the organization, or to think it is the whole answer when it is only part of the solution.

LOOKING AHEAD

There is a new science that can be applied to organizations today. Applying it effectively, however, requires understanding that change is now inevitable and will occur faster than ever before, that the constant winds of technological change impact organizations in unpredictable ways, and that economic shifts due to political and social change impact different industrial sectors differently. Organizations must understand that an event that occurs locally no longer has just a local impact, but rather has to be viewed in a much broader context. A monetary crisis in one country is not an isolated event: it impacts currencies and government policies in many countries. The world is so interdependent that the effects of every event are magnified by the effects of every other event.

In other words, the ground rules have changed, and if business is to survive, it will have to adapt to these changes and the next and the next. The only way out seems to be to restructure organizations so that they can deal with the global forces that are continually buffeting them. For reasons that will be made clear in the next chapter, the organizational form that is most suited to adapting to these constant changes can be found by looking at developments in the realm of the science of chaos and complexity.

According to chaos theory, "a small change in input can quickly translate into overwhelming differences in output." Thus, the "butterfly stirring the air today in Peking can transform the storm systems next month in New York."[8] This image has been applied to an examination of chaos by Edward Lorenz, a scientist looking at weather systems, who mapped the intersections of air pressure, temperature, and wind velocity over time. What emerges is a pattern that makes it clear that a change in any one of those forces impacts the other two. A three-dimensional graph of the relation of these forces over time resembles a butterfly (or mobius strip, or a loosely tied ribbon): lines looping around a central point, never quite following the same path, but always returning toward the central point. (See Chapter 2 for a much fuller explanation of this concept.)

The basic ideas concerning growth and change that are being explored in this new science are already finding application in the world of economics, where investors are using them to develop a set of tools to help people understand the complexities inherent in today's stockmarkets.[9] Those investigating chaos theory also have found medical applications involving the circulatory and respiratory systems.

In business, the rapid movements a business organization makes around a central point—its reason for being an organization—in response to the impact of outside events on its governance, its technology, and its leadership create a butterfly shape. The changes that cause the organization to loop back and forth around that point may be the result of decisions made by leadership in response to economic, financial, business, or social developments; advances in technology; or the regoverning of the organization in response to changes in technology or leadership. Since achieving success in business requires managing complex organizations in an increasingly complex global economic environment, we believe that ideas from this new science can be used to fashion practical management tools that will help organizations successfully compete in the rapidly changing business universe.

The second part of chaos theory that we incorporate involves the concept of complex adaptive systems; that is, the ability of organisms to respond to change by adaptation. Because the organization of the future must be free to move in new directions, it must be lean and poised for growth; it must have employees who understand and have the skills associated with its core competencies as well as the ability to transmit those skills to affinity workers (those hired under temporary contracts, arrangements with alliance partners, or from agencies); and it must house the institutional memory and the knowledge of key processes. When it grows, however, this new organization must expand in such a way that it can retrench when necessary—without creating turmoil for itself or for those who are, even temporarily, its employees.

This new organization will be led by people who understand their own abilities and their own limitations, people who understand that openness to learning is the best form of leadership. And it will have leaders at every level. The structure of the organization will be held together by technology—communications as well as information technology (IT)—used to its fullest and understood by all.

CREATING THE NEW ORGANIZATION

A decision to move an organization toward this new form requires commitment, and it requires abiding by a set of seven principles designed to ensure that the organization neither descends into the stagnation that comes with order (the cause of the downfall of several major organizations) nor spins out of control into chaos (the cause of the downfall of many small- to medium-sized businesses that try to expand too quickly). These principles (explained in greater depth in Chapter 12) establish the boundaries within which the new organization moves in response to the changes that buffet it, and they serve as the building blocks for developing the specific rules a given organization will put in place to ensure it grows in the right way at the right time and retrenches with the least harm to present and future workers and customers.

THE PRINCIPLES GOVERNING ORGANIZATIONAL SUCCESS

1. **Set ethical standards and do not accept deviations from them.**
   Build an organization based on trust, honesty, and integrity.

2. **Establish a social contract.**
   Set expectations and conditions of employment with current, future, and temporary employees.

3. **Maintain a strong, lean organization based on core competencies.**
   Avoid permanently adding people and positions that don't relate to those things that are the keys to the organization's success.

4. **Develop leadership skills at every level of the organization.**
    Work with selected individuals to help them develop the
    skills needed to make the organization run when lean and
    expand when appropriate.

5. **Be open to learning, encourage experimentation, and be innovative.**
    Constantly try new things based on information garnered
    from suppliers, customers, successes, failures, and experts in
    your and other sectors, nations, and institutions; that is, to
    return to the quote that opened the chapter, "experiment
    and . . . learn from mistakes."

6. **Avoid restructuring when you should be regoverning.**
    Frequently assess your strategic and operational governance
    models (these will be explained in Chapter 6) to be sure
    they match your scope, size, and structure.

7. **Ensure connectivity.**
    Build human and electronic communications and informa-
    tion networks that tie together people and offices, enabling
    rapid response and collaborative work regardless of time
    and location.

These seven principles provide the boundaries that keep the butterfly organization from descending into order or flying off into
chaos. They ensure its integrity as it swirls around, reshaping itself
to remain competitive, to achieve growth, to maintain its position
as a force for national economic growth as well as corporate growth.
How an organization becomes and then maintains life as a butterfly is the subject of this book.

THE JOURNEY TO COME

The evolution into a flexible organization is not simple. Today's
organizations will not enter a cocoon and be transformed from caterpillar to butterfly. It will require a conscious decision on the part of
leadership. Moreover, the larger the organization, the harder it will be,
but it does not all have to happen at once. Remember, it is an evolutionary not revolutionary process. The first step is understanding the

nature of the new organization and the interaction of the forces that help it fly—governance, technology, and leadership. The second step is understanding the principles that maintain the organization.

THE SHAPE OF THE FUTURE

The two chapters that comprise Part I of the book explore the forces that will determine the shape of the new organization.

Chapter 2 looks at organizational history and shows the relevance of the theory of complex adaptive systems to organizational structures. It explores the interaction of the forces of weather that gave birth to the Lorenz butterfly and then shows how the interaction of the forces of governance, technology, and leadership shape and reshape organizations.

Chapter 3 explores the problems involved in navigating the organization through the shoals of complexity, concurrency, coherence, and connectivity. This exploration also looks at the importance of dynamic thinking—the ability to think concurrently about the long-term effects of changes on organizations, the holistic effects of those changes, the ways in which the organization's culture can be opened to change, and the integration of business and IT strategy—as well as the different types of networks that tie the organization together.

GOVERNANCE IN ITS MANY FORMS

The three chapters that comprise Part II focus on the organization's governance structures because the way in which the particular butterfly that is your organization will be structured impacts not only leadership, but technology, which sometimes drives and always complicates organizational transformation. Technology, particularly information and communications technology, is more than just an enabler, allowing direct and immediate access to information. It allows communication across and up and down as well as among and between organizations in ways that confound some forms of governance and encourage others.

Chapter 4 examines ethical governance, the foundation in values that makes it possible for an organization to assume the butterfly shape. While issues of compliance are involved, trust, accountability, and responsibility both to employees and stakeholders are at the heart of ethical governance.

Chapter 5 looks at those issues of external governance that impact the new organization, particularly the responsibilities of those who serve on boards for helping to maintain the flexibility and anticipatory capability of the organization, as well as the expanded role of the board in guiding the new, more complex, rapidly moving organization of the future.

Chapter 6 explores the issues of strategic and operational governance. Deciding on the form—from holding company to federalist—and structure needed to accommodate changes in direction will be a major issue in the new organization, one that will require careful management. The chapter also looks at operational governance, exploring the ways businesses are structured internally, including governance differences at various levels of the organization, to show the problems that a multiplicity of governance models creates—and how those problems can be solved.

INFORMATION AND COMMUNICATIONS TECHNOLOGY COMES OF AGE

The two chapters of Part III explore the relation of information and communications technology to the organization, looking both at the impacts of changes in governance on the information technology group and the role of the technology leader as enabler of the electronic network that holds together the many disparate parts of the butterfly organization.

Chapter 7 explores how the new connectivity between organizations and between employees at all levels is enabled by and makes demands on technology, raising the complex issue of accommodating many governance models to ensure responsiveness to an organization's current and future strategic needs and flexible size. The chapter explains the difficulties of ensuring connectivity between units and divisions in organizations that move to multiple governance models during the transition to new organizational forms.

Chapter 8 examines the role of the head of technology, a dangerous occupation in terms of tenure. It looks at why the position of chief information officer (CIO) is so problematic and discusses the role these leaders will have to play to make the new leadership needed by the flexible organization possible.

LEADERSHIP FOR THE NEW AGE

The four chapters in Part IV explore leadership in the dynamic organization. Understanding the new, mutable form is not enough; ensuring that it works is critical—and that requires a strong enough vision to take on the challenge of moving the current organization to the new form. It means convincing shareholders and boards that the upheavals will bring rewards. It means believing so strongly in the transformation that you can convince the organization to change its culture and accept changes in the role you yourself play.

Although leadership within an organization begins at the top, leaders at different levels also have strong impacts on their divisions, their functional areas, or, in organizations that have turned to cross-functional teams, the teams they lead. Thus, no matter how solid the arguments in favor of a plan for the future, for adopting new techniques or processes, for developing new products and services, or for literally changing what the organization does for a living, unless there is strong, but not forced, support from all the organization's leaders, the plan is likely to fail.

In thinking about the issue of leadership, it is important to remember that there are many different styles of leadership. Leaders may be delegators of authority, they may be dictators, they may be consensus builders. Moreover, their style impacts the internal structure of the organization. Often, what are regarded as failures of leadership are a result of a mismatch between leadership and governance structure.

Chapter 9 looks at some of the ways organizations have changed in response to the demands of the world outside, particularly the development of teams and empowerment, both of which are initial steps in spreading leadership skills through the organization. The chapter then explores the skills needed by the core workforce—those who combine hands-on skills for doing the work of the organization when it is in a period of waiting for an opportunity for growth with the leadership skills needed to guide those who join under temporary arrangements of various kinds. And it looks at the value and importance of the affinity workforce, which joins during times of expansion and retrains constantly in advanced skills.

Chapter 10 explores the issues of constructing and leading an organization made up of countless formal and informal relationships,

including the sharing of responsibility and the need for boundary
management. The chapter also looks at the changes in the kinds of
information that leaders need in order to know when and how to
construct and deconstruct various types of alliances at the right
time in a rapidly changing world, where flexibility and responsiveness are keys to survival.

Chapter 11 answers the question, Who is a good leader for the
new organization? It does so by examining leaders who are "exper-
imenters," doing the things necessary for helping their organizations
evolve, focusing on such qualities as honesty, loyalty, integrity, the
love of learning, and the ability to inspire, to think laterally, to
communicate, to delegate, and to bring and accept change.

Chapter 12 examines in depth the seven principles that help an
organization maintain its balance between chaos and order, showing how the principles can serve as building blocks for the complex
adaptive structure that is the butterfly organization. It provides
examples of rules to make each principle work but does not construct a concrete rule base, because the rules should be context
specific; that is, the principles should be considered commandments, not subject to change, while the rules are a constitution,
subject to amendment in response to changes in the world. The
information needed to construct the rules will be drawn from the
material presented in the preceding chapters. For example, these
new organizations will need rules to ensure ethical behavior, rules
to ensure the availability of individuals with core competencies,
and rules to ensure that decisions are made with proper guidance.

The Epilogue looks at the successes the seven principles can
bring and discusses why companies should adopt all seven. It returns
to Filene's concept of the way out:

> Unless I wholly misinterpret the signs of the time, we are in a period
> in which business men, in order to survive and succeed, will be com-
> pelled to adopt the sort of policies that will give us an increasingly
> better social order. During the next ten or twenty years we shall
> come to see from practical experience that there is nothing contra-
> dictory between successful business and social progress.[10]

Filene was far too optimistic. The nation did enjoy social
progress, but it was an outgrowth of both government legislation
to protect workers and the union movement, which, combined

with the strong markets for our goods and services and little competition, resulted in a strong and prosperous middle class. Today, the conditions that led to that prosperity have disappeared. We live in an economy in which information is the single greatest natural resource, competition is global, and a new world order has not yet taken its final form. In *Top Heavy*, Edward N. Wolff notes that "after the stock market crash of 1929, there ensued a gradual if somewhat erratic reduction in wealth inequality, which seems to have lasted until the late 1970s. Since then, the inequality of wealth holdings, like that of income, has risen sharply." In fact, he points out, "Wealth inequality in the United States was at a sixty-year high in 1989, with the top 1 percent of wealth holders controlling 39 percent of total household wealth."[11]

The cumulative impact of these changes is a growing discontent and lack of civic engagement of the American worker. This frustration and despair about the future are reflected in wavering consumer confidence. In many organizations, the result is a loss of commitment and involvement. In politics, the result is such a loss of belief that incumbency may soon be a thing of the past.

Many business leaders will deny that this is in any way their concern. "The business of business is business." Of course it is: the purpose of business is a fair return on investments. If, however, business wants to avoid increased government involvement and whatever may develop in the absence of unions, business leaders must accept that it is also the business of business to help ensure that the workers they employ are well educated and trained, that they are treated fairly, and that they can earn enough to buy the goods and the services produced by other workers. That is the only road to the strong economy that business so desperately needs. That is the way out.

PART I

THE SHAPE OF THE FUTURE

2

ORDER OUT OF COMPLEXITY

Humanity's current institutions are designed to cope only with current problems. The need . . . is to redesign institutions—of government, education, economics, business, and so forth—to bring them into line with the pace and complexity of 21st-century challenges.

Rushworth Kidder[1]

*O*ver the past two decades, the world has changed dramatically. A truly global economy has emerged, with major stockmarkets around the world functioning on what amounts to a twenty-four-hour basis. The international political situation was altered radically by the end of the cold war and has since been troubled by a seemingly endless series of outbreaks of ethnic and religious violence around the globe. Scientific and technological advances have become a daily occurrence, facilitated by the technology of the day before. The breaches in the social contracts between citizens and their governments, employees and their employers, and individuals and the family have created uncertainty, resentment, and even fear.

Chaos, turbulence, whitewater are all used to refer to the condition the world is in, and nowhere is that description more true than in business. In this world, new products become commodities in months, and technological innovation is history before it takes hold; a competitor is tomorrow's alliance partner in one area and still a competitor in another. Organizations have been relentlessly searching for new ideas, new leaders with new ways of leading, new ways of doing work, and even new work to do to deal with the speed and complexity of these changes. Stakeholders, especially large institutional investors and boards of directors, are intervening more frequently in the management of the companies in which they have an interest. Leaders are searching for ways to satisfy their multiple constituencies. Serious and complex questions about what organizations should—and can—do to ensure that they will prosper in the future have been raised. And so have questions about the very nature of organizations.

Large organizations have tended to be very formal, legal entities, with management and operating structures that adhere to a fairly limited range of models. They have boards with chairmen and executives in charge of various functions—administrative, financial, marketing—and it has been easy to describe the roles and responsibilities of those who are part of the organization. Those who worked for these organizations were loyal to them, and the organizations provided steady employment in return. These large organizations are what come to mind when we think about business because they are the organizations responsible for such an overwhelming part of any national economy.

Over the past few years, as the economic picture has altered, organizations have responded by instituting a wide range of changes in the hope that they could thereby increase profitability and productivity, and achieve competitive advantage. Organizations acquired newer and newer technology, outsourced, downsized, formed strategic alliances, flattened their structures, turned to Total Quality Management, replaced their chief executive officers, created teams on every level. Each of these so-called solutions brought some immediate rewards, along with turmoil within the organization. None brought permanent increases in productivity or profitability. Worse, in many cases they carried costs in terms of growing disaffection of the workforce and the loss of core competencies.

The simple truth is that there is no single, best "solution." Indeed, we believe that the solution is the ability to anticipate and then adapt to each new development as it occurs. For leaders, that means being able to change the way they lead to meet the needs of the moment (for example, to be risk-takers at one moment and conservative at another). For organizations, it means having internal flexibility in terms of structure, culture, and management; it means being able to mutate, for example, from hierarchical to flattened governance structures in various parts of the organization, and then back again, and from small, permanent staffs to huge workforces, and then back again. Impacting all of this—and being impacted by it—is information and communications technology. Leadership and governance must be facilitated and enhanced by the right use of technology and the use of the right technology. It means understanding what technology is available, how much of it you need now and how much you may need in the future so that your technology skills and platform are ready to expand when appropriate.

As we will show in the pages that follow, the ability to understand the interaction of leadership, governance, and technology and to respond to the effects of changes in any one of these on the others will determine the future of those organizations that produce the goods and services that mark our civilization. The wisdom and flexibility involved in anticipating and responding correctly and swiftly to events outside—and then to the effect of the response within the organization—require dealing with levels of complexity. The inescapable truth is that the changes necessary to become so fluid that you can survive require a new understanding of what constitutes an organization and an understanding of the organization as a complex adaptive system. By that we mean understanding the organization as something that is changing and evolving in response to forces that impact its basic elements.

EXPLORING FORM AND STRUCTURE

There have been numerous attempts to determine the form that organizations will have to take to survive the turmoil of the modern world. Peter Drucker sees the new organization as one that is "infinitely flat," a replacement for the command-and-control hierarchies of the past with their many managerial levels. This new organization will be information-based, depending on knowledge specialists working together in some way. Organizations will make a transition from the flow of things to the flow of information.[2] Charles Handy envisions the new organization as a "shamrock," three separate domains, each equivalent to one of the leaves of a shamrock. The shamrock organization is controlled by a very lean coordinating body, which may or may not be considered part of the leaf that is the heart of the organization, containing those who embody the organization's core competencies. The second leaf is filled with contract relationships with single persons or organizations that are paid for project results, and the third is a flexible workforce paid for doing specific jobs.[3]

Many more such forms have been suggested, ranging from cluster organizations to federalist to volunteer. In addition to these more familiar forms, James Brian Quinn describes the "starburst," which is similar to a conglomerate; it, however, tends to sell off units, allowing them an opportunity to avoid the contradictions inherent in their being entrepreneurial within a bureaucratic structure. Quinn also explains the "spider's web . . . highly dispersed nodes of service operations [that] interact with each other directly and frequently . . . [through coordinating committees] without formal authority" and the "inverted pyramid," in which everyone works to support the people who have contact with the customer.[4] In a 1994 article in *Fortune,* John Huey says that "business is moving to organize itself into virtual corporations: fungible modules built around information networks, flexible work forces, outsourcing, and webs of strategic partnerships."[5]

At first glance, each seems a useful and valid form for dealing with a turbulent, competitive business environment. When we examine each carefully in terms of a possible change in, say, the economy, however, we find ourselves deciding that it makes more sense for a company to follow a different model than the one that seemed right on first glance. When, in turn, we test the new one against different conditions, yet another seems to make more sense. The point is that no one conventional model can be adapted to meet all possible contingencies. The new organization will have to have the adaptability to take a new form almost at will, with just the right mix of leadership, governance, and technology to meet the next competitive challenge, the next technological development, the next economic cycle.

When we started describing what we thought this new organization would look like, the image we first turned to was a butterfly. Looking back, the image seemed useful because the butterfly was a form that evolved from a caterpillar, a creature that moved along slowly and steadily before its metamorphosis into a form that could glide through rough winds as well as fly from flower to flower. We saw the management team/visionary leader at its head determining what to do and when, and then conveying that message to the rest of the small, permanent organization through the spine. The wing veins were the wires of technology through which these messages were sent. Those receiving the message were empowered to do whatever was necessary to provide the strength needed to flap the wings in response to the winds encountered. The point was that while the organization had to maintain just enough muscle not to damage its core competencies during periods when gliding along was advisable, it would have to have in place sufficient resources to quickly build up muscle to deal with opportunities for expansion as they developed. The muscle would come from having in place partnerships, alliances, outsourcing arrangements, and temporary workers.

The more we thought about this image, however, the more we realized that we too were falling into the trap of structure, we were merely creating yet another variation on a theme. The natural human desire for order, for what is familiar and therefore comfortable, makes all of us contemplating these issues try to give the future a definable shape. We see the need for change, but we want the change made to result in something with parameters we can describe.

In *Dynamic Planning*, we discussed change management, emphasizing that the classic theory of how to manage change was no longer valid. The time had passed when unfreezing the current culture, introducing a change, and refreezing the culture was a usable methodology. We called instead for unfreezing the culture, introducing the necessary change as part of that process, and then opening the culture to the concept that each change introduced was itself temporary—something that would hold only until the next change came along. Today, everything changes so quickly that the time it would take to refreeze converges with the need to once again unfreeze, making refreezing pointless.[6]

The more we worked with organizations to help them set business and technology strategies, the more we realized that the elements of the business we were trying to describe were right, but the reasons for deciding that they represented a butterfly were wrong. The shape had nothing to do with the elements of an organization. Rather, the image had to do with the way the organization had to adapt to accommodate the effects of changes in the world around it. The problem was that we were thinking of the wrong butterfly.

A VARIABLE FORM

Our butterfly is not the butterfly of the fields, but one that is recognizable only in its broadest outline—the butterfly of chaos theory, a computer-generated image (see Figure 2.1). Known as the Lorenz butterfly, it was created in the early 1960s when Edward Lorenz, a meteorologist at Massachusetts Institute of Technology (MIT), used a computer to graph the points at which three variables of weather (temperature, air pressure, and wind velocity) intersected at given points in time. What Lorenz was doing was tracking variations in weather patterns over time by graphing them in three dimensions. Most of us are familiar with two-dimensional graphs. In such graphs, one axis, say, the horizontal one, represents time (in months) and the other, the vertical axis, represents the figures for average temperature each month. The same technique can be used to plot the other weather variables over time. The graphs of these variables could be overlaid to obtain a collective picture of temperature, wind velocity, and air pressure at each of the points in time (see Figure 2.2). The problem is that such

Figure 2.1.   The Lorenz Butterfly.

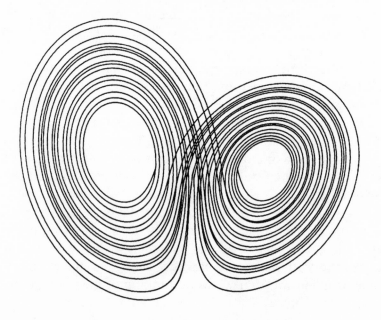

Figure 2.2.   Examples of Two-Dimensional Graphs.

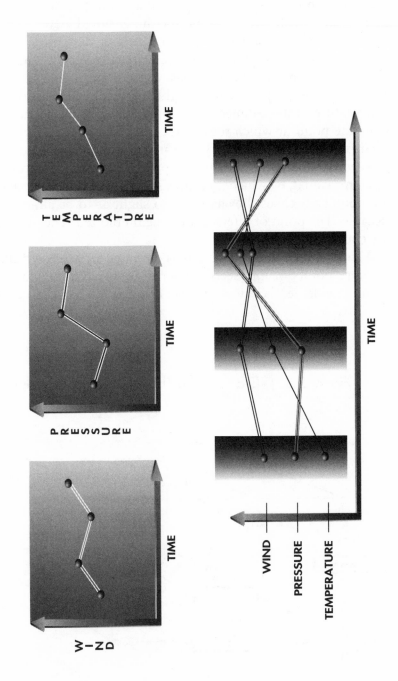

two-dimensional graphs cannot display the relationship of each variable to the others. To gain a good understanding of the way they impact one another requires a three-dimensional view.

In a three-dimensional graph, one axis or dimension, say, the horizontal axis, represents wind velocity; the vertical axis represents air pressure; and the third axis, which in three-dimensional representation is perpendicular to the other two axes, represents temperature. A three-dimensional approach makes it easier to determine the point at which these three meet in time (see Figure 2.3). That point is then plotted. Then, at the next interval chosen, the three variables—wind velocity, air pressure, and temperature—are again measured, by which time at least one is likely to have changed, although sometimes the change is so slight as to be almost unnoticeable. The point of intersection is again plotted. Then the points are connected by a line.

Although the lines that Lorenz's computer drew seemed chaotic, as more points of intersection over time were entered, a pattern began to emerge: there was order in chaos. The shape that emerged

Figure 2.3.   Example of a Three-Dimensional Graph.

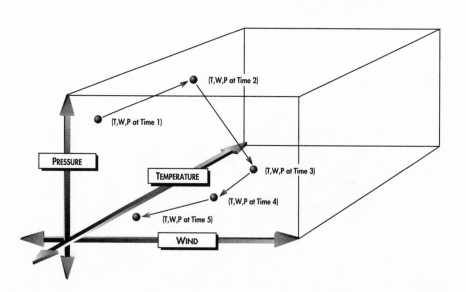

always stayed within certain bounds, never running off the page but never repeating itself, either. It traced a strange, distinctive shape, a kind of double spiral in three dimensions, like a butterfly with its two wings. The shape signaled pure disorder, since no point or pattern of points ever recurred. Yet it also signaled a new kind of order.[7]

What was unexpected, and what Lorenz's graphical representation emphasized, was that the very smallest of differences in the point of intersection that result from any, even infinitesimal, change in a single variable has startlingly large implications. In his book *Chaos*, James Gleick describes this phenomenon as the "butterfly effect," because of the shape of the pattern of intersections. Gleick explains that what Lorenz had discovered was a classic example of the notion of "sensitive dependence on initial conditions"—that is, "a small change in input can quickly translate into overwhelming differences in output." In other words, according to Gleick, the "butterfly stirring the air today in Peking can transform the storm systems next month in New York."[8]

The three-dimensional computer graph of the points representing the intersection of the three variables over time created a pattern that looped and turned widely no matter how minute the changes in the equation representing the point of intersection. It turned out that what appeared to be small, hardly noteworthy variations translated into chaotic swings. In the real world, think of small unpredictable events that have large ramifications; for example, a flat tire is a small event, unless it happens on an expressway during rush hour, tying up traffic for miles.

ORGANIZATIONAL IMPLICATIONS

The butterfly shape, created by mapping the effects of three variables upon one another, dovetailed with our concept of the three critical variables in every business: leadership, governance, and technology (that is, information and communications technology as well as other forms of technology used in producing a product or service). As we shall show throughout this book, a change in leadership has an impact on governance and technology; a change in technology may in turn have an impact on the leadership style and attributes of the organization's leaders; and a change in governance has an impact on the role of information and communications technology and leadership within the business (see Figure 2.4). Changes in these variables impact the shape of the organization, but however chaotic the forces buffeting it, the organization, though extremely fluid, is still recognizable as an organization.

In *Leadership and the New Science*, Margaret Wheatley studies the relationship of the science of chaos to organizations. She points out that systems that constantly reshape themselves in response to events are not only fluid but self-organizing and thus self-renewing. But she imposes a condition:

> An organization can only exist in such a fluid fashion if it has access to new information, both about external factors and internal resources. It must constantly process this data with high levels of self-awareness, plentiful sensing devices, and a strong capacity for reflection. Combing through this constantly changing information, the organization can determine what choices are available, and what resources to rally in response. This is very different from the more traditional organizational response to information, where priority is

Figure 2.4.   Three-Dimensional Graph: Technology, Leadership, Governance.

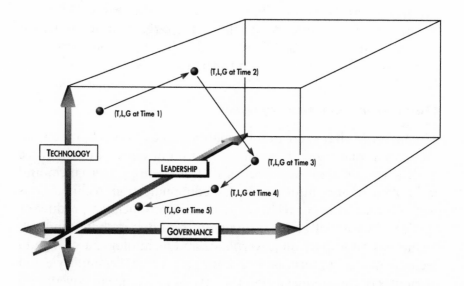

given to maintaining existing operating forms and information is made to fit the structure so that little change is required.[9]

The point is that small changes in leadership, governance, or technology in response to events will lead to significant changes in the business. But, in organizations as in nature, so long as boundaries are maintained, there can be order in the chaos. This notion has been applied to economic cycles by Hyman Minsky, who observed that systems that are "multidimensional, nonlinear, and time dependent" are by their very nature unstable. His point is that although the dynamics that mark our capitalist economy lead to the "development of conditions conducive to incoherence—to runaway inflations or deep depressions, . . . incoherence need not be fully realized because institutions and policy can contain the thrust to instability. We can, so to speak, stabilize instability."[10]

The same rules hold when it comes to businesses. In response to changes, for example, the organization may increase or decrease in scale or scope, and these changes must take place quickly. The principal characteristic of our butterfly organization can be summed up in the word *dynamic*, which we define as changing and active, accepting all structures as temporary. But the dynamic organization remains an organization; the "thrust to instability" is somehow contained.

To understand this requires some further exploration of chaos theory. In chaos theory, unpredictability (that is, the inability to state with any degree of accuracy what will happen next) is different from randomness. This can best be illustrated by the game of "heads or tails." If a coin is tossed in the air, when it lands, one side or the other will be facing the floor—the side of the coin with the picture of a head on it or the reverse side, known as tails. Although we don't know ahead of time which side will face up—that is, we can't predict the outcome—in the course of flipping the coin one hundred times, we could predict with a high degree of confidence that it will turn up heads about fifty times (in reality, it may be forty-nine to fifty-one). Each time the coin is flipped the result is random (it is as likely to be heads as tails), but over time, the outcome is predictable, an equal number of heads or tails. In chaos theory, although any single event has random, unpredictable results, the results of events over time become more predictable and seem to have order.

THE DYNAMIC ORGANIZATION

Dynamic organizations "maintain a coherent identity throughout their history. Stasis, balance, equilibrium—these are temporary states. What endures is process—dynamic, adaptive, creative."[11] Remember that in chaos theory the variations that are mapped take place within boundaries, points that contain most of the possible fluctuations in movement. Our dynamic organization varies in leadership and governance, in form and structure, but the shapes it takes all fit within boundaries, which we believe are external and internal rules—some written, some understood—that control the behavior of the organization and those within it.

The shapes that this new organization takes are the result of the intersections of governance, technology, and leadership as they change in response to external events. For example, leadership on one level sets the logic, the vision, the direction of the organization; on another it enables processes. Technology enables and facilitates leadership and governance, but how much technology an organization uses is driven by leadership and governance.

In the pages that follow, we will examine these three components of the butterfly organization in depth, exploring such questions as, Who controls it? Who leads it? Who decides on its shape at any given point in time? Within that shape, what governance structures are put in place? How does technology fit in? We also will explore the boundaries that ensure that the butterfly does not veer off into some other realm, some other space, exploring questions that are similar to those that set the boundaries of human behavior, preventing total anarchy from destroying civilization. For example, no matter what form of government—monarchy, democracy, republic— a people chooses, underlying that government is a set of beliefs and principles. If businesses are going to adapt continually to ensure they always have the right shape needed to glide through the turbulent winds of the modern age, they will have to be certain that they never breach the boundaries.

THE STEPS ON THE EVOLUTIONARY LADDER

The key to future success lies in accepting that the need to deal with chaos is now a norm. Trying to change or modify the old organization by creating alliances, empowering employees, or adding new technology onto current frameworks won't work. The old edifice will dominate, preventing evolution into the new permeable shape needed for survival. As James Brian Quinn says in *The Intelligent Enterprise*:

> If managers merely replicate past practice, as companies did when they installed electric motors in multilevel mill factories, they will miss the power of new technologies to redefine the entire business in relation to all its environments. To achieve maximum benefit takes a thorough reconceptualization of the business as a series of interconnected knowledge-based and service activities—and a willingness to reorganize and refocus management around these activities in ways the technologies now permit. The processes of change will be very uncomfortable, but the payoff can be extremely high. And the cost of not changing may be comparable to that extracted from manufacturers who did not make the transition to electricity properly or in time.[12]

Of course, no organization can start again from scratch. Products have to be made and services performed while changes that go to the heart of the corporation—involving image and reputation as well as governance, leadership, structure, and the role of communications and information technology within the enterprise—are taking place. The only hope for success is to find ways to make those changes as smooth as possible.

CONCLUSION

"Morphing," the graphics technology that allows a face on a film or video to be changed into another by manipulating the picture so that the shift appears seamless, may be a good image to keep in mind when thinking about the evolutionary process that will result in the butterfly organization. This evolution will result in an entity that is constantly changing form but, like the morphed face, retains certain basic characteristics albeit in different shapes and sizes.

Traditionally, those in charge of a corporation oversaw the operations of what was a very structured entity. Tomorrow, although there will still be overarching entities that exist because they provide a means for manufacturing or developing products or services profitably, these organizations are not going to have set structures, set numbers of employees, set quotas for production of products. Flexibility and responsiveness to context (that is, what is happening in the world economy, politics, demography, and consumer perception) will determine their shapes at different moments in time. Managing all the threads that pull the organization together, that ensure connectivity of the parts, that help manage the complexities involved, that give the organization coherence, requires an ability to address many issues concurrently: it requires extraordinary foresight to navigate the shoals of order and chaos.

3

NAVIGATING THE FOUR C'S—
COMPLEXITY, CONCURRENCY,
COHERENCE, AND CONNECTIVITY

*Complex systems constructed such that they are poised on the
boundary between order and chaos are the ones best able to
adapt by mutation and selection. Such poised systems appear to
be best able to coordinate complex, flexible behavior and best able
to respond to changes in their environment.*
Stuart A. Kauffman[1]

*T*he coordination of the relationships between governance, leadership, and technology will determine the way the new organization responds to changes in the world. This coordination involves
understanding complexity; being able to think concurrently about
the effects of the impact of numerous events; understanding that
there are mechanisms that must be in place for the organization to
maintain coherence and be a recognizable entity; and ensuring that
the connectivity needed to exchange information about developments outside and within parts of the organization is in place. The
new organization, much like a ship navigating stormy seas, must
find ways to coordinate these elements if it is to deal successfully
with the complexity it encounters as a result of waves of economic,
political, social, and technological changes.

COMPLEXITY

The twentieth century, which marked the full blossoming of the Industrial Age and the transition to the Information Age, is also, according to historian Barbara Tuchman, the Age of Disruption, marked by two major world wars, the discovery of nuclear fission, and the first travels into space. In other words, it is an age of major events and major advances, a time in which everything changes and then changes yet again. The effects of many of these changes on the global economy have been severe, bringing an increasingly rapid and seemingly continuous series of challenges to corporations, government organizations, and institutions of every kind.

The result of these challenges and the strategies that have been employed to meet them is an increased level of complexity within organizations. For most of the century, complexity—what little there was of it compared to today—was generated by the need to do more (sales, marketing, services, and so forth) with more (financial and human resources, technological capabilities, and so forth). More recently, complexity has been created by the continuing need to do more, and to do it better and more efficiently—but with fewer traditional resources.

For example, in the private sector, businesses have had to cope with low or, in some cases, no domestic market growth; the markets that they deal with have demanded more (for example, better service to accompany a product and higher-quality products); and the demands have changed constantly, increasing and decreasing in response to outside forces. Businesses have stretched to become global, only to face global competition—and the competitors are fierce. To survive, companies are striving to become best in class in every market as the ability to sell second-rate products and services off-shore is rapidly disappearing. In the public sector, a tighter economy has changed the public's ability and willingness to support government programs at the same time that it has created a need for help, leading to cries for the reinvention of government. And not-for-profit institutions are facing the challenge of lower contributions and lower rates of return on endowments, which demand changes in the way they operate and the way they connect with their supporters.

Complexity is also increasing as technological advances (primarily in information and communications technology) continue at an incredible rate. What wasn't possible five years ago or was prohibitive because of cost is the norm today, raising critical issues about investment in future technologies. Since there are no indications that the pace of these technological advances will slow, and since their costs drop rapidly shortly after they are introduced as the promise of yet another generation of advances begins to be heard, being first to invest in a new technology is no guarantee of a competitive edge. At the same time, allowing the competition to invest first while waiting for the cost to fall can result in competitors determining which of the available current technologies will prevail, becoming the standard to which everyone will have to adapt.

The decisionmaking facing leaders also grows increasingly difficult and complex because these advanced technologies have multiple impacts on organizational structures. Communications technology and executive support systems have eliminated layers of management, increasing the time demands on remaining executives and increasing the number of people in the organization who can easily communicate their opinions directly to top management. Add to this the effects of time compression stemming from the rapidity of the influx of new possibilities, and you have leaders trying to deal with increased complexity with less time for trend watching, discussion, and contemplation—all the elements important to successful management. Moreover, much of the work of an organization is now done across functional areas and in conjunction with alliance partners, outsourcers, suppliers, and temporary employees outside the core organization, forcing managers from many different divisions and organizations to deal with different cultural norms, different expectations, different professional standards and jargons, and, when global players are involved, different languages.

The cumulative effect of this increased complexity is that conventional notions of strategy and structure are no longer relevant for achieving the balance between order and chaos. As noted in the last chapter, the organizations most likely to be able to walk that line, to be able to shift rapidly in response to changes in the external world, will be what we call butterfly organizations, those organizations that have internal flexibility in terms of structure, size, processes, culture, and management. Because they rarely maintain the same form for long, butterfly organizations are works in progress. They are dynamic organizations that are able to respond to threats from direct competitors, from within their industrial sectors, or from the world outside (social, political, economic, or technological) by accommodating the effects of those threats through changes in leadership, governance, or technology—or any combination thereof. They are prepared for those changes to impact, in turn, their scope of business, their core competencies, their size, and their relationships with stakeholders, customers, alliance partners, outsourcers, and so forth.

The name butterfly organization is a form of literary license: these dynamic organizations are shape shifters, in need of a new name each time they change. However, they can be defined as organizations no matter what shapes they take, and as organizations they are bound by certain rules and adhere to certain laws that keep them looping back and forth over time around a central point. The result is that, as an organization reacts to changes, it shifts form, moving along a trajectory that produces a butterfly shape, hence the "butterfly organization." The major point Stuart Kauffman was making about poised systems—in business terms, dynamic organizations—was that they had the ability to "coordinate complex, flexible behavior and . . . respond to changes in their environment."

What we are dealing with when we discuss butterfly organizations is more than a "complex system"; it is a "complex adaptive system"—that is, according to Murray Gell-Mann, "a collection of simple parts that interact to form a complex whole capable of learning about and reacting to the outside world."[2] More, according to John H. Holland, who, along with Kauffman and Gell-Mann and other members of the so-called Santa Fe group, has been laying the groundwork for thinking about complexity, "a complex adaptive system has many levels of organization, with agents at any one level serving as building blocks for agents at a higher level. . . . Furthermore, . . . complex adaptive systems are constantly revising and rearranging their building blocks as they gain experience. . . . [And] all complex adaptive systems anticipate the future. . . . [N]ew opportunities are always being created by the system."

The true nature of these systems, according to Holland, makes it meaningless to talk about them as ever reaching equilibrium. "In fact, if the system ever does reach equilibrium, it isn't just stable, it's dead." The only thing that the agents of, say, the economic world—the systems analysts, the electricians, laundromats, factories, and mills—"can do is to change and improve themselves relative to what other agents are doing. In short, complex adaptive systems are characterized by perpetual novelty."[3]

Given that organizations are complex adaptive systems, it stands to reason that they inherently have the capability to anticipate the future and create new opportunities. The critical issue that must be addressed is how to put in place the mechanisms for unlocking this potential within an organization. We believe that the key to taking advantage of the changeability, and thus adaptability, of these systems, is a new way of thinking, one based on a set of four principles that, when internalized in such a way that they are thought about concurrently, result in what we call dynamic thinking. It is a way of thinking that must become second nature to everyone in the organization because it makes it possible for people to welcome change, to step into unfamiliar territory with cautious anticipation, to aid in the process of adaptability themselves. Indeed, internalizing these principles of thinking will enable those who help shape and reshape the enterprise to constantly extend the bounds of conventional wisdom to accommodate the discontinuities and nonlinearity that mark the Information Age; they will become leaders by improving themselves relative to what other agents are doing, and thus be able to lead their organizations to competitive advantage.

DYNAMIC THINKING: THE TOOL FOR MANAGING A COMPLEX ENVIRONMENT

A key to managing the new organization is dynamic thinking, which is based on four interrelated principles: long-term thinking, holistic thinking, openness to change, and business and information technology integration. In *Dynamic Planning*, we showed how these principles were the underpinnings of a new framework for planning. However, as we have interviewed leaders at all levels of business (as well as in the public and nonprofit sectors), it has become evident that these principles also have to be the basis of all thinking in—and about—the organization if it is to become flexible enough to adapt quickly to the chaotic forces that constantly batter it. Dynamic thinking is concerned with developing the mental models of the organization, which is a necessary prelude to actually creating the new organization.

LONG-TERM THINKING. When thinking dynamically—for example, deciding whether to take a new direction, to become a provider of logistics instead of a just a provider of transport, or to produce products through a new process—one must look at the implication of the decision in the long term. First, the organization should have some vision or collective understanding of what it wants to be at some future point in time; that is, it should always be trying to achieve an objective so that making a decision about a product or service can be measured against that objective. At the same time, given the world around it, the organization must understand that the goal set today may have little or nothing to do with the world as it will be tomorrow. Thus, when deciding how much to invest in the new product or process or service, care must be taken to ensure that if the world changes before you put it in place, making the product useless, you have not so tied up the organization in pursuing it that you have no resources with which to move in another direction. Organizations must maintain a "what if" mentality.

HOLISTIC THINKING. Holistic thinking means accepting that everything is impacted by and has an impact on everything else and thus never thinking about a problem, or a solution, without examining it in the context of the organization as a whole. It involves achieving an in-depth understanding of the enterprise across the value chain (administrative functions, financial, marketing, sales, or human resources that support the functional areas of the organization) and down into those functional areas (manufacturing, warehousing, new-product development). It means knowing the directions in which the organization must move to keep a competitive edge so that when, say, a process is determined to be in need of reengineering, the effects of reengineering it on other processes and on employee skill sets is given consideration. It also may mean investing in a totally new technology even though the one in place seems to be doing the job—or not jumping on a new technology bandwagon as a result of a belief that further change is likely because of trend watching. In addition to looking at the problem and the solution in the context of the enterprise, in the new flexible organization holistic thinking means taking a broader view of customers, suppliers, and other external parties the enterprise may deal with in order to understand the effects and/or implications of both the problems and the proposed solutions on them as well.

OPENNESS TO CHANGE. Openness to change is a necessary prerequisite for thinking dynamically. It requires examining new ideas and new technologies and new products with an open mind, exploring their benefits and costs, and deciding which would provide value to the organization without worrying about the personal consequences of the change. It means being able to overcome the fear of the unknown and explore the world looking for innovative ideas— something that is impossible when people are determined to maintain the status quo. An organization that is incapable of dealing with change on an ongoing basis simply will not survive.

BUSINESS AND INFORMATION TECHNOLOGY INTEGRATION. In a truly dynamic organization, the business side does not determine what strategy to follow and then call in the technology side to ask it what technology can support the strategy, and the technology side doesn't decide to buy the latest technology because "it will be useful someday, if. . . ." The business and technology sides work together to determine which option is best for the company, given available or developable technology, and the business side is made aware of technological advances that might have an impact on business. The role and importance of technology to business does not have to be proved; it is understood.

These principles should be so thoroughly internalized that, when applied to a question about, for example, the impact of a new technology, they are thought about almost simultaneously, and whichever is thought about first, the person doing the thinking begins to consider the next principle—and the next—almost concurrently, never quite completing the cycle, always waiting for more information to add to the equation. Once this way of thinking is second nature to those who set strategy and policy, it takes far less time for those in the organization to react to discontinuities, to new developments, new threats, new opportunities.

CONCURRENCY

Dynamic thinking requires concurrent thinking, an extremely difficult way to approach problems because it eliminates clear beginnings, middles, and ends. In concurrency, there are numerous discontinuities, and processes are nonlinear. When it comes to exploring the three parts of the butterfly organization—leadership, governance, and technology—concurrent thinking raises the question, Which aspect of the three forces that are so busy pushing against one another is dominant? Is it leadership? After all, doesn't the organization's leadership determine its governance and decide on how much and what technology will be in place?

The new answer is counterintuitive: Not necessarily. Technology has changed the equation. For example, leadership decisionmaking plays no deliberate role when a technology put in place for one purpose is used or adapted for another—at no extra cost and often without anyone deciding that this is what will happen. The result in such a scenario is that governance may end up being changed because this new application of technology allows connections around layers of management, which in turn ends up affecting reporting, hence, governance structures and rules. But another scenario is a change in governance structure as a result of a leadership decision. To support the new governance structure chosen by the organization's leaders, new reporting technologies may have to be put in place. But then, once the technology is in place, it may enable the birth of a new service, which may end up changing the nature of the business. Say, the new service results in the creation of a new division that grows so dominant in terms of profits and success that its leader gradually assumes power or, conversely, the original leader sees that this is a division that should be set up as a wholly owned subsidiary, with its own leadership. The nature of the new organization may make a different style of governance necessary, and, in turn, each additional change brings another change.

Leadership may also be driven from outside the organization, a result of changes in the world that force new modes of operation, giving increased power and responsibility to leaders who once played a lesser role. For example, deregulation of an industry may necessitate putting in place a strong marketing and sales arm that plays an increasingly important part in organizational decision-making. At that point, the influence of those leaders who attained their positions because of their relationships with legislators responsible for public oversight and regulation of the industry diminishes considerably. The interactions that cause such changes are complex and interconnected: the world in which organizations operate is not a world in stasis.

THE FORCES CONVERGE IN THE REAL WORLD

The grocery industry provides an interesting example of the complexity facing organizations today. The post–World War II growth of the supermarket as an alternative to butchers, bakers, green grocers, and stores selling "dry groceries" such as tissues and soaps was impressive.[4] Supermarkets quickly dominated the grocery industry because they offered low prices and one-stop shopping in a very efficient, self-service environment. Then in the 1970s, the industry growth rate began to fall as a result of slower national economic growth combined with a trend toward eating out, a response to the sudden availability of numerous types of fast-food restaurants. The 1980s brought further problems as wholesale clubs, supercenters, and mass merchandizers such as Wal-Mart and Kmart, which had been purveyors of general merchandise, joined the grocery business, rapidly achieving a substantial market share through aggressive pricing policies combined with operating efficiencies made possible through reengingeering and the use of technology.

What these new entrants had done was find a way to streamline the supply chain for providing products to consumers. Success in the industry is dependent on the smooth operation of that chain, the set of steps that brings staple foodstuffs, dry goods, and fresh foods to the checkout counter. The traditional supply chain starts with vendors and manufacturers, such as Kellogg, Nabisco, and Johnson & Johnson, which are known as suppliers; moves to distributors, such as A&P, the Kroger Company, and Stop & Shop, often through brokers and wholesalers; then is trucked to the retailers, the local stores that sell the products to the consumer for household use. Suppliers and distributors warehouse products and all use transportation, usually trucks, to move the goods through the chain. The process has been marked by numerous inefficiencies resulting in overstocking of some products and shortages of others— and a mountain of paperwork for tracking and billing goods as they move through the chain.

In the 1970s, technology, especially bar coding and scanning, began to play an important role in the process. The technologies that simplified recordkeeping and allowed for more efficient replenishment of supplies based on information collected at the point of sale made a great deal of headway into the industry. At the same time, the industry also put in place technologies for such things as inventory and financial management. But, because the mindset of these companies was focused on the value of the technology in replacing manual systems—that is, using technology to solve specific problems rather than trying to use it to deliver or collect information across the supply chain—the potential of the technology was never fully explored. Technology strategy reflected the hierarchical organizational structure dominating the industry. Moreover, the industry culture was very secretive, with little trust among the players within a category as well as across categories.

As the wholesale clubs and mass merchants became new entrants in the grocery arena, they were able to achieve significant efficiencies—reflected in lower prices—by applying principles that were in place in the mass-merchandise retail sector, including the use of technology for improving ordering and payment. The companies offering these lower prices were rewarded by increased market share. In recognition of the advantage these groups had gained, in the early 1990s, the Grocery Manufacturers of America, Inc., set up a working group to "study the mass merchandising industry's model system for procurement, marketing, and distribution."

To its surprise, the group found that "complex and out-of-date business policies and uncooperative relationships between trading partners" were as much a problem as their failure to use the technology they had in place to the fullest or to adopt new technologies. The task force concluded that what was needed first was a basic change in the "relationship of trading partners along the supply chain."[5] The industry group called for its members to begin a new initiative, to be known as Efficient Consumer Response, or ECR.

ECR demands better use of technology, by all the members of the supply chain, to tie together electronically all the components of the chain so as to create a timely, accurate, paperless information flow that matches product flow to consumption seamlessly. However, the technology needed to do this requires all the members of the chain to adopt certain standards to ensure technology compatibility and share a great deal of information; therefore, if ECR is to bring the rewards expected, the leaders of the industry must accept a new cooperative style of working, and see to it that this becomes the culture of their organizations. Moreover, because the technology must operate across the members of the chain, there will have to be a change in organization structure to put in place people to direct and manage these relationships.

Those members of the grocery industry who have decided to move in the direction of ECR are already forming alliances with a few select other members. Over time, these alliances will link together. Each of these steps will involve more technology, more working across organizational boundaries, and further changes in leadership style. The mindset of the leaders in the grocery industry already has changed dramatically; they have come to accept the fact that they face continual threats—and not just from new competitors moving into the neighborhood. They recognize that there also are threats from the outside world over which they have no control (economic trends or environmental and health concerns, for example) and from the industrial sector (general merchandisers deciding to sell groceries, prepared food deliveries) as well. And, of course, their new awareness has brought them to quickly accept the coming challenge from technological developments; for example, some members of the supply chain have begun using new interactive telecommunications technology to provide home grocery shopping.

New entrants to the field using new technology drove the leaders of the grocery industry to reexamine their approach to technology. In turn, this examination revealed the need for a change in leadership style. These changes led to the adoption of technology that changes organizational structure, and that in turn is opening people across the industry to additional new ideas that will bring further changes.

CONCURRENCY REDUX

Examining what is happening in the grocery industry reveals just how the effects of governance, leadership, and technology wrap around one another, appearing at times concurrent. This is what makes it so difficult to decide which to look at first. However, since books are still presented in linear rather than concurrent form, one of these aspects will have to be the point of entry for an exploration of the butterfly organization. A key to where to start may be found in examining two other concepts that are a part of the thinking that needs to be done about chaos and complexity to fully understand the way the butterfly organization maintains its balance in the midst of all the chaos that surrounds it.

COHERENCE

Creating a butterfly organization will prove extremely difficult because the choices that such organizations must make for their long-term benefit are often detrimental to employees and owners (whether they be shareholders, private individuals, or citizens) in the short term. Indeed, these changes may stretch the organizational form so much that the internal and external rules that comprise the boundaries that keep the organization from veering off into chaos instead of moving back toward the points that give it coherence will be breached.

The external rules and regulations are legal and regulatory, and comprise the organization's boundaries and give them legitimacy. They are also the will of the owners of the organization, its shareholders in the case of a business, contributors in the case of nonprofits, voters in the case of governments. The rules and regulations component—corporate governance—can be thought of as the organization's constitution, to which the other component, the internal rules and regulations, or bill of rights of the organization—ethical governance—are appended.

THE EXTERNAL BOUNDARIES

The organization's constitution may take one of a number of different forms, but basically a constitution is that set of rules and regulations that governs its formation and establishes it as a coherent body with rights in and responsibilities to the larger world in which it functions. Briefly, that constitution, in the case of a business, includes the rules of incorporation under which it chooses to form, and the regulations of the securities market on which its stocks are traded; in the case of a government agency or bureau, it starts with legislative mandates; in the case of a not-for-profit organization, the tax codes under which it is set up and its bylaws.

Shareholders can replace leaders they believe are acting in a way detrimental to profitability, just as voters can replace elected officials they believe are wasting their tax dollars in bloated, ineffective bureaucracies, and supporters of not-for-profits can decide that their leaders are enriching themselves rather than promoting a cause. The external boundaries must be maintained through both adherence to the law and communications that build understanding of the shifts in organizational form and the benefits these shifts will ultimately bring.

THE INTERNAL BOUNDARIES

The internal boundaries present a somewhat different problem. Many organizations will have an extremely difficult time achieving cultures marked by dynamic thinking unless their leaders first make certain changes in the way they treat their employees. First, leaders must recognize that most employees are not currently able, financially or emotionally, to accept the costs of frequent swings in numbers of employees and levels of employment as well as in pertinent skill sets. If employees are to accept such impermanence in employment as a part of their lives, mechanisms will have to be put in place to make the costs of those changes bearable. For example, since future employment security will come from the acquisition of the skills necessary for continued, lifetime employability rather than guarantees of lifetime employment, organizations are going to have to participate in providing training and retraining.

Creating a culture with this kind of mindset is a change from the norms that prevailed in business as little as a decade ago, a time according to many when "the notion of culture was not a legitimate topic for bottom-line executives to spend time on." Today, they might say that there is far greater understanding that it isn't until an "organization has established a powerful set of shared values or guiding principles [that] everyone can be mobilized quickly, and their full potential unleashed toward achieving excellence."[6] Indeed, social philosopher Sissela Bok says that today, if organizations are to survive, leaders "will have to take moral principles into account. . . . Trust is, if anything, absolutely as important as the ozone layer for our survival."[7]

To ensure they achieve a reputation for ethical governance, the kind of reputation that will make it possible for them to attract skilled employees who will stay with them through the end of a specific project when they need them, organizations will have to put in place rules for employment security, as differentiated from job security. This requires that they recognize that the costs embedded in programs that ensure some degree of economic protection after termination, training programs during and after employment, and the continuation of some level of benefits during layoffs are more than made up for by savings in outplacement and expensive buy-out packages, as well as, perhaps most important, the benefits of reputation in attracting loyal, trained employees when the time comes for new growth.

THE ANCHOR

Now that we have noted the boundaries that keep the organization from veering off and loosing shape, the other point of reference that needs exploration is the anchor around which the organization twists within its allotted space, the center that gives the whole coherence. After all, without it, we would have something that looked more like an unraveled ball of string than a butterfly.

Coherence is provided through the extensive and constant communications—mostly electronic—that take place externally (between the organization and the state, the organization and its owners) and internally (between individuals and among groups, teams, alliance partners, and outsourcers). These communications webs are responsible for many of the shifts that take place in the organization's shape, and at the same time they prevent the organization from crossing the line to chaos because they ensure that the shifts that are taking place are understood and responded to within the framework of the rules and boundaries that serve as the constitution and the bill of rights of the organization.

The various meanings of the terminology employed in discussing these connections creates some confusion. Part of the problem is the meaning of the word *network*. The dictionary definition of a network is a "fabric or structure of cords or wires that cross at regular intervals and are knotted or secured at the crossings."[8] This term was adopted by the business world, where the concept is known as networking, which is defined by Leif Smith and Patricia Wagner as "a pattern of human interactions characterized by a process of information exchange usually leading to other human interactions and/or material/service information, monetary or spiritual exchange."[9] That definition is from 1981. Eight years later, as technology became more pervasive, K. Hugh Macdonald defined business networks as "systematic relationships between various individuals, organizations, or enterprises normally paired in 'seller and buyer' relationships, in a value system. The phrase," he adds, "is used to imply commercial relationships rather than electronic connections. In practice, whether for efficiency or convenience, business networks are supported by technical (communications) networks used for exchanging information."[10]

When turning to a discussion of the electronic connections, the phrase used was *IT-based business networks*. Today, electronic connections are so prevalent that those who write and think about these issues usually use the term *business networks* to mean electronic networks. In addition, these electronic networks no longer support just the traditional "seller and buyer" relationship, but have expanded to support "cooperative" arrangements between alliance partners. These arrangements take the form of cross-process integration—for example, the cooperative effort between engineering and design processes when the two processes are done by different organizations. The arrangement is one that focuses more on the sharing of competencies for a common purpose rather than a traditional buyer-seller relationship—in this instance, both parties share and derive value from the cooperative relationship. In many ways, this type of relationship is the heart of the butterfly organization.

CONNECTIVITY

The last of the C's to be navigated is connectivity. One can hardly pick up a paper or a business magazine without reading something about connectivity. But what is connectivity? Telephone company advertisements talk about the miracles to come in the not-too-distant future that will allow you to conduct a meeting in remote locations through wireless video conferences using your laptop computer as a telephone, fax machine, or video receiver as needed. Another view of connectivity is the ubiquitous Internet network—a global expanse of computers strung together by telecommunications lines. Connectivity is the ability to sit at home in New York or Telluride and access computers and databases in Zurich, Switzerland, or Austin, Texas. It is the ability to send electronic messages to any one of fifty million people on the Internet. It is the ability to pose a problem on the network and get global answers.

Connectivity is so powerful that it can change industries, even industrial sectors; it is a pure example of the way technology can impact leadership and governance. Walter Wriston, former chief executive officer of Citibank, points out that "a brand new international monetary system has been created. Unlike all prior arrangements, this new international system was not built by politicians, economists, central bankers or finance ministers. . . .

The new system . . . was created by technology. . . . [It] is not a place on a map; it is more than 200,000 monitors in trading rooms all over the world that are linked together. With this new technology no one is really in control. Rather, everyone is in control through a kind of global plebiscite on the monetary and fiscal policies of the governments issuing currency."[11] Developments such as these mean that an event that occurs locally no longer just has a local impact but, rather, has to be viewed in a much broader context. A monetary crisis in one country is no longer an isolated event—it literally impacts currencies and government policies in many countries.

LEST WE FORGET THE HUMAN ELEMENT

Although connectivity is a necessary condition for electronic information exchange, it is not sufficient. This brings us full circle to one of the earliest business uses of the term *network*. The nonelectronic counterpart of connectivity is human interactions, the personal connections people make and use in the conduct of their business. The difference that is most important today is that these interactions—which still take the form of relationships between co-workers, among groups of co-workers, in teams, across and up and down the organization; among and between members of different companies through partnerships, alliances, associations; and with institutions, organizations, and communities with whom the company and its members deal—ignore space and time. People can interact without ever having met, they can work together in real time in different locations, and they can reach across barriers of rank as well as place.

Although the lack of the personal touch does not make communication impossible, there has been a growing realization among those responsible for building these networks, such as Bill Raduchel, the chief information officer of Sun Microsystems, that "you can't have a virtual conversation unless you have real conversations. The indispensable complementary technology to the net is the Boeing 747."[12] Indeed, although the number of such face-to-face meetings necessary for establishing and maintaining relationships seems likely to decline, eliminating them altogether requires finding new ways to build understanding and trust between people.

CONCLUSION

The need for one-on-one meetings relates to the issue of trust, which, as noted earlier, is at the core of building the butterfly organization. Trust is something that must permeate the organization, moving across and up and down its layers and extending outward to alliance partners, suppliers, customers, and community. To succeed, the new organization must build and maintain an impeccable reputation as an organization that always behaves ethically.

The best analogy for the way in which ethics, trust, and integrity must become part of the fabric of the organization comes from the science of chaos and complexity: it is fractals—shapes created in nature or by a computer when mathematical formulas are repeated back on themselves millions of times, forming complex, infinitely replicated patterns akin to those in nature.

The best example of a fractal is broccoli. Each of the individual florets is a miniature of the cluster of florets that comprise the top of a stalk, and a cluster of stalks—or a head of broccoli—is simply a larger version of the smallest of florets. Margaret Wheatley points out that "the very best organizations have a fractal quality to them. An observer of such an organization can tell what the organization's values and ways of doing business are by watching anyone, whether it be a production floor employee or a senior manager. There is a consistency and predictability to the quality of behavior."[13]

In a world of complexity and chaos, unless people believe that the organization they work for is fair, unless traditions of loyalty and caring are hallmarks, unless values are considered important, there can be no trust. The starting point for creating such trust is developing a code of ethics that governs the organization, that inspires and guides behavior at all levels. Ethical governance is the foundation of the butterfly organization. It enables and it strengthens everyone within the organization. How it is built and how it works are the subject of the next chapter.

PART II

GOVERNANCE IN ITS MANY FORMS

4

CREATING A PATTERN OF TRUST

Trust is the fabric that binds us together, creating an orderly, civilized society from chaos and anarchy. . . . Trust must be carefully constructed, vigorously nurtured, and constantly reinforced.

Frank K. Sonnenberg[1]

*T*he issues involved in governance go far beyond the rules and regulations that give an organization legal standing. Governance involves control, accountability, responsibility, and authority—areas that are often only vaguely understood or defined. It is critical to how well organizations perform, determining the nature of relationships within the organization as well as between the organization's representatives and those outside. The dynamics of these relationships will determine how well an organization can shift directions in response to external events.

The key to how control, accountability, responsibility, and authority work within an organization is ethical governance—those beliefs, values, and morals by which the organization lives. They shape its internal culture, and its image to the world. They make up the framework that supports and promotes trust in organizations, a quality whose importance cannot be overestimated.

Remember Sissela Bok's statement that "trust is, if anything, absolutely as important as the ozone layer for our survival." When it comes to nations, she says that "trust is diminished every time a government is unreliable with respect to information."[2] W. Edwards Deming says that

> trust is mandatory for optimization of a system. Without trust, there can be no cooperation between people, teams, departments, divisions. Without trust, each component will protect its own immediate interests to its own long-term detriment, and to the detriment of the entire system. The job of the leader is to create an environment of trust.[3]

The leader, of course, is not the only one with such values, but unless leaders make it clear that such values are the organizational norm, those who hold them will have a more difficult time standing firm against those who do not. That is not to imply that one manager, driven, for example, by bottom-line pressure that leads to an unethical choice can turn an ethical organization around. But one manager who hints to employees that he will favor anyone who can cut costs and whose staff reacts by doing something unethical can be the start of a slide down the slippery slope to unethical organizational behavior. The only way to prevent incremental growth of lax standards is to ensure that those who work for such a manager know that the organization's leaders do not countenance such behavior, and to provide mechanisms for reporting that behavior without repercussions.

Behavioral standards must be established from the top. When they are, they will be reflected in the actions of salespeople to customers, the organization to the government, the boss to the secretary, the janitor to the computer operator, the guard at the gate to the sanitation worker coming to pick up the trash. In fact, at that point trust becomes so completely woven into the fabric of an organization that it makes a consistent, clear pattern, repeated in the smallest part of the design, much as the pattern of a single broccoli floret is replicated in the cluster of florets that make up the stalk, and the stalks that make up the head. It is only when trust becomes a fractal, the basic belief system governing everyone's behavior, that it can stand as the recognizable hallmark of the organization, the inherent way it conducts business, the basis for its reputation.

The benefits that accrue from such a reputation, as we shall see, are many. An organization with a reputation for honorable behavior toward its employees, shareholders, customers, and community is an organization that can be flexible, because it can attract the kind of workforce and strategic allies it needs when it needs them. Such an organization also has the ability to do new things, introducing new products and services more easily because people trust that an organization with a good reputation will stand by its products and services, even those it has never offered before. And perhaps even more important in an age of technology, such an environment allows the establishment of electronic as well as personal relationships; it makes it possible for the core organization to communicate quickly and openly with national and international partners. In other words, trust is the prerequisite for developing the new organization: it is the critical quality that enables the easy and rapid shape shifting necessary to remain competitive in this age of change.

ETHICS ENTERS THE MAINSTREAM

The groundwork for defining and creating the standards of ethical governance that will form the backbone of the new organization was laid over the past two decades. The explosion of interest in ethics in the 1970s and 1980s was prompted by Americans' disgust with the "permeation of the fever of corruption and white-collar crime in American social institutions."[4] The cries of "moral bankruptcy" were the result of the behavior of those who damaged the environment and refused to pay the costs, those who violated the public trust using public funds for their own purposes, those who made millions on Wall Street by circumventing the law. The illegal dumping of toxic wastes in the middle of the night, Bophal, and *Valdez*; senators and congressmen facing indictment; and hubris-driven leveraged buyouts, Michael Milken, and Ivan Boesky all became increasingly offensive as we became aware of the intransigence of the worldwide economic downturn marked by layoffs and downsizings, flattened organizations, and constant media attention to the new, seemingly permanent mid-level unemployment. The American people were dismayed by what they saw as greed and avarice among leaders at the same time that the social contract between employee and employer was being torn to shreds in far too many organizations, with no hint of replacement.

This crisis of confidence led to efforts by the business community to clean its own house. Today, close to 10,000 of the nation's largest corporations have in place formal codes of ethics.[5] By 1993, more than 500 courses in business ethics were being taught. Andrew Stark noted in a 1993 *Harvard Business Review* article that "fully 90% of the nation's business schools now provide some kind of training in the area. There are more than 25 textbooks in the field and 3 academic journals dedicated to the topic. At least 16 business-ethics research centers are now in operation."[6] In addition, there are numerous nonacademic journals and newsletters devoted to the exploration of ethical issues that concern business managers; conferences and seminars on the subject are common; and a new category of manager has come on the scene, the ethics officer. One firm in three has named someone to this position, and one in five has a department set up to monitor ethical performance and provide training in ethical behavior.

Those constructing the new organization are going to have to understand what is involved in ethical governance, the benefits it provides, and how it can be woven into the organization if they are going to succeed.

WHAT IS ETHICAL GOVERNANCE?

Ethical governance involves creating an understanding of the moral and legal obligations and duties, principles of conduct, and values that are expected to guide individual and professional behavior. Creating this understanding—and ensuring that these principles and values are interpreted consistently—involves both the setting of examples and the spelling out of boundaries that help people make ethical decisions when confronted with ethical dilemmas. Ronald Sims of the College of William and Mary points out that the challenge is especially difficult "because standards for what constitutes ethical behavior lie in a 'grey zone' where clear-cut right-versus-wrong answers may not always exist."[7]

Part of the problem in dealing with ethics is the lack of a specific definition. For example, Richard C. Bartlett, vice chairman of the Mary Kay Corporation, divides ethics into virtue ethics and obligation ethics, explaining that "virtue ethics is a group of enduring universal values like honesty, caring, respect, loyalty, and fairness. Obligation ethics consists of the rules of ethical behavior, laws and canons that we humans have devised over the centuries. Rules and laws come from without, and are applied to us from outside ourselves."[8] John Drummond, coauthor of *Good Business*, a handbook on corporate ethics, says "practical ethics means taking decisions based on the shared interests of all stakeholders in a company—employees, customers, shareholders, and the community."[9] In *Framebreak: The Radical Redesign of American Business*, Ian Mitroff, Richard Mason, and Christine Pearson describe the organization based on ethical management as one that is "in the service of humanity" and one that has a "fundamental moral and ethical responsibility to treat employees as whole human beings . . . to make quality products and deliver quality services . . . to get their products and services to all who are in ethical need of them . . . to control technology in the service of the social and environmental good . . . to aid and serve future generations."[10]

Ethics are basically a compilation of those common beliefs, such as the Golden Rule, the Ten Commandments and other religious precepts, the moral codes taught us by our parents, our religious institutions, our schools, that govern the actions of the majority of citizens. Violating these guidelines usually makes us uncomfortable. In organizations, ethical governance is built upon a combination of the level of compliance with legal rules, the ethical beliefs of leaders, and institutional history.

When an organization does not have a positive, clearly communicated ethical climate, the response to ethical dilemmas is often unethical behavior. To correct for this lack, government laws and regulations have been put in place covering many areas where violations frequently occur. Companies that want to avoid penalties, therefore, "are rushing to implement compliance-based ethics programs. Designed by corporate counsel, the goal of these programs is to prevent, detect, and punish legal violations. But organizational ethics," Lynn Sharp Paine of the Harvard Business School goes on to say, "means more than avoiding illegal practice, and providing employees with a rule book will do little to address the problems underlying unlawful conduct."[11]

Organizations must understand that their actions in terms of compliance help form their employees' conceptions of acceptable ethical behavior. When organizations put in place rules that go beyond the demands of compliance, they are sending a strong message to their employees. (It is unimportant what the motive for that behavior is, although there are ethicists who would say that if they are doing so in order to prevent even stricter compliance standards from being enacted, there is little virtue in what they are doing.) Organizations that choose to do no more than meet minimal compliance standards are also sending a message about their ethical expectations. And, of course, organizations that then violate such standards, often rewarding employees for such behavior by promotions, send a clear signal to others in the organization that misbehavior in the organization's short-term, bottom-line interest will be tolerated.

Companies that encourage a "get away with what you can" behavior in one area end up with employees who have low ethical standards and cannot be counted upon to behave with higher standards when it comes to their behavior toward the organization itself. When employees with high ethical standards find themselves working for organizations with low ones, they do not give up their own standards. In a weak job market, when they cannot find another position, they keep quiet about their beliefs but do not violate them; they accept career stagnation rather than act dishonorably, waiting for the moment they can get out. There are also those who, after staying quiet for a time, find themselves so dismayed by what is happening that their sense of ethics finally pushes them to "blow the whistle." The whistleblowers are those whose internal pressures overcome their fears, who take actions that allow them to once more live with themselves.

The point that organizations must keep in mind is that most people have a strong sense of ethics and want to succeed while maintaining those values. Therefore, they will choose to work for and with organizations that have a reputation for ethical behavior. Since the flexible organization will be seeking to attract the best workers and alliances when they need them, it is in every organization's interest to build a reputation that will attract such workers.

According to a report by the Woodstock Theological Center's Seminar on Business Ethics, becoming an organization with a culture of trust depends on the ability to maintain an ethical climate:

> It is both the setting in which all the multiple large and small transactions of the groups and individuals involved in the firm take place

and the net effect of those transactions. The explicit rules and implicit understandings that govern all those transactions are built on precedent, constantly evolving, fluid, flexible, living, repetitious, and organic. So, an ethical climate is either developing or deteriorating, enriching itself or impoverishing itself.[12]

If we are right about the shape that organizations must adopt to survive and grow in the future, and the fact that trust must be a fractal permeating such organizations, then the question becomes one of finding ways to ensure that ethical governance is the organizational norm.

THE BENEFITS OF TRUST AS A FRACTAL IN THE NEW ORGANIZATION

Why should the new organization focus on ethics and trust? First, the new organization must be able to contract and expand in size rapidly. To do so, it must have a reputation for fair dealing that will enable it to expand its workforce when it needs it. Second, it must have the ability to launch new products and services, even outside those usually associated with the organization. To do so, it has to have a reputation as a provider of quality and customer satisfaction. Third, the new organization must be able to band together with other organizations in a seamless fashion, which requires establishing connectivity between members of the organization and others with whom it must deal across halls, streets, states, and nations, at times even allowing others to become a virtual part of the organization with open communication between all parties. To do so, the organization must have a reputation for integrity that will allow others to trust it and that will attract partners with similar reputations.

THE FIRST BENEFIT: THE ABILITY TO EXPAND AND CONTRACT

Work will get done in the new organization through some combination of a small permanent workforce, supplemented by what we call affinity workers—contract, part-time, and temporary workers—and by alliances with other organizations that will be responsible for doing specific tasks or the work of certain functional areas. This set of arrangements will enable the new organization to expand or contract painlessly—and if done in the right way, will be as painless for employees as employers. What it will take is developing a new work pact, or social contract.

RIGHTSIZING THE WORKFORCE. The work arrangements of the future represent an enormous shift in what Americans think of as the social contract between employer and employee. In the Industrial Age, employees devoted themselves to organizations for long periods of time in return for security, seniority, and benefits. This comprised an implied social contract that held the fabric of organizational life together. Unfortunately, the ability of companies to maintain their side of the social contract depended on their success. And so, over the past decade, as businesses found themselves in a new environment, fighting to survive, those companies that took great pride in their ability to provide lifetime employment began to do the unthinkable, downsizing and then downsizing again, often flattening their organizational structures to ensure the greatest savings. Organizations replaced chief executive officers, seeking turnaround artists to stem their losses. In their rush to survive, desperate companies discovered that cutting the workforce increases profits, and turned to it repeatedly as a means to present a stronger financial picture.

In devising the new relationships, employers must remember how painful these actions have been for those with white-collar, managerial positions with companies such as IBM and Xerox who had achieved a comfortable level of success that they thought was permanent. As part of companies that had developed cultures that encouraged the belief that every employee was a member of a corporate family—and once a member, always a member—they are now among the disinherited.

Of course, this belief was, for most Americans, a kindly myth. There was, in the best of times, a group with far fewer skills who faced periods of unemployment throughout their working lives. For these workers, permanent lifetime employment was never a reality. Instead, they eked out a living, managing from paycheck to paycheck, settling for a day's pay for a day's work. Today, however, even that limited contract is disappearing as technology makes unskilled labor less and less essential, making many of those laborers part of a permanent underclass—a fact that will have an effect upon employers. The demographics of our nation, particularly the coming retirement of the baby-boom generation, will make for shortages of skilled labor that this underclass may have to fill.

How can they be educated and made a part of the workforce—a development that would, by the way, have the advantage of lowering taxes, as they no longer needed food stamps, Medicaid, and welfare. (This is, however, a leadership, not governance, issue and will be discussed in Part IV.)

What is clear is that the new organization will have to find ways to replace the implied social contract with a new contract that makes clear from the outset that the only guarantee is employment, with some assistance for education or training, that will ensure employability when the current employment is terminated. It may be the only way to again inspire people to give of themselves, to feel a loyalty to the organizations for which they work, even if this work is only part time or for short periods.

SETTING THE CONDITIONS. The workforce of the new organization will have a number of tiers. There will be a group of core employees who have general leadership and administrative competencies that are needed to run the corporation and people who embody the skill sets that are key differentiators of the organization's core competencies—say, skills in design or marketing or manufacturing processes. In addition, embedded in that core will be people who can quickly train others in any specialized skills needed by the organization. This core group also is the repository of the institutional history of the organization and the carrier of its values.

The core group will be responsible for finding, hiring, and directing the next tiers of workers when they are needed—long-term contract workers, temporary noncontract workers, and part-time workers (including workers who are on premise, those who work in temporary sites, and those who work off site or from home). The core employees will also be responsible for paring down the expanded workforce when necessary. There is a caveat here; as the butterfly organization adapts and changes strategies, today's core skills may become obsolete. If, for example, a company in the transportation business becomes a logistics company, the skills needed at the core can change. This means that even those who constitute the "core" group must be learning—indeed, the importance of retaining the keepers of the institutional history might force butterfly organizations to insist on constant education for core employees. For many, this very real benefit may often feel like a chore.

The need to assemble an additional workforce can pose many difficulties. For example, as more and more organizations adapt this expansion and contraction process, competition for very skilled employees, especially in new technologies, will pick up. When competition becomes intense, the organization's ability to attract workers it needs for short-term or part-time assignments or for shifts at difficult hours will depend on its reputation for fair dealing as well as the terms of the formal arrangements and contracts it develops to manage these relationships. The better an organization's general reputation, the more that potential employees respect it and want to be associated with it, the easier it will be to attract those employees who are most in demand.

Employees, aware that they will need to constantly upgrade their skills and that the only job security lies in being the best trained, most productive, adaptable employee available, will seek employment with those organizations that offer educational opportunities, whether in the form of in-house training or by financing advanced training in colleges and vocational settings. They will also be looking for outplacement arrangements and health-care coverage as well as pension funds that are portable; these will be built into contracts as the competition for a given employee increases.

The issues that arise with portfolio employment—that is, people with specialized skills who work for different companies during the course of any given week to obtain a full week's employment— also have to be addressed. These were not issues when temporary or part-time workers were low-skilled individuals hired to do clerical tasks or manual labor. Today, the temporary worker may be a lawyer hired to work on a large case for several months, or an accountant asked to crunch some numbers related to a prospectus for taking a company public. How can confidentiality be maintained in these situations? What must employers do to protect competitive information and proprietary knowledge when employees work for multiple organizations? What rules have to be put in place? How much will an organization's own ethical values shape these people's behavior? How can you communicate these values to people who aren't on premises very much?

The answers to most of these questions will lie in constructing contracts that spell out obligations on both sides. Temporary and part-time workers will have to accept certain rules and standards of behavior—for example, adhering to rules of confidentiality that can protect the various organizations with which they work—that will have to be clearly spelled out and balanced by what they receive in return.

Trust is the key. People will choose to work for organizations they trust to do the right thing. An article in *Employment Relations Today* argues that this kind of "employee trust is built on concrete acts of good faith, continuity, and consistency in leadership's words, actions, and commitment to fair employment security practices." The article lists among those actions "continuing company commitments to (re)training; access to relevant performance information; clear performance objectives and standards; and useful involvement in supervisory and managerial planning and decisionmaking."[13] Together, these rules will serve as boundaries for keeping the organization intact, enabling it to swing only so far before moving back around the central core that gives it what shape it has—that keeps it from veering off into chaos.

UNDERSTANDING THE NEW REALITY. Employers are already exploring the issue of the social contract between employee and employer. One example is what happened when Central and South West Corporation (CSW), a major public utility holding company in the Southwest, recently restructured in the face of deregulation. As they explored the issues involved in changing the organization to increase its ability to function in a competitive environment, they realized that they would have to streamline the organization and acquire people with new skills—not just now, but again and again in the future.

E. Richard "Dick" Brooks,[14] chairman of the board, president, and chief executive officer of CSW, said that when contemplating a reorganization that would mean reducing their workforce they had to face up to the implications of the fact that many people who came to work for a utility believed they had made certain trade-offs in return for job security. Brooks said that the retrenchment had "broken an unwritten pact—full lifetime employment." He explained that before they took this action, management spent a great deal of time working out a severance arrangement. Looking back at the decisionmaking process, he added that his employees "were responsible for our success, how could we just let them go?"

Brooks and his four direct reports (who constitute a management team, each of whom has major responsibility for operational

areas of the business) set up an employee task force to make recommendations on how the reorganization should be handled.
Management accepted almost every recommendation made by the
task force. Moreover, the task force's involvement helped bring
acceptance of the decisions among those who remained: it wasn't
just those in charge—those who had the large salaries, who didn't
understand "real life"—who had made the decisions.

The result was a $100 million package that involved early retire-
ment, a continuation of benefits, up to eighteen months of financing for retraining for those who were not of retirement age, and a
reduction of some 1,100 employees, about 12 percent of the workforce. (While there was a bottom-line effect on share price, the
company was able to maintain its record of unbroken dividend
increases for forty-three years.) The goal behind their decision was
to be able to say that they were establishing a new pact, one based
on fair treatment but not lifetime employment. It was a way of
sending the message that the company was still a good place to
work. Indeed, even after the event, when a CSW employee won
over $19 million as his share of the Texas lottery, he explained to
reporters that he wasn't going to quit: "Work is a priority in my life,
and CSW is like my family."

CSW's leadership devotes a great deal of thought and energy to
ethical governance. One result is this decision to develop a new
social contract with employees. They believe that this decision,
which includes a determination to stress enhanced education and
training, will make it possible for them to make the many shifts in
direction that may be necessary in the future.

ADDITIONAL FORMS OF RELATIONSHIPS. The second route to flexible
size is to form relationships with other organizations. Some will be
pure contractual relationships: for example, "we would like you to
manufacture this kind of widget for us for the next two years and
we will buy all you can make for this set price." Others will be far
more flexible: for example, "we want to achieve a greater market
presence as we expand, but we can't guarantee that we will expand
at any given rate or for how long we will be in the expansion mode,
but we'd like to buy a minimum of marketing services during that
period and will provide some warning before curtailing the effort."
The forms these relationships take, which will be explored in Chapter
9, are not what is important here; what is important is the role of ethical governance in an organization's ability to set them up.

The more these arrangements are relationship driven instead of contractual, the more necessary they are as speed becomes critical—the more important reputation becomes to the ability to establish them in a timely fashion. The less investigation, the less negotiation and legal hassles, the faster the start up, the greater the gains. If you have an idea for a new service, you will not have many months to take advantage of its being new. Now that new product introductions can take weeks instead of months, the ability to aggregate resources is critical—and that is likely to become truer with each passing day.

The more an organization is known for integrity, honesty, loyalty, the more attractive it will be to others with similar reputations. When the organizations with the strongest reputations come together, they will find it easier to structure loose relationships quickly. In these instances, trust is a result not only of image in the marketplace but also of reputation as conveyed through personal networks. Organizations with leaders who are known for their integrity will be able to shift to the butterfly form most easily. Indeed, the first general moves in this direction are to be found in the growth of what are being described as virtual organizations, increased strategic alliances, and various outsourcing arrangements.

THE SECOND BENEFIT: GROWING IN NEW DIRECTIONS

The new organization is going to be constantly moving in new directions, investing in the manufacture of new products, or developing new services in response to changes in the world. To remain a butterfly organization, it must strive to avoid the acquisition of numerous plants to manage and equipment to amortize, the growth of large marketing and sales divisions responsible for numerous different kinds of products, hiring thousands of employees to work on new product lines. To remain flexible, it must find ways to do new things without adding burdens for the future that will be costly to shed. Inventiveness is going to be the mother of success in the future.

Most of the time, these changes will be handled by acquiring companies, setting up subsidiaries, and forming joint ventures with other organizations in order to avoid expanding the core organization into a massive bureaucracy with numerous reporting layers. The ease with which partners for these ventures can be found, the willingness of people within the core organization to go off and become part of a new subsidiary, and the ability to attract the funding needed to enable some of these decisions will be dependent on reputation. Is the organization trustworthy? If I go off and set up a subsidiary and it doesn't work out well, what can I expect? Who do I want to partner with? How can I attract a partner I can trust?

The value of reputation is clear: the reputation of American Airlines' computer reservations system allowed it to set up a subsidiary that provides technology consulting; Peoples Natural Gas in Omaha had a reputation for well-mannered, knowledgeable service representatives that allowed it to successfully set up an appliance repair service; Caterpillar successfully established Caterpillar Logistics based on its reputation for being able to ship its own equipment around the world quickly. These companies had a history of living up to their promises; they provided quality; they were considered "good" companies. Their reputations laid the groundwork for successful expansion into new areas.

THE THIRD BENEFIT: ESTABLISHING CONNECTIVITY

Many of the arrangements made to move into new areas will involve sharing information electronically, which often means allowing others access to systems that contain confidential information, which in turn raises the issue of trust. The same issue arises in terms of employees who rely on the organization's technology for the performance of their jobs. Rules of ethical governance, clear explanations of expectations, and a sense of fairness and trust will be critical to the ability to establish these connections which serve as pathways linking the butterfly organization together.

As more and more people work together over networks, building trust is presenting a whole new set of issues. Some people are finding that they feel very comfortable working with individuals they have never met; they trust them to behave properly until they prove themselves to be untrustworthy. They tend, however, to be employees who have spent a great deal of personal time on the Internet or with on-line services communicating and establishing friendships electronically—and they still represent a minority of employees. For most, it is extremely difficult to trust someone they have never spent time with, cannot make eye contact with, have never "gotten to know." As a result, building business networks that are electronic instead of personal presents problems that have to be explored and resolved just when organizations are placing greater reliance on these communications technologies as a routine way of conducting business.

ESTABLISHING AN ETHICAL CULTURE

The first step in building the ethical culture that lies at the heart of the new organization is to establish a baseline. The starting point is compliance. Senior management must assess the rules that affect the organization—rules about health and safety mandated by OSHA; legislation and legal precedent governing discrimination of all sorts such as the Americans With Disabilities Act; professional codes of conduct that may apply to employees such as those governing underwriters; legal precedents such as the rules governing insider trading; environmental regulations such as those governing dumping or emissions; state and local worker protection laws. Then, leaders of the organization must make such rules known: "Under the 1991 U.S. Criminal Sentencing Guidelines, a corporation found guilty of wrongdoing may be subject to tenfold penalties unless it can demonstrate a host of specific measures directed at compliance."[15] And they must make clear that violations of these rules and regulations will not be tolerated. That is the baseline.

Creating understanding of the minimum standards, making certain that people know that violations will not be tolerated, presents difficulties even at baseline levels. For example, how does an organization deal with issues such as age discrimination in hiring? What does an organization have to do in addition to making a statement that such discrimination won't be tolerated and sending out information about the value of older workers? In other words, what does it take to raise the bar? When an organization is intent on ethical governance of the highest order, it must devote a great deal of time and attention to the issue.

Creating an ethics program that merely addresses requirements and rules is not enough. It is important that issues usually thought of as "intangibles" also be addressed. These intangibles are humanistic values based on conscience and personal ethical norms. In evaluating the ethics program put in place at General Dynamics, Richard Barker found that there was confusion about the goals of the program, which was designed to build "trust between the company and its customers, suppliers, employees, shareholders, and the communities in which the company functions." The program included a hotline that was devised to allow employees to express problems and receive advice about questionable behaviors. The designers of the program wanted to ensure that "employees understood the rules of the game regarding proper personal and business conduct" and that lines of communication were open for discussion of issues in this area.

Although the program did bring results, there were negative responses. Some employees felt that the very existence of such a program impugned their own ethical standards. Others felt it was a waste of time because they had no decisionmaking power. Others felt that the emphasis on reporting unethical behavior was a problem, disliking the idea of "snitching" on fellow employees. In the formal evaluation, General Dynamics concluded that "many questions that escalate into issues of ethics would arise less often if common civil virtues like trustworthiness, loyalty . . . and respect were practiced regularly."[16]

Indeed, a survey of actuaries who are accredited as Fellows of the Society of Actuaries indicated that their "own personal moral values and standards were of the most help in making ethical decisions." But they added that "the fact that their immediate boss does not pressure them into compromising their ethical standards" and that they were working in a "company environment/culture" that does not encourage them to compromise their "ethical values to achieve organizational goals" were extremely important to their ability to act in accordance with their values.[17] That raises the question of how an organization can ensure that such consistent ethical standards become the ethical culture of the organization.

MAKING IT HAPPEN

Organizations can do a number of things to ensure that ethical governance is the organizational norm. They can emphasize their credos, put in place codes of ethics and ethics officers, establish ongoing education and training programs clearly backed by management, redefine rules for compensation to include ethics in performance assessments, put in place procedures for dealing with violations, and perhaps most important, make it clear that management has an involvement in and commitment to ethical behavior.

Such things are necessary not because people need to be told what is ethical, but because they need to understand the complexities involved in ethical decisionmaking in a business environment in which ethical decisionmaking is seldom a black-and-white issue. It can take weighing and balancing a number of competing ethical concerns. They also need the assurance that their company will back them in their efforts—and desire—to act ethically.

For example, when Levi Strauss decided that it had no choice but to move an operation abroad because it could not continue to price its product competitively unless it did so, a number of ethical issues had to be confronted. The strategic decision to relocate some of its manufacturing abroad was made to ensure survival. It meant, however, abandoning a portion of its American workforce. In making the decision, the "greatest good" principle prevailed. The company decided that its survival ensured far more jobs for Americans than the 1,100 lost by the move.

After the move, however, the company stepped on another ethical landmine. It discovered that some of its foreign suppliers hired child labor. In one case in Bangladesh, the "contractors admitted . . . that they hired children and agreed to fire them." But the contractors also made the point that many of these children's incomes were the key to their families' survival. After evaluating the situation, Levi Strauss reached a compromise, paying for schooling for the children as well as their wages until they were of legal age, at which time they would return to work full time for the contractor. The costs were not huge, and Robert Haas, the president of the company noted, "such actions pay dividends in terms of brand image and corporate reputation."[18] Although, as mentioned earlier, there are ethicists who would call this a utilitarian approach and therefore not an ethical decision, actions taken for mixed motives that do no harm and much good are a fact of business life and not grounds for condemnation.

STARTING POINTS

An organization's credo and management's ethical leadership are important for the reputation of the organization, but they are not enough to ensure the internal strength that is needed to keep the butterfly organization from veering off course, to help it to adapt to constant change. It often takes considerable education, training, and the establishment of policies concerning violations and formal

mechanisms to enhance understanding and build an ethical corporate culture. In order to determine exactly what to put in place,
it is necessary that each organization do an "ethical audit."

CREDOS. The organization's credo, which conveys a company's ethical values and its mission to those outside the organization, is the
most visible statement of the organization's beliefs. If employees
believe that management takes the credo seriously, it can inspire
employee pride and a desire to live up to the values it espouses. In
the case of Johnson & Johnson, walking into its New Brunswick,
New Jersey, headquarters immediately lets you know how seriously the organization takes its statement. It is carved into a gran-
ite block that sits imposingly in the reception area that all
visitors—and all new employees—pass through.

Resembling nothing so much as our collective image (from art and
motion pictures) of the tablets on which the Ten Commandments
were carved, it is impossible to ignore, and although it is long, it is
almost impossible not to read, containing such statements as: "We
believe our first responsibility is to . . . all . . . who use our products and services. . . . We are responsible to the communities in
which we live and work and to the world community as well. We
must be good citizens." Of course, the strength of the image is
enhanced by the way Johnson & Johnson handled the discovery in
Chicago that its over-the-counter medication Tylenol had caused a
few deaths due to tampering: it immediately withdrew the drug
from the marketplace nationwide, issuing its own warnings through
the media, at a cost of over $100 million.

WALKING THE TALK. Given that ethical governance is a managerial
responsibility, reinforcing the beliefs expressed in the credo is the
job of the organization's leaders. Those leaders who are most effective at transmitting their values and beliefs are not embarrassed to
speak out on what many call soft or "new-age" beliefs.

Although there has been a change over the past dozen years as
more and more business leaders have come out in favor of social
and environmental concerns, the distance yet to be traveled is evident in the fact that many of these leaders attract media attention
for what is clearly still unusual behavior. *Fortune, Business Week,
Inc.,* the *New York Times,* the *Wall Street Journal* try to understand
the personalities behind and analyze the costs to their businesses of

the social consciousness of a Robert Haas (Levi Strauss), an Anita Roddick (Body Shop), a Ben Cohen and Jerry Greenfield (Ben & Jerry's), or a Gun Denhart (Hanna Andersson). The rationale behind this coverage is that these firms are still considered unusual; in all too many organizations, the first step to ethical governance must be "to break the custom of silence to make possible the assertion of ethical concern."[19]

There are organizations whose leaders' strong values have precluded their maintaining the "custom of silence." They are not involved in the kind of "change-the-world approach" of a Roddick, but they do deliver clear and consistent messages to their employees about the behavior expected of them as representatives of their organizations and of citizens of their communities and the world. Dick Brooks, mentioned earlier, says that he tells his employees that they can't go wrong if they ask themselves the following series of questions when facing an ethical dilemma:

"Would I want what I am doing to be done to me?"

"How would I feel if what I am doing appeared in the newspaper?"

"Would I want my spouse and my kids to know what I am doing?

He added, "It really boils down to, if it doesn't smell right, it probably isn't right, so don't do it."

He conveys this message to his employees in his speeches and through corporate communications vehicles. It is what he believes, and when he says it, it is clear that it is what he believes. It sets the tone for the ethical governance that is a hallmark of CSW. And his organization thrives in that climate.

CONCLUSION

The role of ethical governance in the transition to a flexible organizational form—to becoming a complex adaptive system—is clear. It is also clear that the responsibility for ensuring that an organization is governed ethically lies in the hands of those at the top of the organization. From stakeholders (such as large pension funds that offer their investors the choice of "social funds" that are comprised of the stocks of organizations that, for example, show respect for the environment) to members of the board (who today often set up social responsibility committees) to leaders (who inspire their organizations with the vision of a future in which "good business policies will be found to be good social policies"),[20] decisions are being made in the belief that doing the right thing is the way of the future. The message is unmistakable: Ethical governance is the first step to good corporate governance.

5

ENHANCING THE ROLE OF THE BOARD

Corporations are not simply bundles of physical assets, they are legal structures whose role is to govern the relationships among all the parties that make special investments in the wealth-creating activities of the firm.

Margaret Blair[1]

Sitting on top of the management of the company, working within a framework of laws, regulations, and judicial decisions, is the board of directors. The way members play their roles—accepting and delegating responsibility, accountability, and authority for the organization's success—influences the way the organization is led and controlled at the very highest level. The members of the board are often called on to serve as arbiters when the goals of the owners of the business (its shareholders) and those who control it (senior management) come into conflict.

The primary responsibility of the members of the board to shareholders involves the creation of wealth. They are responsible for seeing to it that the actions of management, especially the chief executive officer (CEO), increase the value of the company's stock. Today, when the board fails to meet this demand, large institutional investors will try to force action. Indeed, the California Public Employees Retirement System (CALPERS) holds special

meetings with the boards of directors of companies that are not performing well to demand that they take action, such as the removal
of the chief executive officer. At the same time that board members
are pushing for immediate results, however, they are also responsible for the long-term survival of the company, which may at
times call for actions that will, in fact, adversely affect short-term
profitability. This particular balancing act becomes more difficult
as organizations become increasingly flexible and adaptable, often
expending huge amounts to make changes that will pay dividends
only in the long term.

Described in this way, board membership leaves something to be
desired. There are rewards, financial and psychic, but there also are
dangers, financial and to one's reputation. Moreover, as an organization begins to function as a complex adaptive system—that is,
as it becomes ever more flexible, changing size and what it does for
a living—its board is going to have to accept the need to change or
augment its own composition to ensure that as a body it has the
knowledge and experience needed to understand what is happening outside and what kinds of changes will be needed inside to
respond.

The board will have to alert management to those events and see
to it that management's responses are appropriate, especially when
the appropriate responses may involve a loss of control. It will
have to spend more time communicating to shareholders the need
for and the costs and benefits of the resultant changes in direction. And it will have to support and enhance the development of
ethical governance, which is, as seen in the last chapter, critical to
the organization's future.

Although the board needs to play a larger and somewhat different role in the new organization, it is important that it not cross
the line to management. It is not, for example, up to the board to
reformulate the strategy of the enterprise but rather to expand the
thinking and, ultimately, the vision of senior management, thus
ensuring that senior management has the information necessary to
drive strategy in the right direction. The board should aim at focusing senior management's concerns on what the organization should
do, rather than what it knows how to do. The board should aim
at providing senior management with a multifaceted understanding of the world beyond the present competitive environment. The
board must open senior management to an understanding of the

constantly changing external world, and it must itself respond to those changes, often by shifts in membership that will bring in expertise when and as needed. The board, too, must become a butterfly.

THE DEVELOPMENT OF BOARDS

Although most organizations begin as personal endeavors by single individuals or small groups, as they grow in size, a major change takes place, as described in Adolf A. Berle, Jr., and Gardiner Means's landmark 1933 study of the corporation:

> The typical business unit of the 19th century was owned by individuals or small groups; was managed by them or their appointees; and was, in the main, limited in size by the personal wealth of the individuals in control. These units have been supplanted in ever greater measure by great aggregations in which tens and even hundreds of thousands of workers and property worth hundreds of millions of dollars [in 1933 dollars], belonging to tens or even hundreds of thousands of individuals, are combined through the corporate mechanism into a single producing organization under unified control and management.[2]

When this change from individual control takes place, management becomes the responsibility of overseers—a board of directors and the senior management of the enterprise. In theory and law, the board's job is to protect the shareholders' property and oversee management. The contradiction here is that while "the cornerstone of US corporate democracy is the shareholders' right to elect the board, . . . this usually amounts to ratifying the board's nominations (which the chief executive officer will have played an important part in formulating)."[3]

The controls on management stem from Securities and Exchange Commission regulations that impose "administrative rules on corporations designed to assure fair and timely elections for directors, as well as to make sure that the corporations disclosed all pertinent information to dissident shareholders,"[4] and from certain standards of conduct arising from legal precedent. In addition, there are external forces that impact, to varying degrees, corporate

governance. For example, the union representing automobile workers is affected by the costs of its members' health insurance: not only
must the union's officers bargain over the benefit levels with their
members' employees to ensure the satisfaction of their members
with union management, they must pay the benefits when union
members are periodically laid off. Since they are so involved in the
issue of the costs and coverage of medical benefits, they have fought
for and won representation on the board of the major medical
insurer of those in the automobile industry—Blue Cross and Blue
Shield of Michigan. Alliance partners and major suppliers whose
futures are affected directly by the success of an organization also
are increasingly concerned about governance decisions and thus
seeking representation on boards.

Another set of players—though not board members—who have
an influence on boards, according to Edward S. Herman, are the
"various levels of government [that] tax, subsidize, restrict, and
control business, in some cases impinging directly on matters as
basic as pricing (rate regulation, informal interventions into price setting) and the direction of investment (zoning, required pollution
control devices, limits on acquisitions)."[5] Yet another force is the cit-
izenry, including public interest advocates and environmentalists,
who often manage to bring their voices into the boardroom through
acquisition of stock—and at times through board membership.

RESPONSIBILITY, ACCOUNTABILITY, AND AUTHORITY

Going back to the turn of the century, Ambrose Bierce defined the
corporation as "an ingenious device for obtaining individual profit
without individual responsibility."[6] Shareholders derive profit without assuming any duties; instead, they delegate those to a board. If
they do not like the way the board, as reflected by the company, is
performing, they can take action; instead, they tend to simply sell
their shares. Traditionally, only large stockholders and, recently,
large institutional investors have accepted responsibility of any
kind for the long-term future of the organizations in which they
invested. By law, shareholders have the authority to remove members
of the board if they believe that they are failing to act in their best
interests, but more often, they force the board to remove the CEO.
Indeed, as Leo Herzl and Richard Shepro point out, "Shareholders

and markets are much more interested in CEOs than directors."
They note that the CEO is usually the chairman of board meetings
and completely in charge. Moreover, the CEO generally controls
"both the agenda and the flow of information to the directors."[7]

Thus, although shareholders can replace board members and
boards can replace CEOs, the CEO has been considered the most
powerful player. However, the balance seems to be shifting.
Shareholders have become increasingly likely to demand that boards
deal with issues such as CEO compensation and tenure. Paul
Ingrassia noted in the *Wall Street Journal* that "after decades of
somnolence, boards finally woke up to confront inept, ossified
managements, challenging them either to change or depart. When
the dust had settled, the CEOs of General Motors, IBM, Kodak and
Westinghouse had lost their jobs. And a new activist era in corporate boardrooms, in which directors would hold senior executives
accountable for their performance, got under way."[8]

While such accountability, on the surface, often has merit, the
question of how the board can measure CEO performance poses
problems that will become more difficult in the context of the butterfly organization. If flexibility and agility—speed of action—are
key in the butterfly, what does a board do about a CEO whose
investment strategy for future growth hurts the bottom line at the
moment? The idea of maintaining a "reasonable" return on investment—sufficient profitability to bring competitive dividends and a
favorable bottom line each quarter—concurrent with long-term
investment in infrastructure and expansion may be incompatible.
Deciding on the proper balance between profitability and investment—and obtaining a consensus for that decision—will be an
even more critical board responsibility in the new organization,
especially when the organization is involved in more and more
temporary relationships with other organizations.

WHO SERVES—AND WHY?

The new organization is going to need a much more diversified
group of outside directors. Moreover, it will have to make frequent
and rapid changes in board membership in response to changes in
the strategic direction of the organization. If a domestic organization, for example, decides to expand into the international market,

a director with relevant experience can play an important role. Finding the right people to serve, with the help of board members, will therefore be an important part of the CEO's job in the new organization.

Finding the right board members requires a certain understanding of why people agree to serve on boards. Traditionally—and still overwhelmingly—the motivation is friendship with the CEO who asks them to join. For most board members, it also expands their range of contacts and provides opportunities for the exchange of information. Being a board member is considered prestigious; invitations to join boards are made when people have achieved a certain degree of success and recognition for expertise in the world outside. Many have something important to contribute to the organization. Some bring an awareness of social or environmental issues. Investors, suppliers, or business and alliance partners may bring a perspective that ensures that their interests are being represented. Minorities and women promote diversification by serving as reminders to the company to admit more of their race or gender into important positions.

For many, there is also a financial component. Board members of large corporations can receive as much as $50,000 for their service, as well as stock options. The latter reward is favored by many who believe that members need to be actively involved in overseeing the health of organizations on whose boards they serve. Warren Buffett of Berkshire Hathaway says that a "good director is one who has a meaningful financial stake in the venture. . . . There is nothing that makes a director think like a shareholder [more than] being a shareholder."[9]

The rewards, however, must be weighed against risks. After all, for someone who decides to serve on a board to gain recognition, there is danger that the organization may perform so poorly that it is the victim of a takeover, making the board members look bad for presiding over a failing company. According to Eugene Fama and Michael Jensen: "There is substantial devaluation of [the involved directors'] human capital when internal decision control breaks down and the costly last resort process of an outside takeover is activated."[10] And serving on a board that does not stop malfeasance, which seems to have been the case at United Way when its president William Aramony spent the charity's funds on personal luxuries, tarnishes the image of those who serve.

There are financial risks as well. While most organizations carry directors' liability insurance, insurance does not prevent board members from countless hours spent in giving depositions and making court appearances. Moreover, as many who joined boards have discovered, there is often little one can do to really challenge management decisions that can lead to legal problems. Robert Monks and Nell Minow point out in their examination of the issue of board accountability that "directors are not picked for their ability to challenge management." Even when they are, success is not guaranteed. Ross Perot "was brought to the General Motors board just to bring the skills and experience that had made his company, EDS, so successful. When he tried to give the board the benefit of that skill and experience, CEO Roger Smith paid Perot $742.8 million" to get him off the board—over $6 more a share than the stock was worth on the day of the trade.[11]

The development of a more flexible organization, however, will require the CEO to adapt to a less autocratic relationship with the board than has historically been the norm. The CEO is going to have to go outside the usual circle to find members, in part to broaden the knowledge base contained on the board and in part to ensure that the board is more likely to challenge senior management's assumptions. Shareholders, in turn, are going to have to be sure that the CEO accepts the need for a board that acts more like an owner than a mere investor.

MAKING THE NEW BOARD WORK

As an organization becomes more complex—multinational, involving more or different lines of business, new partners and new alliances—the board needs to spend more and more time helping set strategic directions, overseeing fiduciary matters, reviewing executive compensation, and addressing social and environmental issues, all while considering the return to investors. This is a full-time agenda, but board membership is not a full-time occupation. Committees are therefore set up to provide advice and counsel in special areas, and to report to and gain general board approval for their recommendations. They also serve to ensure independent judgment when it is important; for example, the compensation committee is usually made up of outside directors.

Organizations that are changing rapidly to remain competitive need to review the structure and composition of their board committees to ensure that they are prepared to provide the oversight and advice needed as they continue to evolve.

THE AUDIT COMMITTEE

Jonathan Charkham, in his comprehensive study of corporate governance in five different countries, addresses the need for and responsibility of audit committees. He says that these committees became prevalent in the United States in the 1970s in response to financial abuses, adding that the Securities and Exchange Commission (SEC) made them "a listing condition in 1978 and stipulated that they should be a composed of outside directors (thereby changing the shape of American boards)."[12] Today, almost every organization has an audit committee.

In 1992, as part of the wave of concern about corporate governance, the Committee on the Financial Aspects of Corporate Governance (the Cadbury Committee of the United Kingdom) issued a report that laid out two main principles: managers "must be free to drive their companies forward but exercise that freedom within a framework of effective accountability." Moreover, that accountability must be to outside directors who "should bring an independent judgement to bear on issues of strategy, performance, resources, including key appointments, and standards of conduct."[13]

Proliferating globalization and alliances, acquisitions, and mergers across international borders will increase the role and responsibility of financial oversight committees. A study project by Price Waterhouse commissioned by the Institute for Internal Auditors highlighted the issues that audit committees will face:

• International operations, which will require an understanding not only of foreign currency transactions, but will be complicated by the current lack of generally accepted international accounting principles

• Joint ventures and partnerships, which will require oversight

• Environmental liabilities and exposures, which require preventive and remedial actions, as well as involve penalties

- Improved monitoring of management estimates, particularly those that result from restructuring and recurring items such as retirement benefits

- Expanded involvement with computer-related controls, given the security issues that rise from the extensive use of networks across loosely organized relationships

- More involvement with and reporting on internal controls, an issue that is increasingly coming under public, and SEC, scrutiny, and

- More attention to interim reports before they are filed with authorities to ensure compliance with laws and regulations.[14]

Clearly, these issues are all tied to the changes already taking place in organizations today as they are migrating to the new organizational form of the future. If audit committees move in the direction suggested by the Price Waterhouse study, they will be better prepared to deal with such problems as the costs of managing the constantly expanding and decreasing workforce and the financial oversight involved in working within different alliance structures that will inevitably arise in the butterfly organization.

THE NOMINATING COMMITTEE

As the number of outside directors on boards has increased, so has the number of nominating committees; by 1989, 49 percent of boards had nominating committees, up from 7 percent in 1972.[15] The job of the nominating committee is to review potential new members suggested by the chairman of the board (who is often also the CEO) and on occasion to present its own recommendations. The nominating committee, usually composed of outside directors, tries to evaluate the need of the board for a broad spectrum of expertise and multicultural representation, develop profiles of the ideal candidates, and then evaluate candidates to determine whether they fit the profile. Sometimes outside search groups (Spencer Stuart is perhaps the best known of the firms that specialize in headhunting at the board-member level) are asked to help.

The nominating committee also reviews the performance of current board members and helps bring about the removal of members who no longer perform well. Sometimes, the issue of an aging board becomes a problem, which usually leads the nominating committee to either set conditions of service—shorter terms, for example—or add members. The problem for the new organization will be how to add relevant expertise when necessary without increasing the size of the board to the point that it hampers decisionmaking. (For most companies, board size tends to range from ten to fifteen; larger in the government and nonprofit sectors.)

Another role played by the nominating committee involves the selection of a new CEO when the current one departs—unless there is a formal, board approved succession plan in place. The nominating committee depends on the board to set the criteria for the new CEO, then uses that information to conduct an initial search, often with the assistance of a search firm. In an organization that is striving to become more flexible, the implications of possible future directions and possible future governance models for the selection of the CEO (as well as board members) must be understood.

Indeed, if the organization is going to complete its metamorphosis, the role of the nominating committee will become increasingly important. It will have to focus on being prepared to add new members with broad expertise, often members with different kinds of experience and backgrounds (academics, heads of nonprofits) who will not quite fit into the current board culture. The committee will have to take a harder line on performance criteria for existing members; for example, if decisions have to be made quickly, availability must be a test of performance.

THE COMPENSATION COMMITTEE

The compensation committee is responsible for setting the compensation, including stock options, of senior management and executive directors, including the CEO. In recent years, shareholders have begun to call for caps on the earnings of directors, or at least a clear relationship between their remuneration and the financial success of the organization. These concerns grew vocal enough that the Securities and Exchange Commission set out rules in 1992 requiring reports from compensation committees, or for companies that had no such committees, the entire board, covering, "a discussion of the compensation policies for the executive officers, including the extent to which it is performance based; an explanation of the reasons for repricing the exercise price of options granted to named executive officers, if such options were repriced during the last year; and disclosure of the identity of the members of the compensation committee, identifying any members that are employees or officers of the company."[16]

Compensation is likely to become even more of an issue in the flexible organization of the future. When alliances are rapidly formed and dissolved to meet short-term market opportunities, and as shifts in products become a way of life, quarterly bottom lines may no longer be considered an indicator of yearly returns. Products and markets may come and go in a fiscal quarter; a linear extrapolation of the next quarter's revenues and profits may not be possible because last quarter's products and markets have been replaced with new ones. Under these conditions, new measures of performance and compensation will have to be developed to adequately reward the management of the enterprise for preparing the organization to meet future market conditions and economic cycles.

The responsibility for understanding these shifts in the new world of business and for developing a fair and appropriate set of performance measures will fall on the board in general, but on the compensation committee in particular. CEO compensation in the organization of the future may require a mixed approach, including cash bonuses for quarterly performance, stock options in lieu of increases when the bottom line is flat because of a necessary retrenchment in the face of an economic downturn, or a promised future increase plus stock options when value falls because of an expensive investment aimed at future growth. In all events, the compensation committee will be responsible for communicating these decisions and the reasons for them to both the shareholders and the executives.

THE PUBLIC POLICY COMMITTEE

Since the 1970s, companies have had to become more aware of the world beyond their immediate corporate horizon. The growth of the environmental movement and increasing attention to social concerns in society have driven this change. In addition, some large institutional investors, especially pension funds connected with educational and public-policy-oriented groups, are beginning to play a much more active role as shareholders. For example, the Teachers Insurance and Annuity Association–College Retirement Equity Fund (TIAA-CREF), the nation's largest pension system (over $125 billion in assets), issued a Policy Statement on Corporate Governance in October 1993, which called on corporations to take into account what it calls, "Social Responsibility Issues." Its statement expresses the belief that building long-term shareholder value is consistent with directors giving careful consideration to the common good of the community:

> The board should develop policies and practices to address the following issues:
>
> The environmental impact of the corporation's operations and products.
>
> Equal employment opportunities for all segments of our population.
>
> Open channels of communication permitting employees, customers, suppliers and the community to freely express their concerns.
>
> Effective employee training and development.
>
> Evaluation of corporate actions that can negatively affect the common good of the community and its residents.
>
> To prohibit deliberate and knowing exploitation of any of the non-shareholder constituencies.[17]

Murray Weidenbaum, former chairman of the Council of Economic Advisers, says that as a result of such pressures, today "about one out of five large companies have established public-policy committees on their boards. These committees give board level attention to company policies and performance on subjects of public concern. . . . [These committees deal with issues such as] affirmative and equal employment opportunity, employee health and safety, company impact on the environment, corporate political activities, consumer affairs, and ethics."[18]

This new emphasis on the corporation as citizen is likely to grow. Moreover, the results of actions taken by these committees are going to be important mechanisms for establishing an organization's reputation in terms of its ethical values, especially its social contract with its workforce. That reputation, as noted in the last chapter, is going to be a key to the ability to attract skilled workers in the future, when a new, flexible organization needs to expand to take advantage of economic opportunities.

GETTING WORD OUT

Because strategic and operational governance of the butterfly organization, which will be explored in the next chapter, will require rapid and coordinated decisionmaking, multiple channels of communication, from video conferencing to e-mail to faxes, will have to be established; these channels will involve the members of the board, and at times, shareholders, as well as the rest of the organization. For example, there will be times when a CEO seeking to take advantage of a unique opportunity will need quick approval for a greater investment of funds than he or she has authority to disburse without consultation. At times, the board (to avoid the anger that comes from surprises) will have to alert major shareholders to decisions that will adversely affect dividends in the next quarter but may bring major rewards over the next year.

Advanced communications technology, however, can be a two-edged sword: it can also be a mechanism for challenging decisions. Such challenges are already taking place. In the example below, where the organization made a decision that adversely affected current employees, a "rebellion" was mounted.

This case history is from a southwestern-based company, a sales-type organization that had been in business for over thirty years. It is a large employee-owned company (such as Avis and United Airlines), which is becoming more common, complicating shareholder, board, management, and employee relationships. With minor exceptions, the company had a consistent record of growth and profits until the recession of 1991. At the time of the "rebellion," the company's stock was not publicly traded, but was held by present and former employees who received shares as part of their compensation package. In anticipation of growth and the possibility of going public, the board had recently added three external members. The board had an audit committee and a compensation committee.

The CEO, who was a board member—but not chairman of the board—had worked his way up through the ranks and had successfully led the company through the recession, largely as a result of his autocratic, micromanagement leadership style, which worked well to sharpen skills and reduce costs while pursuing the current line of business. As the recession ended and profits rose, however, the company found itself in a position to move from a survival to a growth mode; it was ready to expand, perhaps going public to increase its opportunities to enter related fields, but the CEO seemed unable to switch gears. For example, although he had been encouraged by the board to look for new opportunities for growth, he continually presented the board with carefully constructed negative information about every possible option that was suggested. The board accepted what he told them because of assumption that he shared their goal of corporate growth. In fact, he was treating the board much as he did the company's employees—rejecting their advice out of hand. His actions conveyed his belief that the company was not a democracy: "I know what is best for the company."

The flaw in this logic was that since the "employees" were also the shareholders of the company, it *was* a democracy. Collectively, the employees could exert a lot of power. The problem came to a head just prior to an annual shareholder meeting. The CEO was proposing a number of resolutions for approval, including an increase in the number of shares outstanding in order to position the company for a public offering and issuing stock options to the CEO and the members of the board. These proposals were presented to the shareholders (employees) in the proxy statement. It quickly became apparent that the proposals (which had been agreed to by the board based on information provided by the CEO) were not well received by the employees. They felt that taking the company public would result in the "loss of their company"—that is, the loss of control that, although rarely exerted, was important to them as a concept. In addition, they felt that issuing options to the CEO was totally unacceptable given his increasingly disturbing management style.

As shareholders, the employees had the right to communicate with the board; as employees, there was no way to discuss their concerns with the board given the CEO's management style. Breaking down the wall between the behavior patterns normal to them as employees and the rights they knew they had as stockholders was psychologically difficult. But when friendly attempts to approach the CEO were rebuffed rather brutally, the employees' resentment grew.

The critical element in this story is that everyone in the company has access to e-mail. As their resentment grew, word rapidly spread among the more than fifty local offices (through an electronic daisy chain pattern) that made those who were unhappy realize that they were not alone. As the dissent grew, a few of the on-line voices began to assume responsibility for coordinating the information they were exchanging. These leaders formed an electronic committee and drew up a letter to the CEO and the board, expressing their concerns over the recommendations in the proxy. The letter—approved by hundreds of employees electronically—eventually triggered a dramatic change in the management and the board of the company.

At first, the CEO and some board members simply dismissed the letter, believing that it had been generated by a small group of dissidents; others believed that the employees probably had strong support or could get it before the meeting. The dilemma facing the board was that if the letter represented a majority view, the employees could replace the directors with their own candidates and ultimately fire the CEO. The board was concerned that too dramatic an overhaul of the governance structure could destroy the company. The decision at this point was to open a dialogue with the employees to discuss the issues prior to the vote. The board knew that this course of action would imply that it had little faith in the judgment of the CEO—a message it conveyed rather reluctantly, but out of a belief it had no other choice.

The minute word got out that the board was willing to discuss the issue, the electronic dam burst. Board members were flooded with calls, faxes, and e-mail correspondence at both their businesses and their homes. Later discussions revealed that a "core group" of employees had been chosen to arrange that each board member was contacted by numerous employees, selecting the best performers to make the contact. The notion was that if they lost the battle, these "contacters" were the individuals the CEO could least afford to fire. As the flood continued, the board and the CEO held a number of conference calls to discuss the issue. Eventually, the board had a very clear picture of the problems created by the CEO and his management style.

In an extremely difficult and emotional eight-hour emergency board meeting, which the directors decided to call a "compensation committee meeting" in order to exclude the CEO, options were discussed and evaluated. The members also discussed the fact that if they fired the CEO, the employees could get the impression that the board was weak and could be influenced any time a controversial or unpopular decision was made; yet if the board backed the CEO, the employees could use their personal and electronic network to organize the voting of shares to replace a number of the board members with the intent of taking over the board and firing the CEO. In the end, the board fired the CEO. At the annual meeting that followed, despite the board's actions, the shareholders voted to replace two members of the board.

This example raises numerous questions about the possible impacts of technology, especially communications technology, on power structures. It makes clear the need to govern empowerment by putting in place rules that continue to ensure that, on the one hand, concerns are raised and discussed and, on the other hand, continual real-time second guessing of decisions is avoided.

One way to control such behavior might be to institute guidelines for behavior, such as the twenty-eight-point set of board guidelines General Motors Corporation issued in 1993; the guidelines deal with board access to senior management, but guidelines about access of all interested parties could be added to create a more comprehensive document.

The GM guidelines suggested that board members have complete access to GM's management, but added that "it is assumed that board members will use judgment to be sure that this contact is not distracting to the business operation of the Company and that such contact, if in writing, be copied to the Chief Executive and the Chairman." In pursuit of this, it added that the board should encourage management to, "from time to time, bring managers into the board meetings who: (a) can provide additional insight into the items being discussed because of personal involvement in these areas and/or (b) represent managers with future potential that the Senior Management believes should be given exposure to the board."[19]

John G. Smale, chairman of the board of GM, notes that the guidelines in no way

> represent any shift of power or decisionmaking from management to the board. The GM board does not involve itself in management decisions . . . however, it is appropriate for the board to regularly monitor the effectiveness of management policy and decisions . . . [this] involves asking . . . What are your plans for the future? How do you propose to achieve those plans? How do the results produced by those plans compare with the performance of other companies in your industry? That kind of monitoring requires candid dialogue, not just the review of oral and written reports. And, it can't be effective unless there is mutual trust and confidence between the board and management.[20]

Such trust requires free and open communication not only between the board and management but between the board and shareholders. The need for such a change is being recognized. Although, as Kirk Stewart points out, "public companies still follow Stone Age procedures revolving around an annual report, an annual meeting, and distribution of quarterly reports . . . more and more companies . . . are taking steps to speed up their communications with shareholders." Among the new communications technologies available are PR Newswire or Business Wire, all-day financial broadcasts on CNBC, computer on-line services, faxing, conference calls to as many as one hundred analysts and investors at a time, video conferencing when possible, and, soon, CD-ROM annual reports. The age of real-time reporting to investors has arrived.[21]

But this is only one of the issues created by the new communications technology. Leaders are going to have to deal with the entire spectrum of concerns raised by technology in order to shape the organization of the future so that it does not slip over the edge into chaos.

NEW RESPONSIBILITIES IN A NEW ORGANIZATION

The world in which business operates today is global, interconnected, and unbelievably complex, quite different from the world in the 1920s that Edward Filene thought he could learn about through a yearly vacation tour of Europe taken to discover "*all* the forces, local, national, and international, that promised to react upon and determine future business conditions."

What is needed today is best described as anticipatory capability, the ability to determine which future trends need exploring, which technological advances to investigate, which mergers between organizations will affect the future of your organization. Business leaders today need to expand their peripheral vision, to find a way to see what is happening around them in every direction, almost beyond the horizon, and then to determine which of these events warrants tracking. The surest road to this ability is to tap the knowledge of the members of the board—as newly constituted in the butterfly organization. Given the backgrounds and experiences of the members who will be added, almost on an "as-needed" basis in response to changes in strategic direction, the board should be able to provide a wealth of information about various industrial sectors and global markets. If they are given the opportunity to explore these issues with one another, the result will usually be insights that, together with good instincts, can point the organization's strategic thinkers in the right direction.

The right mix of members—and opportunities for interaction between them—are essential to constructing and running this kind of organization. Richard C. Leone, former chairman of the Port Authority of New York and New Jersey, president and member of the board of the Twentieth Century Fund (the foundation Filene established), and a member at different times of many corporate boards, says that traditionally "corporate boards are defensive operations, while nonprofit boards are active boards." But there is already, he adds, a change under way as boards are expected to be more responsible, in part because of what he calls "increasing transparency"; that is, as the actions of boards become more open to scrutiny because of greater emphasis on procedure and more reporting requirements, the kind of openness demanded of public boards may become a model for corporate boards.[22]

The fact that corporate boards are, as Leone says, less active than other types of boards clearly must change if boards are going to play the leadership role necessary in a butterfly organization. For this purpose, nonprofit boards may well provide role models. They meet periodically to explore questions such as, "What trends and developments should this organization study over the next six months, the next year?" Corporate boards of butterfly organizations are going to have to assume a similar role in the future, focusing on more than current financial performance. It is an expanded role, one that will demand more time and may limit the number of board memberships people assume.

Board members are also going to have to assume some degree of responsibility for seeing to it that the CEO changes strategic governance models when the organization reaches that point in its evolution where command-and-control management does not work. When an organization enters numerous alliances with others, when it has to partner on equal terms with suppliers, or when divisions doing certain kinds of creative project development simply need more empowerment to test innovations, the strategic governance of the organization will have to change. Since this often requires the CEO to trust those under him and many CEOs have traditionally resisted relinquishing any control, the board will have to encourage, if not demand, this change in behavior. Since taking such a position would be extremely unlikely when a board was composed wholly of CEOs, board diversity becomes even more important.

Murray Weidenbaum says that the "corporation is a continually evolving institution in the U.S. economy and, as external requirements change, key elements such as the board of directors continue to adapt and modify their actions. These factors," he emphasizes, "help to explain the fundamental strength and long-term resiliency of private enterprise institutions in the United States."[23] The role of the board in corporate governance is important, but it is only one, as Weidenbaum notes, of the keys to the resiliency of organizations. Another key is, as just noted, the ability—and willingness—of an organization's leadership, including the board, to change the way the organization is governed strategically and operationally in response to shifts in external forces.

6

UNDERSTANDING AND ALIGNING GOVERNANCE MODELS

Where the traditional organization was held together by command and control, the "skeleton" of the information-based organization will be the optimal information system.

Peter Drucker[1]

*O*rganizations, like countries, have governments; whether an organization is the equivalent of a dictatorship, a democracy, a confederacy, a commonwealth, or an empire is the result of strategic decisions made by its leaders about the rules and laws that control the way the organization operates. At one end of the spectrum, organizations have hierarchical command-and-control approaches similar to those of the monarchies of old. At the other extreme, they set themselves up as loosely knit coalitions of independent organizations joined together for financial advantage, an approach not unlike that of the Holy Roman Empire, in which the ruler did little more than collect a percentage of the monies gained through the arrangement.

Strategic governance decisions were once fairly simple, determined by the business of the organization. The business of the organization, however, has become more complex. In the heyday of the Industrial Age, when most of the largest companies were engaged in manufacturing, governance adhered to a simple command-and-control model. Today, organizations have become part of a global economy: leaders find it necessary to set up functional units, site plants overseas, enter into strategic alliances, deal with multiple suppliers, and market to many diverse cultures in many different ways. The result is that no matter what form of strategic governance has been in place at the top of the organization, the necessities of the Information Age require many changes in the way organizations actually carry out their operations, even if they are still in the same business they were in two decades ago.

Problems such as maintaining profitability, achieving growth, and dealing with continuous change result in constant attempts to reorganize and restructure because companies fail to anticipate the need for new kinds of governance to suit new worlds. Organizations today need multiple governance styles at different levels and in different functional areas, divisions, units, and locations. Unless leaders understand the need for—and the effects of—this kind of governance "diversity," they will not be able to help their organizations achieve the flexibility and adaptability necessary to successfully walk the fine line between order and chaos.

In fact, many of the problems besetting organizations arise from new ways of working, such as teamwork or empowerment or alliance partnerships, all of which have dramatic effects on strategic and operational governance. Leaders who insist on adhering to a familiar style of governance at both these governance levels and who make exceptions when they think they have no other choice find that exceptions soon become policy. The result is that, no matter what governance model is supposedly in place, the lines of authority, responsibility, and power soon become blurred, creating problems ranging from confusion to total paralysis.

To ensure the right skeletal structure for the butterfly organization, leaders will have to modify governance models to encompass the changes they themselves support, changes often made possible or driven by technological developments. Moreover, the changes in lines of authority and responsibility—and the delegation of degrees of power to different members of the organization—that accompany these governance decisions must be crystal clear to all participants at all times. Gaining an understanding of the different models and the ways in which the new organizational form forces a multiplicity of models at different levels is critical to understanding how the new organization will be able to stay on a flight path that neither leads to chaos nor descends into order.

THE BASIC FORMS OF STRATEGIC GOVERNANCE

Although no one governance model will prevail throughout the organization of the future, the models that do appear are going to be adaptations of current models, much as the butterfly is a metamorphosis from the caterpillar stage. This, then, requires understanding the models that are in place as the twentieth century draws to a close. There are, in general, five traditional forms: monarchy (this is typically a highly integrated centralist organization), democracy (this is the federalist model), confederacy (this takes the form of a franchise type organization), commonwealth (the conglomerate), or empire (a holding company).

The lines, of course, are not clear-cut. For example, there are companies that could be classified as "high centralist"—that is, *no* decision is made or resource allocated without discussion and consideration at corporate headquarters. There are also "low centralist" companies—that is, companies that are on the cusp between centralist and federalist. In such companies, except for *major* resource decisions, business units have well-defined policies and procedures for most contingencies. Variations such as these often make it difficult to distinguish clearly between models at the various ends of the spectrum, but understanding the basic differences in reporting structures and the way communications flow as a result of different governance models is necessary for developing the technological networks that will be at the core of the organization of the future.

CENTRALIST

The centralist corporation follows the classic command-and-control model that has served as the cornerstone of the Industrial Age. All the decisionmaking power resides in a single leader who cares about and is involved in almost every aspect of the business. The organization has a shared mission, values, and purpose. Policies and procedures are well defined and serve as a very formal and rigid rule base for conducting business. There is a common vocabulary—everyone understands what is meant by an asset, how profits are calculated, and what a customer is.

The command-and-control center is corporate headquarters. It sets the cultural norms of the organization, it makes all decisions about resource allocation, and it controls human resources, hiring and firing management in order to achieve performance goals (as compared to either selling or buying business units). Corporate headquarters provides a high degree of central services that the business units, which have little or no autonomy, have no choice but to accept.

In the centralist, traditionally vertically integrated model, the company owns all of the competencies required to produce a product. Integration of activities is imposed by corporate headquarters in order to optimize the corporate entity, in most cases at the expense of the individual business units. Headquarters sets and controls performance measures, such as return on investment or return on assets, and dictates the development of strategies and plans. In this model, all data/information is perceived to be an asset of the company, and it is corporate headquarters that controls the flow and sharing of information among business units.

Given these characteristics, the centralist governance model may lack the flexibility required for growth in today's environment. It is, however, a model that served this nation well when the issues of competition centered on resource allocation and optimization in a competitive marketplace that was growing and did not exhibit turbulence.

Automotive and energy companies such as General Motors, Du Pont, and Standard Oil Company grew to their prominence under centralist governance,[2] as did such mammoth enterprises as IBM and DEC. As global competitiveness, rapidly changing markets, and a customer focus have become market drivers, however, the model seems to have outlived its usefulness. It is no longer enough to provide a product that is reasonably priced and fairly well made—such products quickly become commodities, with little opportunity for differentiation and small profit margins; global competition requires developing products or services that are exciting, innovative, or, at the very least, significantly changed versions of older products.

FEDERALIST

The federalist model is usually a development from the centralist model, and as a result there are areas of overlap. The business units of centralist organizations are not bought and sold, while in federalist organizations, they may be. For example, a strategic business unit that is developed as a result of, say, the creation of a new product from a research-and-development effort, but is not tied closely to the parent's core business, may be sold. (Buying and selling of companies are not, however, as common as in other forms that will be examined.)

The federalist organization, like the centralist, has a shared mission, values, and purpose. Its policies and procedures are well defined, especially for the shared functions, but as they are adapted at other levels within the organization, they serve as a far less formal and rigid rule base for conducting business. Each unit may define profits and assets as it wishes for its own financial records, but the information reported to corporate headquarters must adhere to common definitions. (The problems that multiple definitions cause for those responsible for information systems will be explored in the next chapter.) Although corporate headquarters provides some central services—for example, protecting the "image" or brand equity of the company in both models—decisionmaking about resource allocation and human resources tends to be given to the individual units in the federalist model. And in this model, data/information is shared across the organization as well as up and down, with individual units often making their own decisions about sharing.

The leader of the federalist organization does not insist on running every aspect of the business and overseeing every decision. Each unit or division is given a degree of empowerment, and the process for strategy formulation is "top down-bottom up." Corporate headquarters sets the strategic direction, reviews the specific business unit strategies, and then explores the alignment between the two. Although on rare occasions it may modify its strategies based upon input from the various business units, the "top-down" view ultimately prevails.

In the federalist model, the business units are encouraged to exhibit cooperative behavior—and a portion of their rewards (that is, compensation) comes from overall corporate headquarters as well as business unit profit and loss. In other words, they are encouraged to walk a line between what is in the best interests of the company and the unit. For example, a unit might make a product that could garner high prices if sold outside the organization, but the item is a component of the parent company's major product. To keep prices down, and therefore competitive, the unit may be asked to sell the product "at cost" internally.

One of the best examples of a federalist governance model company is ABB Asea Brown Boveri, which is described by Percy Barnevik, its chief executive officer, as "a federation of national companies with a global coordination center." According to Barnevik, one of the challenges of running this kind of company is ensuring that it is "radically decentralized with centralized reporting and control."[3] Other companies that have turned to this form of governance through mergers and strategic investments—and subsequently changed from centralist to federalist governance in response to globalization—are Volkswagen and Citicorp. Each of these companies has followed a practice of "acting locally" while "going global." They have had to give power to the "states"—that is, business units in local areas—in order to succeed in a global marketplace. On the other hand, a manufacturer of goods that does little more than sell its products in other countries based on strong brand image, such as Caterpillar, does not face the issues involved in running local business units in foreign nations.

CONFEDERATE

As with the centralist and federalist models, the confederate model tends to have a common culture, shared values and purpose, and a strong image in the marketplace that is normally protected by corporate headquarters. Franchises and associations for the purpose of achieving economies of scale are confederate models.

In the franchise form of this model, corporate headquarters is responsible for providing services such as those related to general image and finance and purchasing in return for an agreed-upon percentage of profits. The menu of a fast food establishment, such as McDonald's or Carvel, is for the most part mandated by corporate headquarters, and the ingredients needed are purchased by headquarters to achieve economies of scale and standardization; recipes for basic products must be followed, but "regional specialties" can be added; there are national advertisements, but prices can vary by region. All hiring may be done locally, with no interference from corporate headquarters, but the uniforms worn and the rules for appearance are set by corporate headquarters. Moreover, corporate headquarters is totally responsible for franchising rules, licensing arrangements, and may even arrange loans.

For the most part, information (primarily financial information) usually flows from the business units to corporate headquarters, although information can be shared among business units (and headquarters) if it helps to achieve synergy—that is, "I will share information if it benefits my business unit." Moreover, each "unit" has its own model of governance—the owner of the franchise may run the business as a dictatorship or set up a federalist team structure; that is his decision. But as an owner, he is required to pay certain royalties and maintain certain standards set by the franchisor that protect the investment of every other franchise holder.

In the association form, there is usually a group identity overlaid on the identities of the various individual businesses that have come together to, say, buy supplies from manufacturers in bulk at discount. Members may be precluded from buying from other manufacturers no matter what deal they are offered in order to maintain the association's purchasing power. Yet each distributor can, as can each franchise owner, run his business under any governance model he chooses. There could be joint advertising of special offers or total joint advertising. They would not, however, tend to share financial information, except as it might affect the dues they would have to pay the association. As a result, the lines of communication must link each business to the association's central offices, but not to one another.

CONGLOMERATE

The next step toward less control and oversight is the conglomerate, a commonwealth model. According to *Fortune* magazine, "a conglomerate must have at least four unrelated businesses, none accounting for more than 50% of its sales."[4] In conglomerate governance, the business units are autonomous and may be in different industrial sectors. Basically, a conglomerate is formed through the process of acquiring companies that have the potential to increase earnings through growth or to reduce costs. These noncore business-related acquisitions are then helped to grow through the infusion of resources and new management ideas from the acquiring company.

In this model, businesses are purchased to "fill out" a portfolio to create an even cash flow or earnings stream (which tends to be the primary motivator) as compared to buying a business because its competencies would add to the existing portfolio of competencies—that is, create synergies among related businesses. Phillip Blumberg, dean emeritus of the University of Connecticut School of Law, says that "in financial matters, conglomerate groups function much like other groups, with a high degree of financial interdependence among the affiliated companies. The economic potential from internalization of the capital market function through substitution of the group for the market for financing purposes has in fact been recognized as one of the major incentives for the existence of conglomerate organizations in the first place."[5]

Although business units are bought and sold to enhance the portfolio, the corporate office would tend not to sell business units that represent its image in the marketplace. The role of the corporate office is to provide some degree of shared services (primarily financial) and, in general, information flows, but each unit tends to set its own strategy. In fact, there is often little in the way of "corporate strategy"—aside from profitability goals.

The late Royal Little of Textron explained that the "key to running a conglomerate well is to give the division managers the authority to run their own shows—but to make sure they are motivated. You must have people who are competent in their businesses, and you don't want to restrict them too much, except for approval from the board of directors for things like capital expenditures."[6] This definition creates some confusion. General Electric is, by *Fortune*'s definition, a conglomerate, having the prerequisite number of diversified units. Yet it is, given the management style of Jack Welch, more a federalist organization. Therefore, it can be defined as on the cusp between "high federalist" when it comes to management style and "low conglomerate" in governance style. This mix of styles often creates problems that result in leaders' decisions to restructure their organizations.

HOLDING COMPANY

The holding company governance model is often called a "shell"—that is, a "company or corporation that exists without assets or independent operations as a legal entity through which another company or corporation can conduct various dealings."[7] It is created solely for the purpose of acquiring and holding the stocks of other companies. Among the more notable of the large holding companies today are Berkshire Hathaway, Kohlberg Kravis Roberts, Mitsubishi, and Barlow Rand. Warren Buffett, who chairs Berkshire Hathaway, one of the most successful of these companies, believes that success comes from investing in a selected group of enterprises that the managers of the holding company know something about. Buffett says that an investor "should act as though he had a lifetime decision card with just 20 punches on it. With every investment decision, his card is punched, and he has one fewer available for the rest of his life."[8]

The board of a holding company is composed of selected members of the boards of the companies that it holds, and the chief executive offer (CEO) is not a major voice in decisions about the disposition of assets. Since the holding company has a controlling interest in the companies it holds, it often replaces their management or finances their growth in order to achieve profits, but the holding company itself tends not to be involved in the management of the companies. In this model, each business unit is totally autonomous, and the connections between companies often go unnoticed. Brand names and images of the individual business units are maintained in the marketplace. There are no expectations of synergy and the only financial information is reported from the "held" companies to the parent.

NEW FORMS FOR A NEW AGE

Over the past decade, changes in strategic governance have become increasingly frequent. These changes were driven first by mergers and acquisitions, then by increased global competition, and finally by efforts to move outside normal organizational forms in response to advances in both telecommunications and information technology. Some of these changes have been deliberate; some have been in reaction to events and pressures from outside the company and therefore occur without much forethought or awareness.

As organizations expand globally, they often cede control to local firms. As they react to downward economic spirals that have made it harder and harder to maintain market share and profitability, they often eliminate layers of management that, in previous eras, were the information intermediaries that kept the command-and-control structure functioning. As they turn to new information and communications technology, formal reporting structures are falling by the wayside. As they rush products to market, they turn to cross-functional teams. As specialized skills become increasingly necessary and the time to train staff becomes too costly, they acquire expertise on a temporary basis.

These changes all impact the strategic governance of organizations. The changes that create the greatest problems are those that attempt to enhance profitability and reduce costs and are not considered in terms of governance. If a company has not moved to outsourcing, not entered alliances, or not hired temporary workers, the governance issue is rarely addressed—even though different levels of the organization may suddenly be working under different governance models as a result of efforts to improve quality or operational excellence. And even when decisions result in work being done across corporate boundaries, if the changes take place on the operational level, their impact on strategic governance may go unrecognized. Changes that are driven by management from the top, resulting in mixes, and hopefully, matches, between strategic governance models across, up, and down the organization—and outward to multinational divisions, partners, and customers—are the most effective.

DIFFERENCES BETWEEN TOP AND BOTTOM

Some companies are moving toward a more federalist model for upper management, for those with specific skill sets that allow them to work at home part of the time, or for employees whose creativity is their core competency. The same company, however, may have a single unit responsible for manufacturing. Only if the product is something that needs assembly, such as a car, will teamwork, which introduces a form of empowerment, spread to that layer of the organization. Line work such as that in a company making, say, hubcaps, is a different story; the work on the line consists of placing metal ingots in slots for the machine that stamps the shape of the pieces, which are then heat treated, polished, packed, and shipped to the end user. These people work in a very centralist environment, the same environment that may have existed since the founding of the company.

Problems will arise if the senior manager in charge of manufacturing asks for suggestions from workers on the line. Unless the ground has been prepared, our experience has been that there is more likely to be a slew of complaints about working conditions or requests for various amenities than suggestions. These workers have little trust in management, little knowledge of the long-term goals of the organization, and little sense that they have anything to gain from putting forth ideas.

DIFFERENCES IN GOVERNANCE MODELS BETWEEN INSIDE AND OUTSIDE

Many companies that considered themselves centralist have moved away from that model without being aware of it. Is a company still centralist if its payroll is outsourced and its marketing is done through a number of strategic alliances with smaller companies? If it has a floating temporary workforce in its information technology division? Such changes took place as companies downsized, right-sized, reorganized, and restructured to remain competitive, but the original governance model was never formally adjusted to reflect these changes.

The changes made as a result of efforts to remain competitive primarily affect the way work is done; that is, they impact the operational level. For example, say that senior management of a company that has traditionally been highly centralist authorizes alliances with a number of companies for the purpose of out-sourcing some or all of the administrative activities of the company (finance, information systems and telecommunications, purchasing, and so forth). The company still has control of the activities and can mandate that no business unit has an option to use any other provider of the service or to develop the capacity to handle the service themselves. To senior management, controlling the actions of the various business units means maintaining centralist control. What they do not realize (until it creates a problem) is that the company no longer has the ability to decide that the service be performed, say, faster this month—without paying a premium for changing the terms of the contract. The centralist model expects total control over business processes, but contractual arrangements preclude this degree of authoritarian decisionmaking.

In the federalist model, each business unit retains a degree of empowerment that allows it to outsource activities in order to achieve its goals. At the extreme, the individual business units could even establish alliances and form virtual companies to develop new products or services, making the business unit, in turn, a holding company within the parent federalist organization. As a holding company, the autonomous business unit could then form a relationship (alliance or joint venture) that followed a centralist model.

Finding leaders who can deal with different models on different levels is essential to the success of the butterfly organization. And so is a new layer of management to control the intersections of the relationships between these different strategic forms. This new layer of management is likely to emerge out of the ranks of those in charge of operations. (This position, aptly titled boundary manager, is explained further later in this chapter and looked at in detail in later chapters.)

The most complex set of changes in governance will obviously affect large multinational companies that utilize different kinds of strategic governance at different operational levels, across cultures and involving other firms.

OPERATIONAL GOVERNANCE

It is clear that the farther an organization moves from centralist to butterfly form, the more operational governance becomes an issue. Whoever controls a functional division of a company controls an operational area. Normally, the style of governance of the whole organization is chosen by the CEO. But when a devolution of authority results from a reorganization or restructuring, it may also result in the selection or incorporation of another governance model in another part of the organization.

For example, a senior executive may tell a line manager that she can "run her operation the way she sees fit." So the line manager establishes relationships with two vendors. With one vendor, the relationship is very unstructured, with little in the way of formal terms spelled out because they are jointly trying to develop a new manufacturing process for a part the line manager needs but does not want to build internally. Consequently, there is a lot of "give and take" with respect to product specifications and manufacturing processes, as long as the required parts are delivered to the line manager on time and within budget. Both parties cooperate in the expectation that doing so will ensure a competitive advantage for the line manager and a "sole-source supplier" relationship for the vendor. In the case of the second vendor, from which the line manger needs more of a commodity product, the criterion are price, quality, and delivery schedules. With this supplier, the line manager has spelled out all aspects of the relationship in formal terms, from the beginning.

The senior executive who gave the line manager governance authority is upset at the way she is handling the relationship with the first supplier and pleased with the relationship with the second vendor: "That's the way business should be conducted." What is wrong with this picture? It is clear that the senior executive did not understand the implications of granting power and authority to the line manager. The words were there, but the underlying understanding of empowerment was not.

THE PROBLEM OF MIXED MODELS

The complications that can be created by changes intended to enhance productivity, reduce the workforce, and increase innovative thinking have led many companies to multiple reorganizations over the past few years. Because of the conflicts that arise when centralist, federalist, and conglomerate models try to coexist within an organization, or when confederate-style organizations work with suppliers that are centralist, projects get delayed and costs rise. When that happens, management often tries yet another new way to organize. The problem, however, may not have been in the way the company was reorganized, but rather in the fact that governance style was not taken into account when making the changes. Learning new rules of governing—*regoverning* not restructuring—may be what is needed.

For example, a West Coast technology company that adheres to a federalist form of governance was setting up a project that involved establishing a cross-functional team composed of individuals from application development, marketing, and sales in order carry out plans to release an updated version of a financial application before a new competitor, a well-known hardware manufacturer, released its first application in that area. The decision to turn to a team structure was made in the hope that it would reduce the time to market for the new product. A senior member of the application development group was assigned the job of project manager, and granted the authority, responsibility, and accountability to accomplish the stated objective. The project was internal in the sense that all of the resources, competencies, and processes needed to carry out the project were contained in the business unit.

It was clear from the outset that the key to the eventual success of the project was going to be how the project manager ran the project. Given the high degree of federalism in the company and in the business unit, the project manager was free to run the project as loosely or tightly as she wanted. This presented an interesting situation because the project manager turned out to prefer tight control over the project team because of both her background in another company and the less federalist style common in the business area she works in. In the federalist model, this choice was allowed.

However, the mandate given the group was not only to enhance the current functionality of the application, but to package and market it in a way that would make a statement about the company as one that was moving in new directions, one that was leading edge. To fulfill this part of the mandate, the members of the team from the marketing department had to spend a great deal of time generating and rejecting and coming up with new approaches in a very free wheeling brainstorming style of interaction. They found it difficult to try to report on their progress in ways the manager could understand, and found the rest of the team's reactions to the ideas they threw out just for feedback disconcerting. Instead of playing with the ideas, the other members would ask them what in the world they meant. The project manager was able to alleviate the problem after attending a standard marketing meeting and seeing how they operated. As a result, she stopped asking for progress reports and instead let them discuss where they were with their parts of the project in far less formally structured meetings. The relatively small size of the team, the fact that they all work for the same company, and their proximity (the sessions that created the problems were held face to face) all made solving the mismatch in style fairly easy. The problem would, of course, have been far more difficult to solve if it involved alliance partners and the team "meetings" were mostly teleconferenced or the work was done on-line.

Let's take another, more complicated example, one that is more likely to be the norm in the butterfly organization—a project involving alliances set up between companies to work on a single project. The company that initiated the project, which we will call Component, Inc. follows a federalist governance model, and the heads of the business units run their units in accordance with the values of that model. This company entered into a major contract to design, manufacture, and assemble a complex component for a major aviation company. Although it had the core competencies and critical processes in place to do most of the work, management realized that additional expertise in designing and manufacturing a key electronic component was required.

In lieu of building or acquiring the additional competencies, Component, Inc. decided to team up with the industry leader in the manufacturing of the electronic part needed—EP Company. EP Company was excited about the opportunity to work with Component, Inc. because it was a way to expand its market—and it thought the partnership with an older, larger company would enhance its reputation. The companies entered into a strategic alliance.

Once the contract was signed, the next step was to form a cross-functional intercompany team (research and development, design, and manufacturing) to manage the project. The initial enthusiasm was high, although both companies realized that this would be a difficult undertaking—it meant sharing not only information, but hard-won proprietary knowledge as well. It also meant trying to tie several project team members together electronically given the various global locations of both companies. Although a challenging task, the CEOs of both companies were committed to the project, and everyone was "fired up" and ready to go.

Making this type of intercompany/intraorganizational project work requires resolving a number of potential problems before the project actually begins. The first group of questions that should be asked are: What type of strategic governance model does each of the companies adhere to? What are the implications of a difference in strategic governance models between them? What are the implications at the operational governance level? Since both companies would be supplying project team members, who would be the project manager? Or should there be a pair of project managers? And how much authority and responsibility would the project manager(s) be granted?

It was inevitable that other issues would arise during the course of the project, but if this first group of challenges had been tackled in the beginning, the project would have gotten off to a better start. The companies, however, were not aware of the dangers posed by the cultural differences between them.

The first problem that presented itself was the choice of project manager. Normally, the company that is responsible for the final product selects the project manager (with the partner company having right of approval, which is usually not withheld so long as the individual has the requisite competencies and skill sets). In this case, however, because EP Company was centralist, it expressed a desire that the project have two project managers, one from each company, so it could maintain more control. Given Component, Inc.'s greater experience with and more relaxed attitude about joint projects, it agreed.

The choice of members also ended up creating problems. Component, Inc.'s business unit leader selected his project manager and empowered him to, in essence, take the project and run with it. The manger began by inviting EP Company's project manager to join him in interviewing people to put on the team. The differences in governance models raised a serious issue here. From Component, Inc.'s perspective, a project manager has the authority to select the best available talent for such an effort. EP Company's project manager explained that only certain employees were available: there was no choice. Component, Inc.'s project manager became extremely uncomfortable after talking with some of the members assigned to the team by EP Company—they were not people he would have chosen.

The next issue involved reporting. In federalist Component, Inc., senior management wanted to be informed about the progress of the project (in terms of prudent project management performance measures), but they were not at all inclined to cross the line to micromanagement. Given the centralist culture of EP Company, however, senior management not only expected to monitor the project on an ongoing basis, but also "manage" the project manager as well.

The problems that arose because of the differences in governance models when it came to reporting were troublesome throughout the project. EP Company's senior management ended up calling their project manager directly to request various types of information about the status of the project on a daily basis (given the importance of the project). Component, Inc.'s project manager was uncomfortable with what he perceived as the lack of faith and time lost while EP Company's project manager prepared detailed reports; it not only slowed down the project, but caused his own team to wonder about his authority. The other problem that continued to cause trouble was the difficulties team members from EP Company had in working as part of a team—because many of them had no previous experience working in a cooperative environment. They often failed to contribute ideas during the team sessions, instead sending memos to their own managers explaining what they thought ought to be happening; their goal was to gain recognition for their efforts with the people they worked for. In their culture, rewards were not based on team performance but managerial review of personal accomplishments.

When the problems began to overwhelm the team, a "neutral party" was sought to remedy the problem. Once the cultural mismatches were understood, management was able to address the issues. For example, Component, Inc. asked its project team leader to spend some time every week reviewing the project with a peer who had spent a number of years in a centralist organization. In addition, EP Company agreed to replace a couple of team members; this time it presented three candidates for each of those positions. This helped the team acquire some sorely needed expertise. In addition, Component, Inc. had someone from its human relations department sit in on the meetings and facilitate a few brainstorming sessions.

When it came to reporting, a compromise was reached. The team provided more reports than the federalist organization normally expected, but fewer than would be ideal for the centralist side. Another solution that was suggested, but was turned down for a lack of an individual on either side suited to the role, was the appointment of a boundary manager—an intermediary between the team and the company management on both sides. Boundary managers are usually senior personnel who devote their time to learning the cultures of both organizations, moderating disputes, and negotiating the rules that govern the relationship. Boundary managers are the equivalent of ombudsmen, keeping the peace by walking in the space between corporate boundaries, a role that will become more critical in the future as companies begin to work together more and more. (The role of the boundary manager, a very new position, will be explored further in Part IV, Leadership for the New Age.)

The project, while successful in the end, took longer than expected, and both sides ended up losing some profits because of the overtime needed to fulfill the terms of the contract. In a similar case of a joint effort, the situation became even more complicated. In that case, the companies engaged in the joint effort discovered that another company had learned about the project and found a way to produce the same component at a lower price. The companies working together decided to launch a marketing drive to emphasize how the combination of their skills made their component the best and most cost effective—far superior to what could emerge from the new player. Their goal was to set the stage for a competitive advantage by stressing that the reputation for quality that each provided when working together was "Quality Plus." Neither of the original companies, however, had a marketing department with the expertise to launch such a major public relations campaign.

They decided to outsource the marketing project. Unfortunately, the company they outsourced the marketing to had a governance style that was totally different from either of the partners'. They selected a company that followed a far more open, confederate style, where the group assigned to the project consisted of a collection of individuals who worked with the marketing company but were independent contractors. The problems that emerged led to the dissolution of the agreement.

BUSINESS NETWORKS

What are developing here are complex business networks between multiple players. As organizations move toward a butterfly form, they will be deliberately setting out to construct—and destruct—the kinds of relationships just described. When complicated by doing business across national borders, the difficulties increase as do the intricacies of the networks that have to be constructed to handle the relationships.

PATTERNS OF DECISIONMAKING

At a certain point, the networks developed create a governance problem that can perhaps be best explained in terms of decisionmaking by critical mass. In an organization, if every manager understands the long-term goals of the company, their decisions will tend to go in the same direction: if certain managers are resistant, they will soon find that the force of the decisions by the others are so strong that they have no choice but to move in the same direction.

Imagine the decision points in the organization laid out on a piece of graph paper with, say, one hundred squares.[9] Each square represents a decision that someone in management in the organization can make. Now, think of each square as containing a domino. Push the first down and as it falls it topples the next in the same direction, and so forth.

In a centralist organization, the goals are clear and most decisions push the organization in a given direction. If, for example, marketing announces a product in the press, manufacturing may be forced to deliver early and customer service may be pushed to hire more employees to deal with the inquires generated. But when two companies work together as partners, the effects of decisions become more difficult to predict because there are areas of overlap.

To return to the image of the graph paper, imagine that you take a second piece of graph paper and lay one corner of it over a portion of the first piece of graph paper. If the directional push in one company is different from the push in the other, conflict can ensue at the point where the overlap occurs. (For example, if another company is making one of the parts needed to manufacture the product that was announced, they may not be able to deliver on that schedule.) The more overlapping pieces of graph paper (the more companies involved), the more likely it will result in chaos.

However, if a company refuses to allow any overlap, continuing to produce its comfortable, standard product, such as the buggy whip after 1925 or mainframes after 1985, it is in danger of stagnation. The ability to grow and to find a way to control the internal effects of the growth through partnering will determine whether the change succeeds or fails.

Since all the people in all those squares, representing all those companies, are going to have to work together, they must establish common ground and understanding. Every individual involved in those networks has to communicate with the others in the network, so that all understand the big picture—the vision and goals they are trying to achieve. Because the numbers are large and the people are spread out geographically, and since many will never directly work together, the rapid sharing of necessary information is the enabler for the business network. This mix of personal and electronic networks as enablers raises the issue of governing the alignment of information technology and business needs in the complex, yet flexible and adaptable organization, and it is the subject of the next chapter.

PART III

INFORMATION AND COMMUNICATIONS
TECHNOLOGY COMES OF AGE

7

THE ART OF ACCOMMODATION

Technology walls are falling. Old computing architectures are being overthrown. The nature and purpose of computing are being radically altered. Like traditional cold war thinking, the old approach to technology is proving to be inadequate to deal with the new world.

Don Tapscott and Art Caston[1]

Technology has as great an effect on organizations as governance and leadership. It is one of the triad of forces that dramatically affects organizational shape and direction. The various technologies brought into the organization, the speed with which they are adopted, and the ability of the organization to take full advantage of the business opportunities they offer all impact the strategy, form, structure, governance, and leadership of organizations.

In addition to providing business possibilities, most of these technologies enable leadership across vast organizational structures, ensuring that the vision and goals of the leaders permeate every corner of the organization. They also allow communication across and up the organization, impacting leadership and organizational structure and governance. At the same time, the changes made possible by these new technologies impact the ability of the organization to deal with the next waves of technology, including the way technology must be governed, and the role of those responsible for technology.

When analyzing technology's place in the organization, it is critical to keep in mind that technology includes both information and communications. Today, technology is not only a means of aggregating and storing information, but a tool for using, analyzing, and conveying it. The noted author Harlan Cleveland sees the effect of this combination as "explosive," requiring us to "rethink the very fundaments of our philosophy—rethink an economics based on the allocation of scarcities, rethink governance based on secrecy, rethink laws based on exclusive ownership, rethink management based on hierarchy."[2]

In the butterfly organization, information and communications technology as a unit serves as the nervous system of the organization, enabling leaders to lead—and to delegate leadership to many levels. It ties together the functional areas, units, divisions, alliance partners, and the often far-flung and flexible workforce that comprise this type of organization.

This chapter will explore:

◆ What is meant by technology today

◆ The historical role of technology in the organization

◆ The effects of technology on organizational structure

◆ The problems facing the technology group as a result of multiple governance models

Understanding these issues will clarify the role of technology in the butterfly organization that is emerging—and will help make clear the role of the technology leader, the subject of the next chapter.

TECHNOLOGY TODAY—A MULTIPLICITY OF FORMS

The technology of the future is a matter of speculation. The word that first comes to mind in connection with technology still tends to be *information*. Yet there is no way to ignore the fact that vast as the changes brought to the organization by information technology were, the changes that will occur as information and communications technologies merge, tying together people and machine, will be far more wrenching. For example, computer technology is said to have changed the world of work, bringing efficiencies that eliminated many jobs; but advances in communications technology added to information technology have eliminated many layers of management, changed the nature and meaning of work, and the ways that work is done.

The executive on the golf course answering a cellular phone, on the beach sending a facsimile via a wireless computer, or in an airplane sending a presentation to someone for a meeting the next day has become a familiar image in television advertisements. We hear about the "portable office" and wonder what it really will mean in terms of the way we live; for example, many of the social interactions that are currently an understood part of the world of work may disappear. Changes in the way work is done will continue for the foreseeable future because of developments such as video teleconferencing; interactive applications that allow joint work, whether designing the wings of Boeing's new 777 or the preparation of a report for the next day's shareholder meeting by the three heads of the major divisions of the organization (who happen to be in Manila, Dallas, and Rio); access to thousands of data bases and experts around the world through the Internet; and advances in technology that are still in the early stages of development.

Given the development of connectivity, of electronic networks that allow instantaneous communication in real time across vast areas, tomorrow may mean working from home or from a temporary office in an alliance partner's local outlet, working in small office centers with teams who are part of the same organization but who you have never met before and may never see again after the project ends, or working in the traditional office setting. What is most likely is that it will, at different times, mean all of those and more.

In addition, communications technology is already changing the nature of competition in many industrial sectors. Retailing, for example, today includes "home shopping." Telephone, entertainment, cable, hardware and software companies are merging—and then separating only to merge with another set of partners. The constant changes are driven by firms trying to secure places for themselves in the ever-expanding world of home entertainment services. Financial institutions are finding new services to offer electronically, and transportation companies and companies that assemble and ship components worldwide are preparing to use technology to become logistics providers. What the future holds is not crystal clear; indeed, we are probably facing even more massive technological advances. What is clear, however, is that we need to take the time now to develop organizations that will be able to respond to the changes that are inevitably coming. That is the road to future competitiveness.

THE ORGANIZATIONAL HISTORY OF TECHNOLOGY

Many of the problems facing information technology divisions today are an outgrowth of their history. Information technology was a latecomer to the organization, entering the business world some forty years ago in the form of computers that served as tools for expediting accounting functions, tailored to speed such chores as accounts receivable, accounts payable, general ledger, invoicing, and many other generic financial processes. Information technology was also a tool for the scientific and engineering groups of the organization, whose systems were not considered an intrinsic part of the organization but rather as the "equipment" of those who used them.

The group using computers for financial functions was under the direction, in most cases, of the chief financial officer. Therefore, the technologists who supervised and maintained them reported there also. Although the computer is now used in every area of the business—for example, executive support, research, design, marketing, human resources management—in most companies this structural legacy still holds.

Another historical legacy is the isolation of the technology group from the corporate culture. In part, it was a result of location. Large computers required a great deal of space and special air-conditioned rooms because of the heat they generated. In addition, in the age of the mainframe, such large systems represented a huge investment that indicated a company was progressive and planning to grow in the future. The computers were therefore on display in separate glass-walled, climate-controlled rooms; after a while, the "glass house" became a metaphor for arrogance and isolation.

The isolation was real; it grew out of the backgrounds and temperament of those responsible for the technology who tended to remain apart from the world of business by choice, training, or inclination. They were skilled experts in a new field, working with equipment that was so much more complex than earlier office equipment and in need of so much maintenance (changes and corrections to applications are called maintenance) that they were hired by the organization to secure their full-time availability. To understand the problems that developed for these technical experts, it is necessary to keep in mind that, although they became employees, they never became an integral part of the organization because of the enormous cultural gap between them and the corporate community. Many were—and continue to be—science or engineering majors hired right out of school, where they had become totally fascinated with and focused on computers. The demands of programming tend to suit those who are willing to spend endless hours by themselves communicating only with the machine. They have little interest in business per se, but rather are in business because that is where the technology jobs are.

When you combine all of this with the fact that computers were introduced at the point at which most organizations were still adhering to a centralist model of governance, the development of a centralized, command-and-control computer environment was only natural. It was further abetted by the fact that there were very limited choices in computing in that early period. For all practical purposes, once a company selected a computer vendor (usually IBM), the vendor's product line for the most part dictated the information technology strategy.

Then three forces came together: the machines became far more understandable to the average user, the economy faltered, and technology made quantum leaps. With the advent of the personal computer, increasingly user friendly applications, and the development of on-line services, users began to understand what computers could do. This understanding was transferred to the workplace, resulting in demands on the technology division for more sophisticated reporting, more information available in real time, and more efficiency in processes of every kind, from design to customer relations. These new demands were met at great expense. Computerization was the byword, and expectations were high.

Then business came upon hard times and somehow the returns expected from those investments were not there—productivity in the service sector just wasn't improving. In the 1980s, while spending on technology soared, productivity remained flat according to Stephen

Roach, chief economist of Morgan Stanley. In fact, it wasn't until the 1990s that real productivity improvements appeared in the service sector, which had invested so many billions in, and depended so heavily on, information technology.[3] New technology was also appearing that claimed to provide far more speed and flexibility, but would cost yet more billions.

Disappointed by the results, frustrated by the time it took for their computer groups to develop applications, many divisions had found someone in their midst who "knew about an application" that could do "most of what we need." The division head went and acquired the software and used it without waiting for the technology division to find time to begin the long and difficult application development process. Then the facsimile machine and video conferencing equipment came along, and the value of electronic communication began to be touted. Not only were information technology departments overwhelmed, but they were often ignored in divisional decisionmaking and then asked to find ways to "connect" to the rest of the organization whatever new technology had been acquired. Chaos was often the result.

Attempts to dismantle the information technology group, however, were always quickly abandoned as executives contemplating such an action discovered upon investigation that technology was woven into the very fiber of the organization in a way unlike that of any other function. This happens in part because what technology provides to the organization as a whole simply cannot be handled by any one division, unit, or area. Those groups see only the applications they use, and have little understanding of how everything is tied together piece by piece to ensure seamless connectivity. It also happens because people have adopted technologies that are so simple they just do not "feel" like technology.

For example, while working with a major hospital in the Northeast, we saw the problem firsthand in the form of a puzzle facing our client, who was at a loss to understand why he was receiving so many complaints about constantly busy phone lines making it impossible for information to be transmitted by modem. Upon investigation, he discovered that numerous lines were being tied up by the use of unauthorized facsimile machines. Given their low price, doctors had simply bought them and plugged them into a telephone line. This disrupted all the old usage patterns, something that had never occurred to those who bought the machines.

The problems that result when various business units in an organization set up their own information services function tend to center on incompatibility. When those groups decide to mount joint projects, the information technology group is asked to find a way to connect the systems to allow the sharing of data and facilitate communications and reporting. It often takes a great deal of time and expense to construct "gateways" between these essentially incompatible private acquisitions.

Outsourcing is often looked at as an alternative to maintaining an in-house information technology division. It has worked for many companies, but the complexity of the arrangements and the need to manage the relationships (as well as the need to be able to handle abandonment—or threats—by outsourcers) require at least a small internal information technology unit. The unit is then charged with overseeing the outsourcing arrangements, translating the technology needs of the organization, and maintaining the core competencies to ensure that the needs of the organization will continue to be met if the company decides to once again build its own technology capability. If done right and for the right reasons, according to John Cross, head of information technology for British Petroleum Company, outsourcing does result in a small information technology organization that can "become increasingly engaged in activities that create real value for the organization, such as working directly with business managers to suggest technologies that will improve business processes, cut costs, or create business opportunities." There are many dangers, however, he adds, including "vulnerability to escalating fees and inflexible services."[4]

Thus, in some form or other, companies are going to have a corporate information technology function. The critical problem facing the information technology group will come from having to adapt to a more flexible organizational form. The group will have to deal with changes that will take place as the enterprise begins to unite with partners with incompatible systems and often partners who need access to some systems because of joint endeavors, but who must be kept out of areas in which they are competitors. Understanding the nature of the organization's relationships with outsiders (and the degrees of trust involved), the business goals motivating these relationships, and the changes in organizational structure these relationships bring will be a major challenge to those who manage the information technology function.

TECHNOLOGY AND ORGANIZATIONAL STRUCTURE

An organization's structure is the choice of its leadership. That choice, however, is limited by a number of factors. It is limited by the nature of the workforce and its culture, which is a matter of education, skills, training, and background. Choice is also limited by tradition; organizations move slowly when it comes to shifting power and authority or adopting new processes, especially those that impact the "pecking order." And it is limited by the ability to communicate, which limited the size of organizations in the past, a restraint that was eased with every advance in communications—from telegraph to telephone, from mail to e-mail. Finally, it is limited by the availability, acceptance, and use of technology, including the communications technology that ties information technology together. These constraints warrant further examination.

Those involved in the formal study of organizational theory have noted that the ways in which "technology constrains and configures organizational action, and how action constrains and reconfigures technology . . . is a critical process, which is not well developed theoretically."[5] Part of the problem of those trying to understand these changes is the almost unbelievable speed with which they take place. Moore's Law, named for Gordon Moore the cofounder of Intel, states that "the number of transistors that can be crammed onto a microchip doubles every 18 months—a process which brings with it a huge increase in power."[6]

Another part of the problem is understanding the constraints on the ability of humans to accept change and become skilled in using new tools and techniques. Those who study the effects of information technology have found that, because of the time involved relative to their expected remaining life in the organization, there is a reluctance on the part of senior managers to use technology. Moreover, once those who do adopt it become comfortable with it, they are reluctant to give it up and begin the learning curve again. People do not change as quickly as technology does.

The problem is exacerbated by technologists who see their jobs simply as installing hardware and software systems. In all too many organizations, they do not include in their definition of implementation the initiation of change management and training and education programs. The result is that the systems tend to be underutilized, if not ignored a good part of the time, reducing the productivity gains. Teaching business users the business advantages of a system is critical to the system's adoption.

Of course, some types of systems achieve faster buy-in than others. Vaughan Merlyn and John Parkinson explain that "human beings are by nature control-oriented. Programmed with a characteristic physiologists call *homeostasis*, people feel most competent, confident, and comfortable when their expectations of control, stability, and predictability are met."[7] Consequently, as James March and Lee Sproull have noted, "Technologies perceived by managers to increase their control, or the stability of systems under their control, are more likely to be adopted by them than ones that are perceived to undermine the social order."[8] The faster change comes, the more necessary it is that people be open to the concept of change itself before considering any specific changes.

Discussions of the electronic superhighway and of virtual reality and other developing technologies are raising a great deal of new uncertainty. The changes brought by one of the earliest pieces of this looming new world, e-mail, are already, as noted in the discussion of corporate governance in Chapter 4, changing corporate social norms. The ability of people at *all* levels to communicate with one another, bypassing normal hierarchical structures, directly impacts organizational form. And technology's role in enabling teams and flattening structures also impacts it. One can only speculate about what impact the next major technological development—as distinct from simply an improvement in what already exists—will have.

At the moment, however, most of the recent, clear impacts of technology on organizational structure are a result of the fact that "in the 1990s, the personal computer is becoming more and more a communications device."[9] By enabling those in organizations to work closely across organizational borders as well as within them, technology makes expansion in multiple directions possible—with allied organizations, with suppliers, with customers, and with specialists. Tying all the business networks into an electronic whole changes organizational structure and impacts governance because it unites so many differently governed entities.

COMING TO TERMS WITH GOVERNANCE

In many organizations, because information technology grew haphazardly, serving particular needs but with little rationalization of the way all the pieces should fit together, the work of the information technology organization was reactive rather than proactive. While this might have been the easiest and fastest way to enhance the systems in place, and while adding separate stand-alone systems for new business units seems to make sense when confronted with impossible time frames, the approach has led to the usual problems that result from the failure to rationalize the development of systems as a whole.

One of the results that is particularly disturbing is the inability of organizations to determine what information and communications technology assets they have and how to evaluate their costs. Executives of several large companies we worked with have admitted that they have no idea how many workstations their companies have, who has them, or what their capabilities are. One division "upgrades," and some of the old machines are given to a division just going on-line, with far less sophisticated users; some machines replace others that are no longer functional; and some just seem to disappear. Then there is the waste that results from the failure to note that applications are being abandoned, and no one is seeing to it that the number of licenses for using those abandoned applications—and the fees being paid—are cut to match. There is also the counting of assets that includes hardware and software brought into the company by employees because "it's just easier than dealing with the information technology group."

Another development that confounds the calculation of costs is the "shadow" information technology department. We saw this at work in a major hospital in the Midwest, where many divisions had independently hired practitioners who were also information technology knowledgeable. The idea was to have these employees deal with their departments' specific information technology needs, explain to the chief information officer (CIO) what their departments wanted, and work with application developers to be sure they understood their groups' needs. For example, a nurse with information technology expertise who was hired by the nursing department for this expertise was able to go into the system and update the forms used for government reports as regulations changed. Her salary was covered totally by the nursing department, although when we met her she explained that between application development and hands-on training of new nurses in using applications, she really was not doing any nursing. There were at least ten such positions, representing a full tenth of the current "information technology staff," but not one appeared in the information technology budget.

These things just seem to "happen." No one intends to build positions in their budget for someone working for another department. No one is setting out to confuse costs or hide assets. The problem lies in the failure to understand the effects of organizational changes on information and communications technology. John Lowenberg, chief executive of Aetna Life & Casualty Company's information technology unit, sees another downside to this unstructured approach. He says that the resultant "inconsistency in the technology forces a lot of artificial support structures."

He speaks from experience. When he joined Aetna in 1989, the company was using more than one hundred different word processing systems and nineteen different e-mail systems, none of which were compatible. As a result, layers of software were put in place to bridge gaps in the systems and employees could not move from one department to another without retraining.[10] At one point, when we were on an assignment at Aetna, one department was waiting to implement a system that involved one hundred new workstations, only to discover that they were incompatible with the platform being put in place by a division with which it worked closely.

Problems such as these are the result of implicit changes in governance that are not recognized and taken into account. The key to effective governance in the butterfly organization is to make certain that all the technological components of the organization are aimed at the same goal, and synchronize and coordinate timing, needs, and lines of command. Matching governance requires that those responsible for information and communications technology in the organization are alerted to changes in the way the organization is governed strategically and the way it is structured. This will happen only when the information and communications technology leadership becomes part of the team deciding on the changes to be made. Instead of being told that they have to connect with Company B to make a new project happen, they should be part of the evaluation process that determines which alliances and partnerships will be pursued. That is the only way to ensure that when the information technology department builds platforms, those platforms can accommodate many partners. Instead of being told after the fact that the company has changed to an empowered, flattened governance style, they should be alerted in advance.

THE DUALITY OF GOVERNANCE

Unfortunately, governance is the most confusing when it comes to the information technology function. In terms of governance, the information technology functional area or division either itself has to adhere to a governance style set from above or select a model of its own, and it has to accommodate all the various governance models within other groups in the organization in order to support them from a business perspective.

The issue does not arise in pure centralist organizations, where corporate headquarters dictates the role of information technology and those responsible for it run the function and provide the technology to the rest of the organization. But the minute a company begins to move from a centralist model, everything changes. In federalist organizations, chief information officers (CIOs), like all other business unit leaders, are empowered to select their own strategic governance models. When, however, they are providing technology systems for any other division or unit or functional area, they have to accommodate the governance models of that group, finding ways to integrate its technology with that of other units so there will be a workable overall technology infrastructure. The result is that the head of the information technology organization needs, more than any other leader in the organization, a deep understanding of the way every strategic governance model (and the variants within models) affects reporting relationships, empowerment, and levels and degrees of access to information.

ACCOMMODATION: THE PATH TO DEALING WITH CONFLICTING BUSINESS GOVERNANCE

The impacts of organizational restructuring on the information technology function, and the changes in governance that usually accompany restructurings, are often ignored until problems emerge. For example, with the use of new communications technologies, leaders can opt for a flattened, empowered organization instead of maintaining layers of middle management to mediate their wishes. Alternatively, they can choose to set up separate divisions, relying on technology to facilitate necessary interaction, such as the conveying of corporate strategy and the reporting structures necessary to track operational performance. When such choices are made, they inherently impact the information technology division; the greater the autonomy granted to groups, divisions, and units, the greater the impact on information technology. For example, Faith Noble and Michael Newman point out that "organization structures can impact the development process so as to alter computer-based systems to a design which is unintended but more consistent with existing organizational arrangements."[11] The effects of these alterations can be extremely costly, and particularly problematic when an organization is turning to buying instead of building systems.

PREVENTIVE MEDICINE

There are companies that strive to avoid these problems. One example is Shell Oil Company, a U.S. subsidiary of Royal Dutch Shell, which was planning a thorough reorganization and restructuring. The parent company had been in business for over a century. However, at the end of the 1980s and into the early 1990s, it, along with all the other players in its industrial sector, was suffering from a fall in demand resulting in a glut in the oil and gas market coupled with the worldwide economic downturn; revenues were flat and profit margins were down. Although the company was very good at formulating new strategies in response to rapidly changing market conditions, it was slow to implement them because of the levels of bureaucracy in the organization. Something had to be done to change the *way* it did business rather than *what* it did for a living. Senior management of the corporation decided that the time had come to restructure.

The planned restructuring was aimed at abandoning the company's traditional, hierarchical, command-and-control style. Management decided that it had to examine the effects of allowing individual business units to have somewhat (the degree was what they were determining) more autonomy. What was planned was a reorganization that would affect control, accountability, responsibility, and authority—in other words, governance.

Once the senior information technology managers were told about the probable direction of the coming change, they realized they would have to work with much more independent groups in the future, which would mean a complete change in the way they currently functioned. In essence, the very authoritarian model by which they worked—"this is the technology you will all use"—was going to have to be replaced with a willingness to accommodate and coordinate the demands of more autonomous business units.

Merle C. Bone, head of information technology for the U.S. division, called us in to address the issue with his senior managers. He wanted them to understand the possible organizational forms that the heads of the various business units might elect and the impact of each of those forms on the information technology organization. The question we were to help answer was: What impact would various changes in business governance have on information and communications technology, and how could those changes be dealt with efficiently and effectively?

The first step was to develop a commonly agreed upon set of definitions for governance models. Research indicated that there had been little formal study of governance in terms that would be useful for this project, given that the team members represented a number of different nationalities because of the company's practice of sending people overseas for experience. (The five governance models developed with this team—centralist, federalist, confederate, conglomerate, holding company—are described in Chapter 6.)

Once this task was completed, the models were reviewed with corporate management. They had reached the point in their own deliberations where, examining the models developed, they were able to state that the company was likely to move from its centralist model to some form of federalist, probably high federalist, model, moving at some future point to a conglomerate model. They thought it highly unlikely that they would change to either a confederacy or holding company model.

The next step was to explore in detail with members of the technology group what they would have to do to accommodate the models likely to be selected, and how they could position themselves to have enough authority to prevent the choices made by the various units from becoming a disaster in terms of the organization as a whole. The best choice for an individual unit may not work well with the choices made by other units. There has to be connectivity. The solution lies, in part, in defining the decisionmaking rights of business units in terms of information and communications technology.

For example, in a federalist model, business units are granted a high degree of autonomy, which leads some units to believe that they are fully empowered to make their own information and communications technology choices. Some might assume that this allows them to set up and manage their own information technology infrastructure (hardware and communications technology); others may choose to empower the information technology unit with the responsibility for choosing and managing the infrastructure.

One of the questions that arises out of the mix of choices is, Who bears responsibility for the cost of the connections of the different infrastructures? Is it a corporate responsibility, or, given that different units made decisions that resulted in different costs, how can those costs be allocated fairly? After all, while a unit may do its own work on its own system, it is still part of an overarching organization, communicating with corporate headquarters, and frequently with other units. This means that the technologies chosen—e-mail, computers, or sets of applications—should be interoperable. All too often they are not. The difficult chore of constructing gateways between these systems, which is a time-consuming and expensive proposition (it isn't as simple as putting a plug into the right socket—not yet, at least), falls to the corporate information technology division. Since these services have to be paid for, and often the costs are charged back to the units, expenditures on "independent" information and communications technology systems are far higher than expected; at times, when this happens, the total amount spent on information and communications technology can reach the level at which it has severe impacts on a unit's profitability.

The questions the information technology group was facing, which had to be put to management, were: Who will set the rules for responsibility for costs? Will it be the head of corporate information technology, the head of the business unit, or a coordinating body? Who will deal with the problems that could emerge if two different units choose different outsourcers to handle their information needs? What degree of authority will corporate information technology have when it comes to setting the rules of information technology empowerment for the various units?

EMPOWERMENT

To answer these questions required defining the various degrees of empowerment—from minimal (least), to constrained, to bounded, to full (most) empowerment. In the process of defining these stages, the consequences of each for the organization were explored with management.

MINIMAL. Under minimal empowerment, the business units can acquire only those resources that are necessary to support the critical processes of the unit (they cannot decide to use, for example, their own financial systems, since such functions are dictated at the corporate level). Even when a unit purchases a piece of hardware or an application for a purpose unique to the unit, if it has to be tied into the system as a whole, the unit does not have the option of asking for help from the information systems side in dealing with the problems that result from its decision. Instead, it would have to pay for the costs of building the connection. It cannot do what it wants to without accepting that doing so has a business cost.

CONSTRAINED. Under constrained empowerment, the information technology group puts in place a set of principles or guidelines each unit must accept. This might include rules governing security, standards, common systems, choice of vendors. Units may request the development of special applications or be allowed to set up independent systems—as long as they conform to certain standards and use certain "approved" vendors. If they decide to find a unique business solution, they may ask the information technology department for aid and assistance, as long as they pay for it, and as long as they are willing to abide by the principles in place. They have the accountability and responsibility for their own information technology within the limitations set out, and if they have enough "in-unit" technological expertise, they may be able to do some things at a reasonable cost.

BOUNDED. Under bounded empowerment, individual units must abide by a minimalist set of rules relating to common systems and procedures for security when the unit ties into common systems or for the selection of an e-mail system. They are free, however, to acquire any applications they want or even outsource, as long as they can make a business case for it—and pay the costs of linking into the corporate network.

FULL. At the highest level of full empowerment, the business units are free to choose any information and communications technology options they want—for example, hardware, communications, personnel, outsourcing, or any combination of these that they need to support their business. It is this level that is the most contentious. In reality, unless a business makes a strategic decision to become a conglomerate (dividing into separate companies, each with its own profit and loss statements, responsible for reporting only financial results to the ultimate owners), full empowerment is virtually impossible. Under almost any other form of organizational governance, data must be shared and information must be managed across the enterprise.

Deciding on the timing for moves along the continuum and putting in place detailed, specific rules and regulations at each stage are critical for success—and must be the job of teams with representatives from both the business and the information systems sides.

In the case of a foreign client that was contemplating total independence for some units (selling them), the temporary higher costs of full empowerment were considered worthwhile. They were moving to a holding company environment, in which part of the assets of the units would be their information and communications technology systems, and so the information technology organization served as a center for helping each unit develop the best system for that unit, regardless of the temporary difficulties of accommodation.

Senior management of this company opted for the highest federalist model, one very close to conglomerate. The CIO put together a coordinating body of users and information technology personnel to determine the exact levels of authority, responsibility, and accountability for the units. The group established what products and services the information technology department would provide, how applications and technology would be selected, and costs for information technology services. The information technology group became a "profit center" whose goal was to break even, but the group was determined to compete with outside vendors to deliver services. The information technology group was drastically cut in size, with many people from the group hired by other units. The information technology group focused on developing the capacity to provide advice and guidance about business solutions, to serve not only as the provider of common systems, but as business consultants.

The changeover to a reduced information technology unit was made as the company began to give its various business units the independence it believed would lead to a more cost-effective operation. The coordinating body that helped determine the degree of empowerment and the rules was left in place to negotiate the costs of various services. The shift worked well, and at last report the new, smaller corporate information technology group was providing the services needed to the various units. However, this shift had a number of effects: there were some early retirements and some employees the CIO would have liked to retain chose to move into the information technology function of various units rather than spend their time dealing with business issues.

FLYING FREE

When it comes to the butterfly organization, full empowerment is not an option. That choice would, in essence, result in paralysis. The butterfly organization cannot function without extensive, sophisticated communication networks that enable the constant exchange of information and allow work to be done anyplace at anytime, often interactively. Moreover, since much of the work is done with outsiders—both the affinity workforce (those who work for the corporation on a temporary or contract basis) and alliance partners and suppliers and customers—a substantial corporate network is essential. Owning the physical communications infrastructure is not the issue; having within the organization people with the competencies and capabilities in strategic planning and management of the infrastructure is. If the information technology leaders are to put in place a body of rules governing standards, platforms, and security to create a network that accommodates all the players as easily as possible, the information technology organization must be made up of individuals with competencies in business *and* technology—primarily, communications technology.

Moreover, since much of what needs to be done to achieve these objectives requires building relationships with players in other organizations as well as with internal units that have different governance styles, the only way the new information technology organization can succeed is through trust. The leader of the information technology group, the CIO, will therefore be responsible for developing strong ties to colleagues on both the information technology and the business side—a tall order, but one that may, as time goes by, end the turmoil that has become, as we shall see in the next chapter, so characteristic of life in the CIO lane.

8

THE CHANGING ROLE OF THE CIO

This whole effort is not about technology, legacy systems or buying more computers. Getting and keeping customers, taking out costs, reducing time to market—you can't do these things sitting over in the corner as an IT guy. You have to do it as a manager, a leader, a business partner who happens to know a lot about technology and knows how to surgically put it in the business in the right places.

Ron Ponder[1]

The changes in the way technology is defined and used make the management of technology—the electronic network and computers that tie together all the communications and information systems in the organization—a very different challenge today from what it was five years ago. At that time, the keeper of the hardware and software that handled the accounting and word processing systems of the organization was head of the information services function,[2] usually a direct report to the chief financial officer, with little opportunity to participate in senior management decision-making in all but the largest organizations.

Today, technology management is, or at least is rapidly becoming, a far more strategic position. It involves finding ways to tie together separate entities (units, people) so that time and location no longer are a consideration in creating, designing, manufacturing, and delivering products or services. It involves managing and integrating

multiple systems representing the technology needs of various parts
of the organization. It involves, as we saw in the previous chapter,
the accommodation of numerous governance models, all of which
must coexist—and be tied together by technology. It involves helping the organization analyze the uses of new technologies to discover new ways to do the same business it has always done, but
better and faster, or to create entirely new businesses through the
innovative use of the technologies it buys. It involves learning to
address security issues that have become extremely complex because
of the need to interact with numerous, and often temporary, partners. It involves finding ways to build capability at a moment's
notice, often in conjunction with other organizations, and building
it in such a way that it can be reduced just as effectively and efficiently. And it involves always being aware of possible advances in
technology so that the organization makes decisions with an eye
toward accommodating new technologies when they are actually
available. Such foresight is a critical success factor because the
advantages from new technologies are greatest for those who are
among the first to make use of them.

The technology leader of tomorrow therefore must be a business-
person first, with all of the leadership and people skills of any
other senior executive. In addition, this person must have the ability to understand technology well enough to know how it can be
used to leverage the business, and well enough to be able to work
closely with the technologists who constitute the players in his or
her division. This is a very different role from that traditionally
played by technology executives, and the nature of this profound
change is little understood, accounting for the turmoil in the field.

The problems of the chief information officer (CIO), while leadership related, are addressed here rather than in the next part of the
book, the part that deals with general leadership issues, because
technology leadership in the butterfly organization presents some
unique managerial issues.

THE FALL FROM GRACE

The demise of the chief information officer has been predicted
for quite a few years now and has been the subject of numerous
articles that recite daunting statistics. In 1991, a study by Deloitte

& Touche announced that the "average tenure of a CIO is only three years and that almost one-third of all corporate CIOs unwillingly depart from their posts."[3] In February 1995, a study by the same firm reported that "the average stay for a CIO with a large company is just five years," while Computer Sciences Corp. noted that "one third of all large companies replaced their top technology executives in the past two years."[4] In April 1995, the statistics looked even worse: "Companies are demanding faster results from their newly hired chief information officers. Five years ago, a new CIO could expect to have at least two years to boot up systems before being booted out. Now that grace period has sunk to just 14 months, according to recent findings by Positive Support Review Inc."[5]

What happened between the CIO glory days of the 1980s, when the CIO was a corporate god of sorts, and this new era in which many CIOs declared a new acronym to describe their current status: CBT—Chief Blame Taker? How feasible are the major alternatives to the CIO that are being studied? But perhaps most important is the question, What will the new, flexible organization, with its constantly changing alliance partners, temporary and at times off-site workforce, multiple and multinational suppliers, customers, and plants need in the way of a CIO?

A SURVEY OF WHAT WENT WRONG

The major reason given for the rapid demise of corporate CIOs is the failure of the technology they put in place to provide expected gains, given the amount invested in it. What does failure mean? Does it mean that the system put in place did not do what was promised? That it did but that there wasn't a commensurate rise in productivity? Does it mean that it took longer than expected to get it up and running, or that it cost more than estimated? In other words, what went wrong?

Whether this failure is real or not, the perception of failure is evident in the turnover rates of CIOs, and in surveys of chief executive officers (CEOs). A *ComputerWorld* survey of Fortune 1,000 CEOs "found that 64% doubted the value of their IT investment."[6] Among the reasons for this perception are the failure to understand governance, strategic misalignment, lack of proper communication, unrealistic expectations, the failure to bring new technologies into the organization in a timely fashion, lack of innovative uses of technology, and a misunderstanding of how costs and value should be assessed.

IGNORING THE GOVERNANCE ISSUE

The need to understand the implications of changes in governance was explained in detail in the previous chapter. It is a major problem that has only recently surfaced, and one that is going to be a serious concern until CIOs recognize that the governance of technology is one of their critical success factors. It is one aspect of a set of problems that fall under a larger head of matching business and technology in planning for the future.

STRATEGIC MISALIGNMENT

In the mid-1980s, academics studying the problems emerging as technology was becoming a major competitive factor in organizations began to point to the need for developing a formal method for ensuring that strategic decisions about technology were aligned with strategic business decisions. Unfortunately, all too many companies did not accept the fact that many of the problems that were preventing them from gaining the advantages promised from technology were caused by the failure of conventional business planning techniques to treat the information technology function as a cornerstone of the business.

When the strategic decisions of the organization are made by the strategic planners without the participation—or even knowledge—of the technology leadership, the result can be a change in strategic direction that, for example, makes an application currently in development useless. That is a small problem compared to those that occur when management changes an organization's structure without informing the information technology side of the house that such a change is going to take place. Or the problems that arise when the IT group puts in place new applications that require new skill sets on both the IT side and the user side without putting in place change management and training programs. Not examining strategic impacts can have an additional cost: failure to discover other uses of the technology. If users understood the technology better and worked with the IT side to explore its capabilities and the possibilities presented by various applications, they could uncover auxiliary uses that would enable the development of new products and services. For example, customer lists maintained to warn of recalls and track warranties also can be used to launch a newsletter or market a complementary product.

Strategic Alignment Modeling (SAM), a process for aligning business and IT strategy, was developed in the late 1980s to solve this problem.[7] It starts from the premise that every change made in the business strategy affects the business structure, the IT strategy, and the IT infrastructure; indeed, any change in any one of these four components has an effect on the other three. SAM provides a formal process for analyzing the impact of possible changes to help determine which ones would be most effective, what they would cost, and what it would take to implement them. Although SAM has been used successfully in numerous organizations, it has been slow to take hold. It requires new ways of thinking and analysis and interaction and thorough communication among all parties—and each requires strong support from the top.

FAILURE TO COMMUNICATE

Technology is still a mystery to many on the business side of the organization. The fact that they can use a word processor or a spread sheet does not mean that they know how those applications are constructed or what is involved when they access data from different places. Their world of computers involves only a click of the mouse, a touch of the keys, the movement of a light pen. These business users have no idea of the complexity involved, no understanding that, for their particular company, accessing data may take building a gateway from one application to another or building an application from scratch because of the nature of the company's data repository. CIOs who do not recognize this situation and deal with it are going to fail.

We encountered this problem firsthand in a benchmarking assignment for the CIO of a major hospital in the Northeast. The CIO was moving the organization to a client/server environment while maintaining the twenty-four-hour, seven-day-a-week availability of the current mainframe system with a very small staff. He had heard enough grumbling about his division's performance to decide that he'd better evaluate the situation. In order to discover the sources of the greatest dissatisfaction, an analysis of the gap between the user's and the information technology group's perceptions of the performance and importance of IT was needed. What eventually became clear was that, in all of the organizations that were benchmarked, user dissatisfaction had more to do with the communication skills of the CIOs and their direct reports than with reality.

Our client had explained to his users that they would be getting a new system—indeed, he had done a very good job of personally selling the system to senior management. But the users had not understood that putting in the new system would impact their ability to have changes made in current systems or get new applications. Our client assumed that the users would realize how difficult and time-consuming putting in the new system was and that therefore making changes to old applications would be a low priority unless critical; more, he could not imagine that his users needed to be told that subsequent application development would be only for the new system in order to avoid conversions—most had no idea what that meant (until he finally explained it). He failed to realize how little understanding users had of application development or technology architectures; he had assumed a higher level of sophistication because so many of them used complex research programs that they had brought with them to the organization.

The findings of the benchmarking study highlighted the communication problem, which led the CIO to take immediate action. Six months later, the intensive dialogue he opened with users began to pay off in terms of better relations; three years later, he was appointed head of technology when his hospital and another merged.

SETTING EXPECTATIONS

Another problem that is all too common is a failure by CIOs to control expectations. In their eagerness to gain approval for projects, and in their enthusiasm for technology that will help them create a leading-edge IT division and gain the reputation for having done so, many CIOs oversell a new technology. If the technology in question also happens to be a buzzword, the business side gets caught up in the hype and fails to ask enough questions; it wants to gain the rewards it assumes must be there—why else would everyone be moving in that direction? There is little interest in the problems that are likely to emerge along the way—until they happen. Then the reaction is bitter. CIOs have to learn to sell realistically.

Many CIOs, for example, fail to make clear that the gains from using technology to automate a process are far smaller if the process is not reengineered first. In the rush to get approval, they will cite benefits other companies have achieved—without explaining that the system was put in place only after processes were analyzed and streamlined. They avoid raising these issues because they fear the associated costs (and time involved) of the reengineering might temper enthusiasm for the technology. Once they get approval, however, they try to convince management to review the processes the technology will automate. Management refuses because they believe that the expensive new toy will do what they need. The gains realized as a result are far smaller than those expected—and everyone is unhappy.

TIMELINESS

Another major difficulty for CIOs is the failure to deliver applications on time and within budget. Although the problem isn't quite as prevalent today as it was years ago, in many companies, especially those that "build" rather than "buy" applications, it remains a cause of frustration. Management does not understand the nature of the problem. Why can a dam be designed and built with a reasonable degree of timeliness? How can Boeing meet "roll-out dates" for new airplane designs such as the Boeing 777—a monument to technological complexity—consistently? What is so different about building IT applications?

It is both a translation problem and a problem of assumptions. First, there is a lack of a common vocabulary between business users and application developers, each of whom unknowingly uses terms that are "jargon" to the other, resulting in numerous missteps. Second, imagine trying to describe all the steps in driving your car from home to the office. Unlock the car door, fasten your seat belt, turn on the ignition. Well, don't you have to put your key in the ignition? Then what about such decisions as shifting lanes because you know an upcoming exit begins to slow down the right lane just around the curve after the Main Street overpass? The programmer needs to know every detail. For the user, there are numerous steps that are so "obvious" they just don't get mentioned. The problems in interpretation and the steps left out end up requiring the programmer to go back into the application to make changes, and each change impacts the lines of code after that change. The result is what seems like endless delays.

While there are now methodologies, risk management protocols, and enough experience to have reduced the delays with certain types of simpler applications, today companies are asking their developers to produce far more complex applications. For example, developing applications such as global communications systems for handling bank transactions anywhere, anytime, anyplace involves millions of transactions a day, and usually the solutions have not been attempted before.

Cost and time overruns are nothing new in business. For example, building the Alaskan pipeline cost double the original estimate and took a year longer than expected; the tunnel connecting England and France was about a decade late. The problem facing CIOs is in part a result of the aura of "magic" surrounding IT: it is supposed to be a problem solver, not a problem creator. If magnetic resonance imaging can see through us, and we send shuttles into space routinely, why can't the CIO easily tie us to our supplier? The answer is simple: IT really isn't magic.

LACK OF INNOVATION IN THE USE OF TECHNOLOGY

Businesses look to technology leaders to be the prime movers in the use of technology, which is why it is critical for technology leaders to avoid personal attachment to specific systems. No organization can afford a technology leader who will do everything possible to cling to an old, comfortable technology. A leader who spends endless time and resources to make an old technology emulate the speed of a new one, avoiding change out of a fear of the unknown or the difficulties involved in learning something new and complex, is failing the organization. This will become even more of a roadblock if the company forms alliances with other companies and connectivity becomes an issue.

The clearest example of this problem is found among CIOs who are virtually addicted to mainframes. These individuals often give themselves away by the way they, literally, stroke the computer while extolling its virtues. For them, the words *client/server* or *open systems* inspire deafness. They don't even hear it when they are told that the mainframe would not necessarily be eliminated by a switch to client/server because of the necessity of preserving legacy systems and the possibility of using the mainframe as a data repository. They are so determined to protect what they are familiar with—and to maintain the control that a large, single system provides—that they ignore all recommendations for change. Unfortunately, when the leadership of the technology group is terrified of change, the organization stagnates.

THE COST-VALUE EQUATION

Among the most frequently heard complaints about CIOs is that they promise improvements from new technologies that simply do not materialize: "We put in all those expensive systems, and we haven't reduced our workforce at all." Today, technology is far more than a tool for speeding up basic clerical tasks, but the reduction of staff made possible by the first wave of technology remains the foremost measurement criteria. Instead, the calculation should include many of the other benefits computers can provide: greater customer satisfaction, new business opportunities, a reduction in product development time, improved supply chain integration, better inventory management, better information for executive decisionmaking, and so forth.

The days of capital/labor substitution as a measure of the value of technology should be history. Unfortunately, establishing new productivity measurements hasn't been a priority given all the other problems facing business over the past decade. Until this happens, CIOs must clarify the business values that new technology *will* provide, even when head count will *not* be reduced.

For example, an insurance company in the United Kingdom decided to reexamine its technology in 1992 when faced with overcapacity in the insurance market. The shakeout that was taking place in the industry made lowering costs while retaining business imperative. The result was a decision to find a way to add technology that would increase customer service and quality as well as control costs. The goals were clear from the outset.

The company's assistant general managers for IT and for a customer service center became the leaders of a team appointed to evaluate the problem. The first step was a work-flow management study. Taking into account the size of the organization (four thousand employees, four administration centers, seventy branch offices, 3.5 million customers); its current systems (traditional IBM mainframe with dumb terminals); and the need to change, they decided to begin with a priorities review. They discovered, for example, that more than 40 percent of the time of those involved in customer service was spent on pure paper pushing, not on the insurance business. After finding ways to reengineer some of the paper handling processes, they began to investigate how and to what extent new technology could alleviate the problem and simultaneously be used to improve customer satisfaction.

Senior management approved the costs of the new technology on two conditions—that the gains in productivity over a five-year period would pay for the investment and that business volume could be maintained by providing customers with efficient, high-quality service. The criteria were reasonable and the costs and benefits understood. The early results indicate that they will be met. The key point is that all the trade-offs were spelled out and all the players understood them.

In the case of an American insurance company in the Northeast, the situation was somewhat more complex. Senior management was determined to move the company ahead on the technology front to make productivity gains that would allow it to grow the business. On paper, the technology would not reduce the total number of employees, but the reduction in clerical jobs would be matched by increases in jobs focused on customer service, which would include cross-selling to increase the organization's profitability. In order to ensure a smooth transition, the unit responsible for much of the clerical work was relocated, which made it far easier to change staff (many did not want to relocate, especially since the jobs were low paid). The staff hired in the new location was more skilled, but because it was a southern location, somewhat lower paid. There was a productivity increase—but not a reduction in overall staff size.

Examining what went wrong with the implementation of new technologies is useful only if the information garnered is used to avoid making the same mistakes again. If CIOs do not learn to deal with, and learn from, these roads to failure, there is no way they will succeed in the butterfly organization, which will require an even more business-oriented form of communication and information technology management.

ALTERNATIVES TO THE CIO

The CEO perception of the CIO and the costs of technology in an era of downsizing have resulted in a number of attempts to dismantle the CIO function or find new ways to manage it. Among the solutions being tried are dispersing the function to divisions, each of which appoints its own information officer; splitting the job between a business leader and an IT expert to ensure a business focus; outsourcing; appointing CIOs who have business rather than IT backgrounds; and not putting anyone in charge. It is important to examine these efforts because many of them point to ideas that might, in various combinations, be workable in the butterfly organization.

THE DIVISIONAL INFORMATION OFFICER (DIO)

InformationWeek noted in 1993 that "at Xerox, Amoco, and dozens of other large corporations, CIOs are working closely with senior management to reshape the IS function." At that time, for example, Xerox decided to put in place unit-level DIOs accountable to the presidents of their respective units directly, but reporting to the CIO on a dotted-line basis. They said that this was being done to ensure that the units could each find the best business solution for their IT needs—developing their own systems or contracting with either outsourcers or the corporate IS group. The idea was that the corporate IS group would maintain a "coherent technology vision, maximize the company's buying power, enjoy a mechanism for sharing best-practices insights, and ensure that the business units don't sacrifice long-term viability by adopting incompatible short-term strategies."[8] In the fast-moving world of IT, one year and one month later, Xerox entered into a major outsourcing arrangement.

The concept of DIO is still around, but formal recognition of the need for technology expertise within units in a federalist organization is not a replacement for the CIO. The creation of this role is, rather, recognition that technology is such an integral part of the organization that technologists with specific business area expertise are often necessary. Where the DIO exists, there is also a CIO who coordinates activities and runs the corporate IT function. The DIOs help at this level by serving as useful conduits of the business strategies being developed in the units, providing information that can be factored into the overall planning for the technology infrastructure of the organization.

MULTIPLE MANAGERS

Given the complexities of managing the IT function, there are those who advocate multiple managers. Splitting the job between an IT expert and a business leader with technology expertise is one line of thought. Another is to integrate key IT personnel into other groups within the organization; for example, an IT strategist should be assigned to the business planning department. Indeed, *InformationWeek* suggests that "the technology group is too important to be bottled up under any single part of the company. . . . IT should," the article goes on to suggest, "be divided according to its four primary functions." Those functions are (1) the provision of data services, which includes the basic administrative functions; (2) business unit relations, which includes the building of applications and should be handled within the business units with outside support; (3) strategic planning, which requires an IT planning group within the corporate structure; and (4) enforcement of rules through the executives of the organization.[9]

This four-part division offers a number of advantages if those in the various groups report to an information technology leader. The danger is that each of the groups will become an IT area fighting for power and playing politics. The role of IT will be too important to the organization of the future to be divided up into components that are not coordinated by a central leader. There is also the problem of duplication of expertise and equipment if the function is not centrally coordinated, which returns us to the problem of governance. How much empowerment should be granted if the function is centrally coordinated?

This problem arose with a midwestern utility company as well as with an international transportation company, both of which had many separate businesses operating under the parent company. In reassessing and reshaping the IT function, the notion of a coordinating body was agreed to by both companies as a way to handle IT. The problem faced by the team restructuring the IT divisions was: If the function were to be centrally coordinated, what degree of empowerment—minimal, constrained, bounded, or full—would be granted to the coordinating body? At one end, the central coordinating body or an IT czar (either a true body of representatives from corporate and the business units or a single individual) could set standards that the other businesses' CIOs would be forced to adhere to. Or the coordinating body could be a "toothless tiger," having neither the authority to set the rules nor to enforce them. At the one extreme, it would be similar to the "centralist" model of IT; at the other, the potential was to have each business unit's IT group function as an autonomous unit.

In the utility company, the decision was to have a coordinating body, headed by the corporate CIO, with the power to take away any business unit's IT franchise if it did not adhere to the principles established by the coordinating body. In the transportation company, the decision was to have the head of the coordinating body serve as a boundary manager, facilitating and negotiating rules and standards, but with limited authority to direct the activities of the individual CIOs. The business units made the final decision. The utility wanted synergy with autonomy; that is, to develop a common system it could depend on as it grew to meet the anticipated deregulation of the industry. The transportation company's decision was based on the possibility of selling off some of the businesses at a future point in time.

OUTSOURCING

Another possible solution to the problems of IT and the drive to streamline the organization is outsourcing. There are a number of success stories; companies that have turned over various functions—such as payroll—or even their entire IT function to outside agencies. The debate over the wisdom of such moves touches on the loss of core competencies, the loss of control, and the danger that the outsourcers can hold the company hostage in the future. The problem for many companies involves the way outsourcing arrangements are handled.

A market survey of 251 CIOs revealed that although 96 percent reported that all they can really do is "predict information technology's capital expenditures, occupancy costs, head count, capacity utilization and price/performance for the next three years, . . . they are signing outsourcing contracts that average about nine years. That means they have no way of measuring their needs and costs for years four through nine."[10] Another problem is the amount of work involved in trying to run the outsourcing arrangements, especially when the CIO leaves because the job just isn't very satisfying after everything is outsourced. In fact, "company executives who've taken the plunge often find themselves negotiating mammoth documents, dissecting the IS anatomy into units of storage, processing, transactions and so on."[11]

These negative effects are not a given. If the IT organization is strong, outsourcing can have a positive effect. In fact, unless the IT function has core competencies and capabilities in IT strategy formulation and management, it probably shouldn't outsource the function until these competencies are in place within the IT function. A strong, though small core IT group is necessary to develop and manage the outsourcing arrangement, and to build new arrangements if those in place break down. It is also necessary if the company is to continue to learn about new IT possibilities. Without such a strong core group, who will assess the technological compatibility of future alliance partners?

Serious consideration should also be given to the type of outsourcing arrangement the organization should structure with its outsource provider. Will it be a standard, transaction-based contract—that is, based upon a cost per transaction processed? Will it be a specialized contract—that is, will the organization require certain terms and conditions from the outsource provider that would normally not be granted to other organizations? For example, sharing of process expertise in an exclusive arrangement? Should the contract be structured as a performance agreement—that is, if costs are reduced by an agreed-upon percentage, the outsource provider shares the benefit with the organization? Or should the arrangement be a strategic partnership—that is, both parties share the risk, rewards, and pain. Although many outsourcers talk about "strategic partnerships" with the organization, few outsourcers are willing to take an equal risk/reward position with the organization considering outsourcing.

In the organization of the future, outsourcing is likely to play a role, but a core IT function headed by a CIO will be in charge. One such example that may serve as a model is the case of John Cross, head of information technology for British Petroleum (BP). Cross decided to outsource all the organization's technology needs, but he did not choose one provider and did not split the IT needs into discrete slices. Instead, he turned the IT over to a consortium of three contractors who were required by the terms of the contract to "work together to deliver a single seamless service" to all of the forty-plus international business units that comprise British Petroleum. The contracts were short term, required the contractors to benchmark their services so BP could be certain it would continue to get the best deals possible, and were set up to keep the IT group, as much as possible, from becoming "full-time contract managers." The process is not yet perfect; Cross admits that BP "learned that supplier management can be a headache." However, he adds, "We are actively repositioning IT to be the service group we envisioned. . . . Our remaining IT employees [150 out of the 1,400 employees five years earlier] are fast becoming internal consultants."[12]

THE BUSINESS/IT LEADER

According to James McGee and Laurence Prusack, CIOs have, until very recently, been "selected for technical acumen rather than political skills. Few CIOs have embarked on initiatives to improve the way information—not just information technology—is used and managed in the business." Now that it has become clear that both abilities are equally necessary, organizations are rethinking the job specifications. "At companies such as IBM, Xerox, Kodak, and Merrill Lynch, recent CIOs have been fast-track executives with records of managing important nontechnological aspects of the business. If these nontechnical managers can master the considerable technical challenges in the creation of an information infrastructure, then it appears that they already have the skills and influence to bring about a political environment in which the information can be shared and used."[13]

The question is whether they can "master the challenges"—or want to. Technology is continuing to change so rapidly, with new technologies on the horizon almost weekly, that a business executive would face the enormous problem of coming up the curve in terms of learning about the technologies in place, and then adding to that an understanding of new and often untested technologies on the horizon. Today, when even technically astute CIOs are finding it hard to keep up, the challenge may be insurmountable.

LET'S TRY ANARCHY

There are even those who are so convinced that the future is here—that everyone is a computer expert familiar with the Internet and able to access everything they need on-line—that they believe the function is one that can run without coordination of any kind. A small start-up company may be able to function with technology that is not formally connected, except perhaps for e-mail or a good voice mail system. The minute it acquires a second site or employees who work at home to augment its workforce, or needs to establish communications with a client, however, it has to connect its technology. And someone has to be in charge to make it happen. The future is not here yet, but when it arrives, the corporate slogan at Sun Microsystems, Inc.—"The network is the computer"—will, with a slight change, apply to all companies: "The network is the company." That day will not arrive as long as anarchy prevails.

WHO WILL MIND THE STORE?

Given that technology must be tied together if the organization is to be tied together, given the speed of change in technology, and given corporate politics, there simply has to be someone in charge. Ignoring this reality would be a lot like saying that when an organization chooses a federalist model and empowers every business unit, there is no need for an executive body—for a corporate headquarters where the overall corporate strategies are set and the financial and legal (and perhaps marketing, human resources, and other critical cross-functional value chain elements) affairs of the organization are coordinated.

The CIO is not going to disappear, but the job as it originally evolved will; the organization of the future, especially the butterfly organization, will need a more highly evolved business/technology leader, one whose skill sets are very different from his predecessor's.

TOMORROW'S TECHNOLOGY LEADER

What will the IT function look like in the future and how will it be led? Merle C. Bone, CIO of Shell Oil Company, predicts that "the combination of information and communications technology will have an impact on the way business is run and structured, giving the organization the ability to bring together knowledge and skills from any part of the planet."[14] Clearly, this will require many changes in the way IT departments work, but that does not faze Bone, who has been with Shell for twenty-one years. Asked why he has succeeded where so many others have failed, he shrugs, smiles, and tells you about the wonderful people he has working for him.

The reasons for his success can be seen in the history of the way Bone's department serves Shell. The IT group has changed dramatically over time in response to changes driven by economic developments in the world. Bone prepares for these changes, and actively searches for any other issues that might have an impact. He regularly sets up strategy groups to evaluate the current business and look for ways to reinvent it using technology; he also searches for ways to change the technology function itself. When these groups come up with interesting findings, senior management listens. This receptivity probably grows out of Shell's long use of scenario planning.[15]

Asked about the problems facing IT leaders today, Bone noted that "in the old days IS told the business what was good for them, while today the business community has become the customer of IT not the consumer of it." He added that in the mid- to late-1980s, when "business problems required a critical mass of solutions, IT leaders were solving the problems with a piecemeal approach." Finally, he says, he and many others realized that their "philosophy had to change to delivering customer perceived value, as opposed to that of a technology company that delivers technology for the sake of technology."

Bone said that as a result of the most recent restructuring of Shell:

> I have twenty people reporting to me directly, five of whom are business customers, and fifteen in my own group. And there are nine hundred who functionally report to me in a dotted line relationship. We view governance in three dimensions. We have product managers, process managers, and the pay-and-performance relationships such as HR. This makes it possible for both parties [business and IT] to discuss and agree upon the value of the output before they begin. But it must not end there. Ongoing discussions between business and IT are necessary.

Contemplating similar questions, Spencer J. McIlmurray of the Gartner Group predicts that the CIO "will be the key liaison to top management, and will be well positioned to exploit technologies and innovations that go beyond the day-to-day operations. The CIO will understand the strategic vision of the company and link the mahogany

paneled offices with the data centers and the end-user help desks."
Unfortunately, he adds, "You don't find folks like this on every
street corner."[16] That, however, is just one part of the problem.
The other part is the failure of senior management in organizations to learn enough about IT or to integrate IT into the business's strategic planning process.

TECHNOLOGY IN THE BUTTERFLY ORGANIZATION

Before discussing the skills and expertise necessary for the IT leader
of the organization of the future—that is, skills needed in addition
to the other leadership skills that will be explored in the next three
chapters—it is important to determine what the IT function will be
expected to provide in the butterfly organization.

Since information and communications technology is what ties
this new organization together, the technology group must be sure
that the right kind of technology is available when and as needed.
It must help the business side determine what will best serve its
needs, introducing new possibilities when technology advances.
As technology becomes more standardized, it must focus on buying
whatever applications it can to both reduce costs and ensure compatibility with potential partners. It may also choose to outsource
some functions that can be performed more efficiently outside—
but it must retain the core competencies to take those functions
back if changes warrant such a move.

The IT group must be prepared to grow, which means switching
to open systems that can expand in far smaller increments than
past systems. It must understand what kind of skills it will need
when expansion is necessary, and where to find them. It must also
ensure that the technology platform has enough capacity for the
onset of growth—and have plans in place for adding components
when needed. But the department must be prepared to bring extra
human resources into the organization on a temporary basis, reserving to itself the administrative duties needed to run on a larger
scale without putting in place a bureaucracy. It must also have in
place plans that will ensure that those brought on board are, when
no longer needed, let go in such a way that they would be willing
to return if needed in the future. And it will mean setting up training programs, possibly internships, to be certain that people with
the next generation of skills needed are in the wings.

The new IT division must be as broadly based as the organization. For example, although it would be possible to run everything from the home office, it is important that core IT personnel be given exposure to other corporate cultures. They may be needed to grow the organization in different locations, overseeing the training and management of people from many different backgrounds. In addition, the IT group in the butterfly organization must include specialists in strategic business and IT planning, human resources, training, and technology—and all must be good communicators who are able to interact with the business side.

The IT function in the butterfly organization will be accepted as a critical core component of the business, and the IT leader will be the peer of the other direct reports to the CEO. Like the organization of which it is a key part, IT will be a complex adaptive system, impacting and being impacted by forces over which it has little control: leadership changes, governance changes, and additional new advances in technology.

The IT groups of many companies that are striving to become more flexible have already begun to take some of these steps. For example, Wal-Mart has led the charge to connectivity across the supply chain, from manufacturer to customer; the grocery industry is rapidly following suit, trying to establish standardized platforms to connect themselves to one another to be able to compete with mass marketers. Consultancies and other service professionals have been setting up such IT groups because of their need to tie together their far-flung staffs, ensuring constant flows of information and communications capability regardless of location and time.

Companies such as the midwestern utility and the international transportation company mentioned earlier are rethinking their IT as well as business structures to ensure flexibility as each contemplates major changes in the business they do. A major multinational supplier of disk drives is enhancing its technology capabilities to improve what it does now and enable it to become a worldwide logistics supplier in the near future. Companies preparing to play a different role in the future are beginning to construct the global, flexible, IT functions they will need to succeed; the evolutionary process has begun.

A major part of this evolution is the result of what IT experts Don Tapscott and Art Caston call a paradigm shift in technology.[17] It involves the availability of open, client/server systems that allow easy and, compared to mainframe technology, inexpensive expansion and contraction as well as amazing degrees of flexibility. This shift in technology is the enabler of the new enterprise—but probably just the first step into a completely new world of networked information and communications capability.

THE CIO OF THE EVOLVED ORGANIZATION

Clearly, leading this new technology group will take a myriad of management skills—most of which will be explored in subsequent chapters. The skills that are unique to the IT group, however, need further exploration; they will be critical to the survival of the CIO and the evolution to the butterfly organization.

UNDERSTANDING BUSINESS. The new IT leader has to understand the basics of business in order to explain the advantages of technology, not in terms of what the technology can do, but in terms of the business advantages it can provide. For example, the more the technology leader understands business, the easier it is to make a case for the value of a specific technology. If she knows that the cost of retaining a customer is 30 percent of the cost of acquiring a new customer, the CIO can use that information to convince management to invest in a system that allows customer representatives to answer customer inquiries during initial calls 90 percent of the time.

MAINTAINING TECHNOLOGY COMPETENCY. Technology is changing so rapidly that CIOs must find ways to assign staff to the preliminary evaluation of technology benefits. These technologists must find ways to focus on the uses to which new technologies can be put rather than focusing on the intrinsic nature of the technology. They must examine technology as business leaders would, relying on their backgrounds plus the expertise and information they can cull from staff, peers, vendors, and consultants to keep them up to speed. Competency means understanding the benefits of new technologies.

UNDERSTANDING NETWORKING ON A GLOBAL BASIS. The information technology leader must develop greater knowledge and skills in the rapidly advancing area of communication technologies to understand how they can be combined with information systems to create global networks for the organization. The standards that prevail in other nations, regulations that might create problems, and information about key players in these areas should be required learning. It will be incumbent on the CIO to participate in conferences and meetings that focus on these issues.

CHANGE FACILITATION. Carol A. Beatty and Gloria L. Lee indicate that "where technological change and organizational change are intertwined, the speed and extent of change relies heavily not just upon the technical skills of middle managers but more importantly upon their commitment to the new culture and their path-finding leadership skills in seeking solutions appropriate to their situation, which will facilitate the transition."[18] CIOs will not be able to help others adapt to the new organizational culture they are helping to create unless they have internalized it, and the same holds true for helping others adapt to new technologies. Comfort with change is a prerequisite to leading others to accept change, and therefore, the technology leader must be eager to explore what is new and convey that excitement to everyone else.

MANAGING SAFETY AND SECURITY. There are two issues here: one is keeping the company's technology physically safe; the other is securing the information contained within the system from tampering by outsiders.

An investigation after a power outage "found that more than eighty-five percent of the largest firms in the U.S. are totally or heavily dependent on computer technology. While the need for contingency planning for these technologies seems evident, the same researchers found that only six out of ten firms currently have a disaster recovery plan in the area."[19] After every earthquake or event such as the bombing of the World Trade Center, there is an upsurge in disaster recovery planning. Getting companies to carry out that decision is like prodding someone to write a will: "We're in Omaha, what can happen here? We're not on a fault, we're too high up for floods, and this is a fireproof building." "But are you sure you don't have a problem with a disgruntled employee? What if a tornado throws a tree through the window and rain soaks through into wires that run under the carpets, shorting out everything or making the building uninhabitable in the middle of your busiest season?" Complete, off-site, secured backup, and some arrangement for emergency space and equipment are a minimum operational requirement; the speed with which everything is done today makes delays in business resumption because of a loss of technology unacceptable.

The issue of security is far more complex and difficult in the world of open systems and the Internet. Although some companies are aware of the problem and "devices originally designed for spy agencies are now standard corporate issue," John Verity of *Business Week* warns that "for every solution in cyberspace, there's always another problem to solve."[20] The more that organizations partner with others and use temporary workers, particularly workers off-site, the more the IT function must focus on maintaining security. Not only can proprietary information be at risk, but systems could easily be sabotaged in countless ways. Strict rules of access to critical systems will have to be put in place and everyone with access will have to be educated to the risks of security breaches. In all too many organizations, employees have volunteered their passwords to us when we announce our intention to work late into the evening "just in case you want something the password they gave you won't let you access." This is a dangerous mindset, and the CIO must accept responsibility for conveying the danger to everyone in the organization.

PROVIDING EDUCATION. John Davis, head of a New York executive search firm that bears his name, says that "these days, CIOs spend 30% to 40% of their gross time explaining the benefits and the reality of information technology to their companies' CEOs, business unit managers, top production people—the whole senior cadre. Educating others is a much bigger part of the CIO's job now than it's ever been."[21] Not only are CIOs responsible for personally educating senior management about these issues, but they are also responsible for overseeing the technology education of every member of the organization—current and future. The CIO must assume responsibility for ensuring that users accept, understand, and are trained in the new technology.

STANDARDS. CIOs facing a truly connected, networked future, where the need for compatibility will be almost overwhelming, must become part of the move to standards. Unfortunately, organizations devoted to setting standards "are not sufficient to address the problem."[22] CIOs are going to have to push to strengthen consortiums, such as the Open Software Foundation, which will begin to produce detailed specifications that companies will adhere to if enough join. It is one road to speeding the connectivity and compatibility that will make it easier to buy applications rather than develop them and to add new technology and tools to existing platforms.

A BALANCING ACT. In *Competing for the Future*, Gary Hamel and C. K. Prahalad say that the goal of business should be "to be neither narrowly technology-driven or narrowly customer-driven. The goal is thus to be broadly *benefits driven*—constantly searching for, investing in, and mastering the technology that will bring unanticipated benefits."[23] One of the keys to doing this will be the technology leader, whose job will be to help shape the organization and move it in new directions.

CONCLUSION

The information technology function will be an integral part of every organization that evolves to the butterfly form. The reason is simple: IT does more than enable; it enhances and even promotes creativity and innovation. Over and over, when you look at organizations, you see that the difference between yesterday and today is speed, scale, scope, and connectivity—all of which are made possible by IT. Information technology supports—and connects—all the functional areas of the business, including manufacturing, financial, marketing, sales, legal, R&D, as well as the workforce (domestic and international, full and part time), alliance partners, outsourcers, suppliers, and customers, no matter where they are located. To lead this function well, however, takes, in addition to the skills specific to a CIO, a new kind of leader with a broader range of competencies, including an understanding of the difficulties involved in helping an organization maintain its stability—without stagnating—as the world keeps changing. The roles of those leaders and the qualities that make good leaders will be explored in the pages that follow.

PART IV

LEADERSHIP FOR THE NEW AGE

9

BUILDING MULTILEVEL LEADERSHIP

Control of a complex adaptive system tends to be highly dispersed.... [It] has many levels of organization, with agents at any one level serving as the building blocks for agents at a higher level ... [and they] are constantly revising and rearranging their building blocks as they gain experience.

M. Mitchell Waldrop, *Complexity*[1]

The butterfly organization will not appear by magic; all the forces in the world will not move organizations to this new form unless leaders, recognizing the value of the ability to shift rapidly from retrenchment to growth and back again, change the way they think about their businesses and their roles in them. Fortunately, this is already happening. Leaders today are being forced by a combination of forceful stakeholders and economic pressure to find new ways to grow the profits of their organizations, without growing their organizations permanently.

Indeed, organizations today, especially those that have eliminated numerous levels of middle management in an attempt to speed decisionmaking, reduce costs, and take advantage of technology, face the question, How will they manage in periods of growth?

The answer to that question involves three areas of leadership. The first is leadership on different levels (from the board to senior managers, operational managers, and team members); the second is leadership over alliances (determining which roads to expansion make sense, how to structure various kinds of alliances, how to manage them, how to break them up); and the third involves the qualities necessary to be a good leader of the new organization (the properties and characteristics of leadership in this developing organizational form). Each of these topics will be explored in one of the chapters that comprise this section of the book.

This chapter will focus on the devolution of many leadership responsibilities to other levels of the organization. It will explore what needs to be done to ensure that core employees—full-time employees who will spend a number of years with the organization—understand the big picture well enough to serve as leaders in the integration of new workers and temporary workers—a group we call *affinity workers*—into the organization during periods of expansion. The core employee is not a lifetime employee of a single organization, but someone who is part of a core organization on a full-time basis for a period of time who then moves on to become a core member of another organization; the affinity worker is someone who is a part of the workplace as either a contract worker, a temporary worker from an agency, or an employee of a firm with whom the core organization is partnering in some way. Efforts at empowerment and teams will be analyzed for clues to developing the right kinds of employees for organizations that may expand, but that want to do so without adding layers of management. But first, some general issues need to be explored that will apply to all three chapters about leadership.

A PROBLEM OF DEFINITION: WHAT IS LEADERSHIP?

In looking at the debates over whether there are differences between leadership and management, the words of Abraham Zaleznik, written in 1977, seem prophetically relevant to the butterfly organization:

> A crucial difference between managers and leaders lies in the conceptions they hold, deep in their psyches, of chaos and order. Leaders tolerate chaos and lack of structure and are thus prepared to keep answers in suspense, avoiding premature closure on important

issues. Managers seek order and control and are almost compulsively addicted to disposing of problems even before they understand their potential significance. In my experience, seldom do the uncertainties of potential chaos cause problems. Instead, it is the instinctive move to impose order on potential chaos that makes trouble for organizations.2

The problem is that if leaders and managers are essentially different as a result of ingrained personality differences rather than training, it will be difficult to develop the kind of leaders needed in the far leaner, less management heavy new organization. Management gurus such as Peter Drucker offer more hope, taking the view that "leadership involves selecting talented subordinates, providing them with goals and direction, and establishing followers' trust by backing up one's words with actions; the management functions of planning, organizing, and controlling represent critical components of the leader's job."3 Scholars such as Elliott Jacques take the position that leadership and management are complementary processes. To them, leadership involves the ability to set the organization's direction by maintaining a focus on its vision and mission while at the same time maintaining a short-term perspective that looks at current performance outcomes.

When spread across levels, functions, and structures, leadership responsibility includes strategic leadership (that is, setting the vision, mission, and goals of the organization) and operational leadership (that is, ensuring that all the tasks involved in meeting performance measures are successfully accomplished). In other words, the leader and manager components are combined. In fact, William L. Gardner III and John R. Schermerhorn, Jr., state that "it is just as important for a department head to maintain a sense of direction and integrate that department with others, as it is for a chief executive officer (CEO) to give direction to the enterprise as a whole. By the same token, it is as critical for senior executives to make sure their direct reports can and do accomplish daily tasks, as it is for the production manager."4

AN ASSEMBLAGE OF ATTRIBUTES

There are those who say the leader provides vision and has charisma that makes others buy into that vision. Those who study leadership characteristics suggest that leaders also need to be skilled

at planning and organizing, problem solving, clarifying, informing, monitoring, motivating, supporting, managing conflict and
team building, networking, delegating, developing, mentoring, and
rewarding.[5] In addition, leaders must be able to establish an environment in which creativity and innovation flourish. The list taken
as a whole is overwhelming, but at various times, leaders need to
have all these skills in order to motivate those they supervise.

In the past, organizational structure meant that most employees
never played any kind of leadership role; they carried out the tasks
they were assigned to the best of their ability, without questioning
and without necessarily understanding how what they were doing
fit into the bigger picture. This was a carryover of the theories of
Alfred Sloan, General Motors's leader in the 1920s. *The Economist*
says that "for Sloan, the job of senior managers was to create a
system that minimized the idiosyncracies of human behavior; for
today's best managers, the job is to encourage those idiosyncracies
and harness them to corporate ends. To do this, bosses are shifting
their attention from designing a single corporate strategy to shaping
general organizational purposes—so that others, lower down the
pecking order, can design micro-strategies for themselves."[6]

Expecting individuals who have spent their lives in a controlled
corporate environment to assume more responsibility and take
more initiative will require communication, education, and extensive retraining. After all, as J. E. Osborne points out, the "demands
on a leader [are] quite different from those placed on a staff person.
The skills and abilities that worked so well in [that] position no
longer carry much weight when dealing with leadership responsibilities. . . . Leadership represents the ability to direct, motivate, and
challenge others." The tools for doing so include defining and
interpreting objectives, assessing the strengths and weakness of
team members, creating a plan for action, obtaining appropriate
resources, arranging training, and using creative problem solving.[7]

The new organization needs leaders who can delegate responsibility to those at different levels—after having trained, mentored, and
empowered them to act within boundaries. An interesting examination of leadership, which pulled together the views of one hundred
top leaders, concluded that "the notion of one omnipotent, all-wise
leader at the top who figures everything out is no longer workable.
The world is just too complex now, particularly in far reaching
global enterprises. A faster pace and advances in technology mean

that we have to get decision-making and problem-solving out of the corner office and spread throughout the organization. . . . We will need visionary leaders, facilitative leaders, inspiring leaders, collaborative leaders—in other words, leaders of all types arising at every level of an enterprise. Leadership is no longer exclusively top-down, but also bottom-up and 'omni-directional.'"[8] The groundwork for developing these skills is being laid in organizations that have turned to collaborative efforts by employees, particularly empowerment and teams. The result of these advances in management is the development of individuals who understand concepts such as loyalty, free expression of ideas, supporting others, responsibility and accountability, and the efficacy of communication across, up, down, and outside the organization—all in the pursuit of the success of the team, project, or company. Such individuals will play a critical role in the organization of tomorrow.

STEPS IN THE RIGHT DIRECTION

The upheavals of the past several years have lead to changes that have opened the door to the training and development of employees throughout the organization in decisionmaking and leadership skills. These efforts arrived in the form of the quality movement that began in postwar Japan, aided by the thinking of Drs. W. Edwards Deming and Joseph M. Juran. The approach to quality adopted by the Japanese led to dramatically improved products that began to threaten U.S. markets in the late 1970s. The result was the adoption of Total Quality Management (TQM) by many U.S. organizations in the 1980s.

Total Quality Management starts from the premise that quality is defined by the customer, who then responds to a perception of quality with increased demand. Implementing TQM, however, requires a strong leadership team focused on quality improvement and willing to devote sufficient energy and attention to changing the organizational culture to one that adopts quality goals and then develops the appropriate systems and methods for achieving those goals.

Quality management holds employees accountable, but only after training them to meet their new responsibilities. It involves empowering employees—those closest to the critical operating procedures in manufacturing and those closest to the customer in service industries—and it involves the establishment of teams to look for additional ways to provide customer satisfaction. This focus on empowerment and teams brought about by the TQM movement spread beyond quality. Soon empowerment and teams became tools for enabling the shrinking workforce (in organizations that now had far fewer middle managers) to do their jobs when there was no one around to convey exact, minute-by-minute instructions.

Empowerment and teams have laid the groundwork for the development of extended leadership capabilities on different levels. In some organizations, they have produced employees who are far more understanding of overall corporate goals and who are prepared to handle much more on their own, without constant supervision. Unfortunately, this ideal, however laudable, is not being achieved routinely. The problem is very akin to the problems with reengineering: there is nothing wrong with the concept, but it does not bring the desired results unless it is carefully integrated into the organization's culture and fully implemented.

EMPOWERMENT

Empowerment is one of those terms that has multiple meanings. The definition that perhaps most sharply defines empowerment gone wrong was offered by a rapidly advancing middle manager in a major insurance company in the Northeast: "Empowerment means overwork." The woman who offered us that definition had been with the company for many years and was at that point in her career where she was being offered opportunities to prove she should be moved to upper management level. We met her when she was assigned to coordinate the team we would be working with on a change management project. When we asked what other changes the organization had been through over the past year, she provided a laundry list—restructuring, quality teams, a second organizational restructuring, and two new technology systems. Then she added "empowerment." When we asked how each had been introduced and what the effects had been, it became clear that the attempts to introduce these changes had been sporadic, rarely explained to the whole organization in any detail, and had little real effect on performance: "Quality—that let us get to know people outside our own areas; restructurings made everyone paranoid for the weeks it took for them to announce who would be 'restructured out'; technology—finding a way to deal with an unchanged work-load while attending boot camp; and then empowerment, which means, so far as I can tell, nothing but overwork."

The problem is that many companies simply tell people they are being empowered and have more responsibility—that they can make decisions. Empowerment is a concept that cannot be announced and walked away from. It requires many changes in the way business gets done. To begin with, it requires a clear definition by management of what it means within the organization. At a minimum, it involves the sharing of knowledge, the development of trust, and cooperation, but with clear boundaries on responsibility and authority. Empowerment requires, according to Martha Slice and Alan Gilburg, "managers, who have been used to deciding and telling what needs to be done, [to] be comfortable with asking for ideas, feedback, and with encouraging innovation and learning from experience and mistakes."[9] People empowered to make decisions have to be taught how to make those decisions, within what limits, and where to go for advice.

Elios Pascual, chairman and CEO of Mack Trucks, Inc., says that when it comes to empowerment it is critical that everyone be a player: "A CEO must engender understanding and commitment through continuous training and communication across the entire organization. . . . The whole organization must understand how the company defines empowerment. . . . Moreover, because empowerment spreads the responsibility for decisionmaking throughout an organization and across functional disciplines, top-level managers, in particular, must be committed to the company's new values."[10]

Empowerment can speed decisionmaking if done right. Problems arise when the culture is not changed thoroughly first. For example, when one Silicon Valley technology company turned to empowerment, it set out very clear rules, including rights to sign off on contracts at different levels. Under these rules, an employee at manager level could sign a contract for outside services up to $15,000; if the contract was over that, director-level approval was needed, and so forth. Although the rules were clearly spelled out, nothing had been done in the way of training. Managers who had been with very hierarchical companies with multiple levels of approval needed for everything worked their way around the acceptance of responsibility by pushing the cost of assignments up: unless the contract was less than $12,000, which they felt was a "safe" number, they tended to push the supplier to add on additional deliverables or expand the scope just enough to push the cost over $15,000, so they could have the contract signed by someone higher up the totem pole. The more freewheeling and entrepreneurial managers, more typical of that environment, would simply ask suppliers to divide the contract into phases, approving $25,000 contracts by virtue of approving two $12,500 arrangements.

The first "solution" did not reduce the decisionmaking responsibilities of the next level of management—one of the reasons for the turn to empowerment; the second resulted in the director level discovering that it had to check total expenditures much more carefully in order to avoid budget overruns. The next move made was a budget cap for each manager, which eased the immediate problem but was not a solution to the difficulties of a badly thought out attempt at empowerment.

The goal of the original move was to empower the workforce, to create a body of workers who would help the organization achieve a higher level of performance. That goal cannot be achieved by layering a concept over an existing culture. It requires changing the culture to one in which people understand that they are responsible for working with the other members of the organization to improve overall performance by sharing knowledge—of processes, skills, failures, successes—and in which they believe that sharing is possible because of trust.

TEAMS

The development of teams during the past decade as a way of working will prove invaluable as organizations move to the butterfly mode. Leaders will need teams at all levels, particularly at the top, if they are to succeed. It is critical, however, when dealing with teams at the top, that leaders give their teams the scope and authority they need to be effective. In addition, teams need to have a common purpose, they must have real tasks to accomplish, and they must have clearly defined performance goals.

Ensuring that teams interact constructively requires limiting team size, sometimes by dividing a large team into subteams. The team members must have complementary characteristics—problem-solving skills, cognitive ability, a focus on detail or administration, technical skills, negotiating skills, and presentation skills. The importance of teams is based on synergy—sharing information and skills, thereby enhancing the possibility of arriving at a sound conclusion, or discovering a new way to do something because of additional information. It is the "two heads are better than one" theory, tempered by the problems that arise from playing politics, from arrogance, closed minds, and negativism that instead result in stubborn adherence to individual points of view.

Finding the right balance when setting up cross-functional teams poses many challenges. Charles H. House and Raymond L. Price, drawing on their experiences at Hewlett-Packard, explain that while "it is a common belief in management practice today that one of the best ways to shorten development cycles is through the collaborative work of cross-functional teams, . . . collaboration among people from different functions is difficult, uncertain, and suffers from too little mutual understanding."[11]

In addition to the problems that arise because of size, politics, the mix of skills, and the problems inherent in developing a common approach and accepting mutual accountability, there is the basic problem of belief in the value of teams. Jon Katzenbach and Douglas K. Smith argue in *The Wisdom of Teams* that what sets apart the best, or high-performance teams, "is the degree of commitment, particularly how deeply committed the members are to one another. Such commitments go well beyond civility and teamwork. Each genuinely helps the others to achieve both personal and professional goals."[12]

Given the value of teams, and the inevitability of conflicts arising within them, Thomas L. Quick points out in *Successful Team Building* that teams must be taught that conflict is natural, that the arguments over issues must not degenerate into arguments betweeen personalities, that they must avoid placing blame, and most of all that conflict is a group issue and must be resolved if the team is to succeed.[13] Leaders must be available to resolve problems. For example, as was pointed out by a manager at Paragon Communications in New York, "Our employees expect us to deal with those who aren't performing. . . . If we don't hold them accountable, it de-motivates the rest of the crew. Teams perform to their level of expectations. . . . The leadership to excel comes from team members and management cooperating to create a work environment that expects and rewards superior performance."[14]

Because teams take a great deal of participants' time, especially teams with concrete assignments, such as a new design for a container, participation on more than two teams at a time is a mistake. When it comes to teams at the senior level, "the complexities of long-term challenges, heavy demands on executive time, and ingrained individualism of senior people conspire against [success]."[15] Given all these problems, the issue for leaders is how to ensure that a team works.

A good way to find this out is to examine teams that fail. The reasons for failure are as numerous and varied as the approach to teams. The complexities of the issue are vast. In working with two different teams set up by a major international oil company in a period of two years, we saw two very different outcomes. The reasons all tie in to the issues set out above. The first team had five members, they were selected for complementary skills, they had a specific goal, they respected one another's skills, and the leader of the team as well as the "owner" of the project helped resolve conflicts as they arose. We were the only consultants working with the team.

Very different dynamics were at work in the second team. It was set up during a downsizing. It had seven members from the oil company and was working with three different consulting groups, each of which contributed members at different times. Some of this team's members had personal agendas that they were actively pursuing, leaving them little time for the team; the team leader was trying to make a name for himself in the organization because of the downsizing going on; two members of the team were part of groups that had been eliminated because of outsourcing, and even though they were told they'd be found "spots," they were more concerned with their own futures than the project's; the project "owner" was close to retirement age and concerned about the possibility of being asked to take early retirement; and one of the members would reach full retirement age before the team completed its work. The purpose of the team was somewhat amorphous, and the team members never took the time to know one another nor set up and maintain comprehensive communications (meetings were frequently rescheduled or held with members missing because people failed to notify others about dates). In addition, many of the members of the team quickly sensed that the team was dysfunctional and therefore decided to try to assume leadership responsibility, creating constant turmoil.

The first team presented its findings on time to accolades, enhancing their individual reputations and ensuring their futures with the company in a period of downsizing. All are still with the company. The second team missed its deadline, but the project, when finally completed, was deemed a success. The problems, however, did not go unnoticed; as a result, the project "owner" was asked to take early retirement, one young rising star was so dismayed by the experience that he left the company, and no one involved wanted to work on a team again.

THE NEW WORLD OF WORK

Empowerment and teams, however, are only one of the building blocks of the new organization. In a world where the amount of information available is so great no one can read enough, learn enough, or experience enough, the need for sharing expertise and knowledge when it is needed and where it is needed is a critical success factor. Peter Senge introduced the concept of the learning organization based on his belief that "individual learning, at some level, is irrelevant for organizational learning." He adds that "if teams learn, they become a microcosm for learning throughout the organization. Insights gained are put into action. Skills developed can propagate to other individuals and to other teams."[16] Teams, in other words, as well as performing specific tasks, serve as learning tools for complex adaptive systems.

It is critical that organizations moving to the more flexible forms of the future make the principles behind empowerment and teams part of their culture. The members of the core organization will have to spread the organization's values and their own knowledge and experience to those who join the organization. In fact, during every growth period, the new parts of the organization will have to be integrated rapidly. The affinity employees brought in to augment the core workforce will, for the most part, be learning what they need to know about processes and procedures and specific systems and the way work gets done from the core workers with whom they are partnered. The core employees will be accountable for motivating those who start out with less interest in the ultimate outcome of the organization's efforts.

Then, when the butterfly organization decides that the time is right to expand into a new area or produce a new product, it will need to acquire a workforce with the necessary skills. This affinity workforce will be assembled from many sources. Some will be freelancers with specific expertise who will work for a limited time if the compensation is right and the "opportunity" costs (of losing critical contacts) are not too high. Some will come from temporary agencies on a short-term basis; some will come from strategic partnering with firms that are underutilizing their current workforce. Some work will be outsourced; some will be done by older, retired workers or workers who for one reason or another have left the full-time workforce.

The possibilities are numerous, as are the pitfalls. *Fortune* magazine believes that "at some point corporate America's drive for flexibility and cost cutting runs head-on into an another key imperative: the growing belief that competitive advantage hinges upon retaining a work force that is motivated, creative, and independent—empowered. . . . That goal will never be achieved by companies operating with a largely disposable work force."[17] And that is the crux of the problem facing those leaders who would create the flexible workforce. How can an organization pull together a workforce that will care about its success, have some loyalty, and be committed to helping the company achieve performance goals—without promising them long-term security in return?

To begin, the leaders of the new organization must recognize that much of the problem lies in the erosion of trust—actually, an erosion of an almost unwritten guarantee of ongoing employment—between the employee and the corporation. Unfortunately, without this, the flexible workforce cannot be achieved. But the implied social contract between employer and employee, consisting of rights and obligations that each expected the other side to live up to is no longer a "given." The ability of companies to maintain their side of the bargain depends on their success. Now that the world of work has undergone a permanent change, there is a new order in place.[18]

In the future, employees and prospective employees are going to have to assume more responsibility for their own futures, constantly acquiring new skills as change occurs again and again. But it will be in the interest of the leaders of organizations to see to it that there will be employees available with the skills they need when they need them. Organizations are going to have to find ways to help make training available and to create environments that will attract the best and the brightest—when they need them. In other words, employers and employees will have to learn to build relationships on a whole new basis. What will employment contracts look like? What will organizations offer in terms of guarantees and benefits? How can employees maintain needed skill sets? What must employers do to protect competitive information when employees work for multiple organizations?

Questions such as these make it very clear that skills, responsibility and accountability, and trust are the essential components of the new world of work. Given the uncertainties about the shape of businesses in the future, the following should serve as no more than a guide to thinking about these issues.

SKILLS

When it comes to skills, the important issues are education and training. Rapid advances in technology over the past decade have automated businesses that were previously labor intensive, eliminating jobs and demanding increased skill sets. For example, after car rental companies trained clerks to handle a user-friendly screen that could answer all sorts of complex questions and calculate exceptions, it only took a few supervisors in distant locations to answer questions clerks could not answer on their own, eliminating the need for supervisors in many locations. Today, a person seeking employment with a car rental agency is expected to know how to use computers because the trainers hired when the computers were first installed are no longer around. How will people acquire needed skills, especially since the skills needed change as new technologies come into play?

Training may have to become an explicit part of employer-employee contracts. Aware that they will need to constantly upgrade their skills, most people will choose employment that allows them to learn and grow. They will understand that the only job security lies in being the best-trained, most productive, adaptable employee available. And because people who have learned this lesson offer employers the most value, employers will want to ensure that these people accept their job offers, even if the position is temporary. Moreover, companies will realize that if they do not invest in their workers, but simply hire those who have been trained elsewhere, there will not be enough skilled workers available when they need them. Thus, the trade-off, or if you will, the new social contract, is likely to involve the availability of training and education, provided by the corporation; for example, the corporation would assume the costs of providing the training in return for certain guarantees, but the training would happen on the employees' own time.

RESPONSIBILITY AND ACCOUNTABILITY

Setting boundaries and maintaining control are the critical elements in relationships with outside organizations, whether they are strategic alliances or outsourcers. For example, the grocery industry is turning to a system called Efficient Consumer Response, or ECR. This involves the building of alliances between various members of the grocery supply chain to eliminate some of the steps involved in bringing the right product to the right customer at the right time. The electronic systems that will be used to facilitate this involve the sharing of information among many partners. Implementing these new systems involves putting together and managing teams from very different businesses that are geographically dispersed, and seeing to it that everyone knows what they are responsible for and what their roles are.

Although each person on these teams performs specific functions, another set of skills is needed to help develop and smooth relationships among team members, to see that each team does the work it is responsible for, to ensure that tensions between the teams don't build to the point that the relationship is endangered. The core employees of the new organizations are going to have to lead and manage relationships such as these.

TRUST

There are land mines in all of the arrangements that will be part of the new organization. For example, sharing systems with alliance partners potentially allows people from other companies to access proprietary information. Temporary workers may work for you one day and a competitor the next. Although this was not much of a problem when temporary or part-time workers were low-skilled individuals hired to do clerical tasks or manual labor, today the temporary worker may be a lawyer hired to work on a large case for several months, or a statistician asked to crunch some numbers related to a prospectus for taking a company public. How can confidentiality be maintained in these situations? Or, say you have an arrangement with a small distribution house to send out your product, how can you be sure that you have advance warning if they are contemplating a merger, are in financial trouble, or are taking on a major new client that will overburden them, making their work for you less efficient?

No matter how many rules are put in place, how much oversight, in the end it boils down to the nature of the relationships built between the core organization and its new partners and employees. The solution is ethical values, clearly articulated, communicated, and enforced.

THE NEW COMPETENCIES

In the new world of work, no one should expect to remain with one organization for a lifetime, although there will be employees who spend most of their careers in a series of full-time positions as "permanent" or core members of organizations. These core employees will be selected for a set of teaching and relationship management skills in addition to their professional skills. Leaders must recognize that these employees are the key to expanding without losing time in extensive training programs. Therefore, the organization must ensure that core employees have up-to-date skills and can teach them to the affinity workers quickly enough to allow start-up while training is taking place.

Since lifetime employment with a single organization is no longer an option, all employees should build resumes that indicate their adaptability, that make clear they have broad experiences, and that their skills—other than their management and administrative skills—make a difference. When it comes to affinity workers, for the butterfly organization to succeed, the question of benefits—such as health care, pensions, outplacement, training—is going to have to be addressed. Portability of plans is already being discussed by policymakers and, as we will explore further in the final two chapters, there are forces that should drive the satisfactory resolution of these issues.

THE CORE EMPLOYEE

The core workforce will have dual roles. Therefore, core employees will tend to be those who enjoy guiding and teaching others, who have the capabilities needed for management and administration. Basically, they are the same people who worked to rise in the organizational ranks in the past. In the leaner butterfly organization, however, managers are not always in demand and the road to advancement is more limited. The opportunities to manage and lead will, however, arise—but core employees will have to maintain the skills that allow them to remain valuable when the organization contracts—the skills at processes and tasks that every organization needs to make its products and provide its services. The rewards for core workers are likely to come from profit sharing during periods of growth and opportunities to be part of steering committees and management teams throughout their careers.

A model for this kind of worker can be found in many of the new technology companies and in companies where specialized skills are so critical that they cannot afford to lose a "star" performer to pure management. At the oil company mentioned earlier, the leader of the first team, the one that worked so well, was a star technologist who had been in the company for more than twenty years. He periodically served on such teams, returning to the technology division when the projects were over. He was well respected by leadership; in fact, he was the one who presented the team's findings to senior management in as professional a manner as any top leader would. The same model is prevalent in many think tanks, where a core group of employees maintains the organization while projects are developed and funding sought; once the projects are set up, many of the core individuals lead the projects because of their specific expertise in the areas. A controller may run a project on finance when one is funded, hiring temporary help to take over many of the accounting chores for the duration of the project. This allows small organizations to function with limited budgets, while maintaining the expertise they need for growth.

In thinking about core employees, leaders must focus on the fact that core workers perform jobs that are related to the organization's core competencies, and do so efficiently and effectively when the organization is in a "holding pattern," waiting for a trigger to growth. Then, when that trigger is pulled, these core workers must serve as the hub around which the organization expands. Thus, core employees at every level will need some leadership skills, including the ability to encourage creativity and innovation, engage in negotiation and collaboration, deal with diversity, train others, and provide boundary management. At each level, they will be expected to be guides and mentors to affinity workers. Like today's middle managers, they will be responsible for communicating senior management's messages and will be held accountable for the success of the groups with which they work. The difference between core employee leaders at different levels and the middle managers whose ranks have been so decimated in the downsizings of the early 1990s is the core employees have leadership skills *in addition* to their basic skills, which are used and kept up-to-date at all times. They are not promoted to a managerial level that supervises large groups of workers, but rather lead small teams of affinity workers while continuing to do their own jobs.

THE BIG PICTURE. Core employees at all levels must understand the organization of which they are a part. They must understand its vision, its strategies, its goals; they must know its history; and they must know what others in the organization do. In other words, they must have a holistic grasp of the business. At the macro level, there is an understanding of the organization's industrial sector and its direct competitors; at the micro level, there is an understanding of the internal organization and processes. They do not have to know how to do every process, but they should know what it takes to manufacture the end product or to produce the service.

In a period of expansion, core employees throughout the organization will be responsible for creating a cohesive, productive affinity workforce. In times of contraction, it will be important that core employees understand the organization's core competencies so that their thinking can generate new value-added opportunities.

ENCOURAGING CREATIVITY AND INNOVATION.[19] During periods of retrenchment, core employees will also be responsible for brainstorming for new ideas, for these are the lifeblood of the new organization. They will be looking for new products and services that can be created, developed, and offered ahead of the competition. In an age where new products are commodities in months, it is the only way to maintain a competitive edge. Organizations are going to have to build cultures that reward innovation and welcome new ideas, that actively encourage exploration instead of disparaging those who choose new paths.

General Electric's CEO, Jack Welch, Jr., expressed the atmosphere every organization must try to create in General Electric's 1989 *Annual Report*: "We want GE to become a company to which people come to work every day in a rush to try something that they woke up thinking about the night before." The leaders of 3M consider the company's "Eleventh commandment" to be "Thou shalt not kill an idea." Creative environments require a belief on the part of management that time spent thinking is not wasted time, that money should be available for experimentation, that learning is valuable, and perhaps most important, that failure is acceptable. Indeed, many companies now follow the Japanese belief that "if you haven't failed, you haven't tried."

Leaders can encourage creativity and innovation by encouraging their core employees to brainstorm in team settings, by reviewing new ideas quickly, by providing rewards for successful innovations, by making a point of evaluating ideas positively (if they are not adopted, the review should be explanatory, not dismissive), and perhaps most important, by never demanding new ideas on tight deadlines. Imposing a schedule on creativity tends to prompt employees to submit ideas that haven't been fully thought out.

NEGOTIATION. Karl Albrecht, the author of *Value Added Negotiating*, says that "negotiating is becoming everyone's business because of the closer relationships being built between companies. . . . [Partnering] has expanded the need for negotiation skills . . . because partners in these relationships come to the table not to win concessions, but to build an agreement that both parties feel is beneficial."[20] Those leaders who negotiate these alliances will, of course, need a very specific set of skills, which will be discussed in the next chapter.

Core employees at all levels will have to negotiate the division of responsibility, the assignment of roles in joint efforts, and the division of the actual workload as the alliances carry out the project for which they have joined forces. James Krantz of the Yale School of Management argues that "an increasingly essential component of leadership—whether this is exercised by formal leaders or others— will be the ability to manage intergroup process and to promote negotiated understanding of shared tasks."[21]

Good negotiators know that they must understand the culture of those with whom they are negotiating. For example, as Frank Sonnenberg points out, when negotiating in Japan, they must keep in mind that "yes" does not mean agreement, but rather indicates that what you said was heard; "in Bulgaria, a shake of the head means yes; a nod, no."[22]

Good negotiators must insist on objectives being clarified before they help people or groups agree on which ones are most important. If one member of the senior management team says that the location of the plant isn't important, and another says "there are ways around location issues," while another says "we want to be global," it is important to find out exactly what each means. Who, for example, will have to spend the most time at the plant? If it's the person who says that there are ways around the issue, further investigation is needed. That person might be thinking that the way around the issue is to keep in touch electronically, actually going to the site infrequently. Thus, placement of the plant *is* important.

Negotiators also must inspire trust by never making promises they cannot keep. For example, if the person negotiating says that they are going to bring a person at a higher level to a session, they must be able to do so. If they can establish their own trustworthiness as well as the organization's, there will be far fewer issues raised because those who negotiate with them will not spend all their time searching for hidden agendas.

COLLABORATION. Effective collaboration between members of a team or organization does not happen by magic. It takes time and care on the part of core workers, and it takes having shared goals, a fairly close match between the skill levels and expertise of the parties, frequent and open communication, establishing basic responsibilities but not putting limits on responsibilities, common work areas (from shared physical space to shared on-line services), an ability to reach agreement but not necessarily consensus, an eagerness to get input from outsiders without feeling threatened by it. And it takes having in place reward structures that take collaboration into account, rewarding people as much for the success of collaborative ventures as people once were rewarded individually for being "stars."

To ensure the success of collaboration, those involved in collaborative ventures must internalize the understanding that collaboration will benefit the whole organization—and therefore them. They must be shown how collaboration speeds and enhances the generation of ideas across functional areas. Organizations would benefit from providing training workshops for core employees to give them experience with facilitating such sessions. Collaboration also requires an ability to listen and think about what someone else is saying without reacting negatively just because something is new, and thus threatening. The old "count to ten before answering" approach is the most important habit anyone involved in a collaborative effort can develop. In addition, learning to express opposition or a negative opinion without implying fault or assigning blame is invaluable if a leader wants people to contribute in the future. Leaders must put in place ground rules covering behavior—such as prohibitions on personal attacks, attendance requirements, and encouraging communications between meetings—when managing such groups.

DEALING WITH DIVERSITY. In the future, companies will have to deal with diversity—cultural, physical, and functional. By the turn of century, the majority of American workers will no longer be white and male. Moreover, as organizations become more global and engage in more and more partnering arrangements, no workplace will be homogeneous. The misunderstandings that arise when people of many different cultures and backgrounds work together must be addressed, if for no other reason than that misunderstandings impede productivity.

The first step must be taken by those at the top. Organizations must put programs in place and address the issue with core employees by sending out memos stating that discrimination will not be tolerated. That is the smallest step. The next step is candid self-assessment, looking at the makeup of the top echelons. Do you have women on the board? Any minorities? Are any of your executives in those categories? This self-examination gets harder and more complex. What preconceptions do you bring to your evaluations? Look at the people you are considering for board membership: When looking for someone to promote, how much do you look for qualities you know lead to success—those similar to your own? For example, if two equally qualified candidates, one male, one female, are presented with a problem to solve, if the male instantly slaps his hand on the desk and says, "You're right! I'll get on it now!" and the female nods and smiles, then both go off and find solid, if not identical solutions, how would they be evaluated? If you are like so many executives (male), you will add to your evaluation of the solution the enthusiasm with which the challenge was greeted; you were taught to respond that way for the sake of the team in high school or college. The initial response had nothing to do with the outcome. Now ask yourself whether, if both had failed, you would have thought, "Well, at least he tried," even though there is no evidence to support that perception. At the same time, many a female manager would have responded very negatively to the male who failed after that enthusiastic beginning: "He's all puff and no substance." Of course, it is almost impossible to avoid an initial reaction, but there is always time to sit and analyze your responses. Over time, you will automatically weigh the factors that color your perceptions into the equation.

In dealing with diversity, it is essential that core employees recognize behaviors that create problems. Cle Jackson, director of human services at Wang Laboratories, says that his company's program for managing diversity is "built upon four basic 'building blocks.' These are awareness of your behavior; acknowledgment of your biases and stereotypes; focus on job performance; and avoidance of assumptions."[23] Formal programs of this type are essential. Core employees not only will have to eliminate their own prejudices to serve as leaders of groups of workers from diverse backgrounds, they will have to know how to spot problems that arise among affinity workers and know what actions to take, even if it is only to recommend that programs be offered to those workers.

HANDS-ON TRAINING. Core employees must not only have expertise and skills in specific areas, but they must be able to transfer them to the affinity workforce. To avoid delays, new employees, chosen for compatible skills, will often have to be cross-trained in real time. The easiest and most efficient way to do this is to create teams, with core employees responsible for training and mentoring new hires. The skill sets involved in teaching include patience, understanding, and an avoidance of playing politics.

Unfortunately, the will to help others is not enough to create a good teacher. Teaching requires communication skills; that is, along with a deep understanding of how things are done, having the ability to explain it—or at times slow down enough to show by example. This is a form of hands-on training that can work in small group settings. Of course, it also requires that the organization be committed to helping core employees renew their skills during periods of retrenchment.

BOUNDARY MANAGEMENT. Boundary management, managing the relationship between organizations or departments or functional areas working on a project or between the members of a team and those to whom they regularly report, is a skill that will become more important as the organization builds various partnerships for expansion purposes. The more partners, the more networks— business and electronic; the more alliances, the more people there will have to be to ensure things work smoothly for everyone involved without creating bureaucratic structures and multiple approval levels. The importance of this issue in the expanding organization will be explored in much greater detail in the next chapter. Boundary management at lower levels involves appointing group and team leaders who understand what must be reported, who are the important players, who is responsible for what, and what information needs to be disseminated to the organization.

AFFINITY WORKERS

The ability to create a butterfly organization depends on having available a large body of affinity workers—a pool of workers available either through agencies, defined time contracts, arrangements with other organizations—with specific skills when they are needed. Since the economy tends to have ups and downs within sectors, there will be times when, say, the chemical industry is retrenching as the retail sector is growing. Many of the skills, such as in computer technology, supply chain management, working with polymers, or back-office skills will be needed in a number of sectors. By ensuring that the role of affinity worker is satisfying—pays a good wage, involves portable benefits, and includes opportunities for training at the end of or during the period of employment— leaders can be sure they will be able to grow when they are ready.

Affinity workers will need, in addition to constantly updated professional skills, the ability to adapt rapidly to new cultures, understanding of and comfort with discretion, confidence in their own value to organizations, and enough enthusiasm to become part of a core for as long as needed. In the future, people will choose to be core or affinity workers. Each will offer advantages. Affinity work offers enormous possibilities for personal growth in a chosen field; it allows more time for pursuing other interests; it is more mobile; it involves less of the trappings of the corporate world in terms of politics, appearance, communications.

SKILLS. Affinity workers must maintain up-to-date, if not "ahead of the pack," skills in their areas of expertise and in computer use. They will have to be constantly searching to see what is on the horizon and build good cases for employers with whom they are associated to include training benefits in new skills in the employment contracts they offer. They also must learn to take advantage of opportunities for learning: their resumes should show the number of new skills they have acquired over the years, highlighting those that can make them good candidates for cross-training to an advanced level. The goal is to display a capability for learning that will make them attractive to employers who recognize they have to cross-train to acquire a large enough staff for a project.

ADAPTATION. Affinity workers will enhance their value by showing that they rapidly adapt to new organizations. They should indicate an awareness of the issues—for example, asking about corporate dress codes—when looking to join an organization. It will be important to have references that reinforce the picture of someone who quickly becomes a team player. The affinity worker must also have well-honed interpersonal skills.

DISCRETION. Because employers are concerned with proprietary information as well as reputation, they will always be more willing to hire affinity workers who have a reputation for loyalty to their current employer. An affinity worker must be careful not to offer information about a former employer that might cross those lines. Maintaining a reputation for discretion will require not gossiping about former employers, being extremely careful about computer passwords, and a willingness to sign confidentiality and nondisclosure agreements without taking it personally.

CONFIDENCE AND ENTHUSIASM. Affinity workers who enjoy the challenge of new positions and the time between contracts or arrangements spent learning will find that there are many rewards in terms of personal growth. As the new organizations grow stronger, they will benefit the whole economy, providing everyone with greater opportunities. As long as fairness and ethics are the foundation of the relationships, affinity work may prove—for those who prefer change and learning—as rewarding financially and far more rewarding personally than more permanent work for a non-flexible organization. The leaders of the butterfly organization have the responsibility of helping make affinity work appealing.

BUILDING THE ORGANIZATION

Bryan Smith, president of Innovation Associates, Toronto, believes that "ultimately, leadership will have less to do with who's 'in charge' and more to do with individual strengths and interests. Virtually everyone will be a leader of something. . . . The point is that all of these individual leadership initiatives need to come together into an aligned, coherent whole."[24] As the next chapter will discuss, this coherent whole will be the result of the partnering decisions of the organization's top leaders, and will require the skills of senior-level leaders in negotiation and leaders at all levels in implementation.

10

CONSTRUCTING THE NEW ORGANIZATION

The corporate leader of the 21st century must understand and accurately interpret the rapidly changing business environment. The fate of every corporation will depend upon the CEO's ability to anticipate the competition and formulate a strategy for surmounting threats that have not yet materialized. Business leadership in the 21st century will entail fighting wars before they occur.

Korn/Ferry International[1]

*T*hose who lead butterfly organizations must take responsibility for making the right choices and timing them right. They must anticipate and prepare to meet threats and seize potential opportunities. They must react to economic shifts, advances in science or technology, and social or political developments. And since they must always make these choices with the knowledge that more changes are inevitable, corporate leaders must learn to construct corporate edifices that can be easily changed in response to events without disrupting the basic organization or damaging its core competencies.

The flexibility an organization needs to be successful requires building partnering arrangements of various kinds, including long-term relationships with suppliers and customers. It also requires "outsourcing, alliances, and joint ventures . . . rather than the traditional model of a parent company with wholly owned subsidiaries. . . . [Such entities] are increasingly becoming the models for growth, especially in the global economy," according to Peter Drucker.[2] These relationships, however, will not succeed unless leaders first assess the leadership, culture, governance, technology, and perhaps most important, the core competencies of potential partners to determine whether there is a fit, and, if there isn't, but the relationships are still deemed necessary, factor in the costs of managing the relationships to overcome the mismatch.

Although some companies have made strides toward the butterfly form and many more have taken some small steps (examples will be presented in the next chapter), most have a long way to go. As noted in the previous chapter, the rules governing relationships with employees in these complex new organizations are not yet in place, especially the rules to protect affinity workers. And the core workforce still has to learn a great deal in order to be a natural and ongoing source of strength to the core organization while guiding those who join temporarily. Preparing core workers to assume their responsibilities will be a major leadership issue. In addition, leaders are going to have to hone certain talents of their own in order to pull together the pieces that comprise the organization. Finally, they will have to draw on the expertise of their (carefully selected) board members for advice and counsel, and draw lines in the sand to ensure that the ethical governance that glues their organization together is not threatened by their choices of partners.

In this chapter, the paths to the construction of the new flexible organization will be examined, beginning with a look back at the mergers and acquisitions of the 1980s and the virtual organizations of the early 1990s, both of which provide a great deal of insight into the problems that emerge when joining organizations. Various other paths to growth also will be explored, as well as ways to negotiate, integrate, and manage these paths, particularly the kinds of leadership expertise necessary for these endeavors.

REMEMBER CONTEXT

Since we are looking at an evolving form, it is impossible to know exactly what it will take to construct it. What is clear is that each organization will probably take a somewhat different path. Some butterflies will emerge when large, powerful organizations move to a more flexible form and decide on controlled growth through managed choices by leadership. This will require an understanding of and focus on core competencies and a long-term perspective and vision, and management will have to put in place rules and governance models as strategies and goals change. These organizations will spend a great deal of time on research and development, constantly seeking new products and new markets. Some butterfly organizations will be the result of a deliberate choice made by new entrepreneurs who recognize that the form provides the opportunity to expand their fledgling businesses with far less risk, and without adding the costly layers of bureaucracy that remove the speed and innovation that mark new enterprises.

As larger, established organizations move toward a more flexible organizational form, which involves reconfiguring skills, people, resources, plants, locations, services, and so forth, leaders will proactively change strategic governance, using technology to construct the web that holds the organization together. Such changes will move companies in new directions (remember that the intersection of governance, technology, and leadership is what causes the organizational oscillation that creates the butterfly pattern), and it is essential that these components be managed properly. In smaller organizations, the complexity of managing the relationships between governance, technology, and leadership poses two major dangers—a loss of vision and the possibility of unwanted acquisition because of poor partnering choices.

COMING UP THE LEARNING CURVE

Two different approaches to organizational growth offer lessons about what to do to ensure that partnerships of varying types work and what to avoid. The first, mergers and acquisitions, while offering a number of lessons in how to pick the right partners, does not lead to the butterfly organization because it is primarily a vehicle for expansion. Moreover, its ultimate aim is integration, which does not easily allow for termination of the arrangement; indeed, the organizations involved become fully entwined, as did the four members of the so-called Big Eight accounting firms that merged, creating the Big Six. Today, for example, it would be impossible to disaggregate Ernst & Young into the old Arthur

Young and Ernst & Whinney. The second approach, the virtual organization, while easily disbanded, does not maintain a core—it is often an organization in cyberspace—and is created more for specific purposes than long-term survival. The most successful "virtual" organizations, however, often seem, like Dell Computers, more butterfly than virtual as time goes on and they develop additional competencies, build plants, add staff, and set up corporate headquarters.

MERGERS AND ACQUISITIONS

The mergers that marked the mid-1980s were all too often driven by greed and avarice or herd instinct overcoming careful reasoning (every apparently successful merger drove yet another leader to enter the fray), which led to numerous catastrophes as chief executive officers caught up in the frenzy to grow their organizations rushed into ill-thought-out deals. The costly financing required and the mismatches between organizations led to bankruptcies and, in some cases, legal problems that became the subject of business press headlines.

The merger-and-acquisition-fever died down for a time, but as companies found themselves cash rich as a result of increased profits from the downsizings of the late 1980s and early 1990s, mergers have once again boomed, but for different reasons. Some companies involved in the most publicized deals (such as Viacom and Blockbuster and Paramount and various regional telephone and cable companies) are looking ahead to the dawn of the interactive age, trying to ensure that they will have the right mix of technology and entertainment to offer on the most popular communications vehicles. Some mergers are in industries such as defense (Lockheed and Martin Marietta) and health care (Columbia Healthcare and Hospital Corporation of America) that are facing economic constraints as a result of government cutbacks. And many are taking place in banking (Chemical and Manufacturers Hanover—and now Chase Manhattan), where mergers are a means of concentrating capital to achieve the asset base needed to become more competitive against far larger banks and financial service providers on a global basis.

The failures of mergers and acquisitions offer many lessons to those trying to expand and grow. To begin, it is important to understand both the financial and strategic reasons for these arrangements.[3] The principal financial reasons for mergers and acquisitions fall into two major categories: fairly immediate effects on the financial position of the company and longer-term benefits through increased size. In the first category are increased stockholder equity, diversification of the portfolio, increased earnings per share, stabilization of the earnings stream, and the funding of high-growth businesses. In the longer-term financial category are rewards through reduced operating costs, economies of scale and scope, consolidation of purchasing power, elimination of wasteful competition, and the ability to spread marketing costs to new and related products.

There are also strategic reasons for entering into mergers and acquisitions. Some companies enter into them because management intuition about the future indicates that others will soon provide clusters of services or products that will make it harder for companies with more limited offerings to compete; that is the rational for the multitude of mergers taking place between technology and entertainment and phone companies. Some are trying to achieve critical mass to enter an arena dominated by large players; some are trying for global reach; and some are trying to penetrate new market sectors. Others are trying to expand their technology base, respond to industry trends, or deal with regulatory changes that will make them vulnerable. Still others are trying to increase their growth or take advantage of a resource overlap. And there are those that are looking to address management issues, either to bring in new management or weed out management that cannot deal with change.

In general, the goal is to achieve synergy. The new, larger organization looks for common distribution channels; tries to create common facilities (for warehousing, headquarters, and so forth); attempts to tie together the promotion of products to enhance advertising and selling; and does everything possible to apply the intersection of management skills and industry knowledge to competitive problems and opportunities. Frequently, however, these attempts fail to bring the desired gains. For example, the Panhandle Eastern acquisition of Texas Eastern in 1989 resulted in a -6.1 percent stock performance as compared to the industry performance over the five years that followed; after Dayton Hudson acquired Marshall Field in 1991, the stock performance of the merged company was less that half that of the industry over the three years that followed; and GTE's acquisition of Contel in 1991 resulted in an 8 percent drop over three years from its preacquisition price, as opposed to an average 13.3 percent improvement by others in the industry over the same time.[4] Of course, some mergers, such as ConAgra's joining with Beatrice Foods and the Chemical–Manufacturers Hanover union, succeeded.

Both the successes and the failures provide clues to how to combine entities; it is, however, important to remember that mergers and acquisitions, unlike the partnerships formed by the butterfly organization, are meant to be permanent.

VIRTUAL ORGANIZATIONS

The so-called virtual organization is a phenomenon that drew intense media attention for the almost obligatory Warholian fifteen minutes. The virtual organization takes two forms—a temporary alliance of various individuals or companies arranged by an entrepreneur or group of entrepreneurs with a vision or an attempt to present the appearance of a larger organization—both of which depend heavily on instantaneous electronic communication. In the first instance, these companies continue to do everything else they have always done but devote some portion of their time, resources, and energy to various components of the production of a new product or delivery of a new service. The difference between this form and strategic alliances is the involvement of those totally outside the organizations who are, in effect, "brokering" the alliances. In the other form, the virtual organization is an attempt by a small, newly formed organization to give the appearance of size, without investment in personnel, plant, and so forth.

The virtual organization exploded on the American corporate consciousness in late 1992, promoted by such management gurus as Roger N. Nagel of Lehigh University and William H. Davidow and Michael S. Malone, authors of *The Virtual Corporation*. The virtual organization that they envision "will seem to be a single entity with vast capabilities but will really be the result of numerous collaborations assembled only when they're needed."[5] Indeed, the virtual organization is not meant to endure. Its core competencies are contributed by its partners. It does not have its own core workforce. It is truly a butterfly of the fields that lives its brief life and dies. A world of virtual organizations seems unlikely, since they tend to rely on tapping into the core competencies of other organizations or—at the very least—experience and expertise gained working in larger organizations. Rand Araskog, head of ITT, points out that the "creative ideas and breakthrough technology" that are the heart of entrepreneurial start-ups come from those who "received their background experience in publicly held corporations."[6]

The concept of the virtual organization and the efforts made to create them can provide lessons for the migration to the butterfly form. Entering into these arrangements teaches organizations how to work together electronically in real time, it helps promote deep understanding of one's own core competencies, it engages people in managing relationships with those outside the organization, and it begins the process of building trust with partners with whom the only connections may be electronic.

EXPLORING THE CHOICES

Organizations enter into partnerships in the hope that doing so will allow them to "collapse the period needed to get a product to market, slash development costs, rein in capital spending, plug gaps in product lines, add valuable skills, enhance images, crack foreign markets, get entrepreneurial firms up and running, and generally enhance competitive position with customers," according to W. Daniel Gibson.[7] Another, far simpler definition is that they are a means for cooperating and forming coalitions based on mutual needs that allow the organization to continue to concentrate on its core competencies. Steve Bergsman writes that "instead of building a grand structure to support principal operations as companies have done in the past, there is a move to contract out to service providers the ancillary, supportive functions while the company concentrates as much as possible on the core competency."[8]

Periods of economic stability provide opportunities for growth during which partnerships of many kinds are used to facilitate expansion. However, these relationships, which will take many forms, must be set up in such a way that they can be left easily, without permanent damage to either side. These relationships include:

- **Strategic Alliances.** These relationships involve cooperation to achieve mutually beneficial objectives, such as development of a new product or technology or penetration of a new market; they usually involve the temporary merging of groups or units from different organizations that share decisionmaking and contribute resources commensurate with the gains each hopes to achieve.

- **Regional Cooperative Networks.** Used successfully in industrial areas of Europe (Sweden's Smaaland, Germany's Wurttemberg, and Italy's Emilia-Romagna), these networks are groups of firms that "cooperate in order to compete—that collaborate to achieve together what each cannot do alone."[9] They involve everything from joint ventures aimed at product development to exchanging product information. The model, which is most effective for small- to medium-sized manufacturing enterprises, is now spreading to Canada; three such networks have been formed in Ontario: the Technology Triangle Manufacturers' Network, the South Western Ontario Manufacturers' Network, and Ottawa Manufacturers' Network. There are also interesting similarities between these cooperative networks and the way Silicon Valley's technology firms interact, which will be examined in the next chapter.

- **Long-Term Relationships with Suppliers and Customers.** These are usually very informal adjuncts to standard sales arrangements. For example, the customer for a given product may, in addition to buying the product, provide information in advance about sales trends. Creating efficient supply chains through such cooperation brings enormous rewards to the players in an industry: Toyota devotes a great deal of time and effort to establishing long-term relationships with suppliers, often working to help them improve their processes and thus lower costs. These relationships play an important part in Toyota's success.

- **Technical Licenses.** These are arrangements that involve one company licensing the right to use another person or company's process, logo, or software for a given time under a fee arrangement, ranging from flat rate to percentage of profits. The arrangement may include an option to purchase. If one company is a technology vendor, the relationship may involve the cooperation of the user in helping the technology company adapt the technology to its specific needs.

◆ **Joint Ventures.** Two or more organizations team up to create an independent, legal entity for a specific purpose. The new organization eventually stands on its own, independent of its "parent" companies. In the butterfly, joint ventures may result from arrangements within the company itself to develop new products or services that are then spun off into independent entities in order to keep the core organization lean.

◆ **Outsourcing.** A formal agreement to have specific responsibilities, such as technology or marketing, performed by an organization that specializes in that function. There are specific deliverables, fees, and timing.

◆ **Contract Work.** This can involve anything from an individual working from home (free-lance), to a small group that bands together, to members of another firm who are "loaned" while that firm is in contraction mode. It involves the performance of specific assignments for given terms.

These are not the only possible variations on the theme of partnering. As companies become more and more global, alliances of various kinds will become more common. As organizations keep experimenting with ways to grow without adding bureaucracies and layers that do not bring value, additional ways to construct these organizational networks will be developed. The key to all of these forms is that they do not change the core of the organizations entering into them; the core changes only in response to major triggering mechanisms, not the formation of alliances. The goal is to ensure that the core organization and the core competencies are enhanced rather than diminished by these relationships.

DOING IT

Although many of these arrangements may be initiated by a handshake, careful consideration must be given to whether and how soon they should be formalized by legal contracts. (In some cultures, such as Japan, arrangements are made without elaborate contracts.) Moreover, these relationships must be entered into only after careful analysis and then managed with care to ensure that they are successful and provide all the parties to them with adequate returns.

These arrangements will not always be at the corporate level. Under some governance structures, functional areas or business units will make their own arrangements, doing all the negotiating and having only the final vetting of the contract done by the corporate legal department. Thus, leaders at different levels must have sufficient negotiating and boundary management skills to deal with the areas of intersection created by these arrangements. In addition, there must be leaders capable of constructing the electronic networks necessary for tying together the various parties to these arrangements.

People skills will be particularly important, according to Van Campbell, vice chairman of Dow Corning, who explains that "you not only have to deal with the business, you also constantly have to deal with the relationship you have with the partner—nurturing it and maintaining high-level contacts, so that when you deal with items of substance you will be dealing with friends, people you understand and respect."[10]

Many believe that partnerships should be structured as long-term arrangements. Van Campbell says that they should be thought of as "lifetime arrangements." But for the butterfly to succeed, while they may be lifetime relationships, both sides must accept that the "arrangements" will be frequently interrupted. Reality has always called for exit strategies since, as Gene Slowinski, George F. Farris, and David Jones note, "partnerships fail for many reasons, including non-performance by the partner, hidden agendas, and changes in corporate strategy. Prudence requires that managers plan for the possibility of these unfortunate occurrences. Exit strategies should meet the test of fairness, while protecting the resources of both parties."[11] In the future, all such arrangements will need to have built-in strategies for termination that protect all parties.

A Case in Point

One area in which cooperative arrangements seem to be critical is technology. Companies in search of that all-important competitive advantage are linking up in new ways with companies that supply technology. This is particularly important for companies that do not want to develop—and constantly redevelop—the internal resources needed to engage in technology research. It also provides an answer for those companies that are reluctant to outsource because they anticipate bringing technology in-house at some future date.

The case in point involved an alliance between Allmerica Financial, a major, fast-growing insurance and financial services company headquartered in Worcester, Massachusetts, and DST Systems, Inc., of Kansas City, a leading developer of automated business solutions and the financial industry's largest information processor.[12] In 1989, the board of directors of State Mutual Life Assurance Company of America, an insurance company under the umbrella of Allmerica, put in place a new management team whose background was not in the insurance industry, but in mutual funds. The board was determined to move the company into the Information Age, and so it chose to search for a leader in an industry that had moved far in that direction. The team, headed by Jack O'Brien, who had a strong reputation for innovative and forceful leadership, immediately developed and began to implement a strategic plan focused on long-term growth of capital and surplus by targeting returns on each core business line and product, reducing operating expenses, and instituting management compensation incentives tied to profitability and growth. At the same time, the company would make continual reinvestments in their core businesses—investments aimed at building service capability and enhancing profitability.

O'Brien's vision was to create a "corporate structure that would increase financial and regulatory flexibility for each of the member companies and enhance efficiency and productivity." He says that he firmly believes that the "only companies that will succeed in the slow growth decade we seem to be in are those that create the organizational strategy, technology capacity, and effective marketing focus to deliver higher quality products, backed by exceptional service at competitive prices." Soon after taking on the mantle of chairman of the board and president, O'Brien, who loses no opportunity to convey his belief in the need to change and grow, brought over a management team he trusted from Fidelity Investments.

The team O'Brien imported included Larry Renfro, who was named vice president of Allmerica, and Robert L. Rutland, who soon became president of the new client services operation that was set up to provide the technology needed by the companies that were being folded in under the Allmerica umbrella. Both had worked with O'Brien before and both shared his basic belief in technology's critical role in every service organization today. At the time, most insurance companies were slowly being dragged into a future driven by technology while devoting enormous amounts of energy and resources to restructuring and restructuring again in the hope of finding a way to cut costs and maintain growth. Allmerica under O'Brien began to charge ahead into technology.

O'Brien named Theodore Rupley, who has a significant insurance industry background, president of a newly acquired company, Hanover, because in addition to his deep understanding of the industry (he was an underwriter early in his career), Rupley had spent enough time in research departments to know what technology could do. Rupley quickly initiated a relationship with Renfro and Rutland, with the goal of finding a technology partner to increase efficiency and improve customer service. They turned to DST Systems, a company well known in the mutual fund industry as the supplier of computerized recordkeeping for more than 32 million mutual fund shareholder accounts. DST's chief information officer, Jim Horan, who is responsible for its overall technology strategy, is expert at leading DST teams in migrating technologies across industries and national borders.

The discussion quickly centered on adapting DST's customer service workstations and automated work distributor to Allmerica's need for an efficient, paper-free environment that would allow accurate and efficient response to customer inquiries, particularly phone inquiries. Horan and Renfro, who had worked together when Renfro was in the mutual fund industry, discussed the processes involved in the insurance business, and both quickly saw the similarities to the mutual fund industry.

At that point, the freedom to innovate that was a part of the mindset of both their organizations allowed them to decide that they would work together. They shook hands and the alliance was sealed, a decision based on mutual trust, and which was supported by their organizations. An interesting side note is that while Allmerica and DST are partners or allies when it comes to the workstation technology and workstation management systems, Allmerica's client service centers and DST are competitors when it comes to financial accounting, each offering the same services to prospective clients.

There were many advantages to both sides from this partnership, which was solidified under a legal contract negotiated while the work was under way. The teamwork involved in the customizing of the DST system led to the transfer of knowledge—the DST team learned about the insurance industry and accumulated more knowledge about process similarities, while the Allmerica team members learned about the system, becoming both future trainers and change agents for Allmerica.

To what can the successful outcome of the alliance be attributed? Although integrating the new business strategy with the right information technology strategy has played an important role in Allmerica's success, remember that it worked so well because it was part of a dynamic plan. O'Brien determined that he would move the company in new and different directions and made that fact clear to everyone: the message that management would not put up with roadblocks to new developments and was prepared to reward innovation was communicated throughout the organization from the top down. Management's focus on looking at problems holistically enabled those looking for fast technology solutions to see the similarities in processes, such as in billing and payment and account updates, and to apply the knowledge gained in one service area to another. And the trust between the organizations that was possible because of cultural similarities paved the way to speedier results.

IF THE SHOE FITS

If the new organization is to grow through various partnering relationships, it will have to put in place processes for deciding when such steps are warranted, for evaluating the value of arrangements before entering into them, and then for developing plans for implementation. The first step is to know enough about yourself to select compatible partners; for example, unless both sides are clear about their own reasons for entering the partnership, understand the core competencies they bring to the table, and are aware of the importance of governance, the partnership is doomed to failure. The second step is to learn to look before you leap; that is, an organization must know enough about potential partners to know their goals are the same. The third step is to make the partnership work once it is initiated.

KNOW YOURSELF

To be certain that a partnering arrangement works, time must first be spent in self-examination. Why do you think the time is right? If it is a large, complex, and possibly risky alliance, have board members been consulted? If it is the result of an instinct about the future direction of the industrial or service sector, has any trend analysis been pursued? If another company has suggested it, have you carefully done your own analysis instead of studying theirs? This is the first level of questioning.

In order to be able to move quickly when the time is right, organizations must have ready answers to the many questions that come up during the self-examination stage.

GOALS. What do you want from the alliance you are contemplating? Is it a chance to seize market share in an emerging market? Are you trying to gain access to a new technology? Do you want to improve skills? Are you hoping to have someone else provide capital for something you want but think too expensive? A clear understanding of what you are looking for allows you to determine when you have succeeded—and when the arrangement can be ended. If you allow the alliance to continue endlessly, there is always the possibility that your partner may try to acquire your organization when it has money to invest or is worried about losing the relationship, or that some in your own organization begin to push for acquiring the partner. The other danger in failing to continually question the value of partnerships is that they will continue when they no longer add value because they have become comfortable. The result is mass for no purpose, something the butterfly organization strives to avoid.

CORE COMPETENCIES. Do you know what you bring to the table? Unless an organization clearly understands its core competencies, it can waste time and effort searching for partners. In *Competing for the Future*, Gary Hamel and C. K. Prahalad define core competencies as "a bundle of skills and technologies that enables a company to provide a particular benefit to customers."[13] Among the examples they give are Sony's skills at miniaturization, Federal Express's capabilities in logistics management, and Motorola's competencies in wireless communication. If you know your core competencies, you know what you have to offer in terms of other products, services, companies, or industries. In the same way, determining what a potential partner's core competencies are allows you to make an informed decision about a possible match. For example, a company whose strength is in customer service might be a good match for a company that excels in new product development.

GOVERNANCE. Have you a clear picture of your internal governance on all levels? Governance mismatches can quickly kill alliances. If you understand your own organization's governance, you will be in a far better position to assess the likelihood of there being a match, or at least the possibility of accommodating the governance style of the partnering group, division, or unit. The adaptability of the technologies of partners in terms of governance is also important and should be kept in mind when assessing the compatibility of the technology itself.

FINANCIAL STABILITY. Is your potential partner financially stable? The first step in evaluating the stability of your potential partner is one that the CEO should formally delegate to the chief financial officer. Even if the leadership of the potential partner is well known and the organization has a good reputation, a thorough, independent analysis of its financial status is necessary. It will serve as a key to any hidden agendas, such as the possibility of the partner putting your company in a position where it can force you to sell your organization to them if they are very cash rich or of their not being able to see the arrangement through if, for example, they are facing financial problems because of recent losses that have not become public knowledge.

A BALANCE OF STRENGTHS. Are you entering the relationship as equals? The knowledge base and skill sets of potential partners must be carefully evaluated to determine if their strengths and weaknesses supplement what you have, and vice versa. An organization should also take into consideration the value of what it can learn from a partner when weighing the value of an alliance.

CULTURAL COMPATIBILITY. Do you share values, purpose, and mission? Partnerships cannot succeed if the cultures of the organizations joining together are incompatible. Values, standards, and beliefs must align for partnerships to succeed. A nine-to-five, on-premises, leave-the-work-behind workforce may not mesh well with a ten-to-twelve-hour-a-day, take-the-work-home workforce.

TECHNOLOGY. Are you on the same technology playing field? For a partnership to succeed, there must be a clear understanding of each organization's technological status and goals. The worst case (lose-lose) scenario is trying to merge two companies with equally strong, state-of-the-art technology systems that are incompatible. When organizations merge, either their technologies must be compatible, or one organization must be looking to acquire the technological know-how of the other in return for an equivalent advantage in another area.

ACTION STEPS

Once both sides determine that the match is right, the deal can be negotiated. (The skills for doing that will be discussed later in this chapter.) Then the organizations can move ahead, but they must do so with care. Unless the following steps are taken, the outcome will be unsatisfactory, if not disastrous.

COMPREHENSIVE INTEGRATION PLAN. It is critical to have a well-developed, comprehensive integration plan for project implementation that includes a timetable for specific objectives, such as combining sales forces or naming people to positions.

TIMING. Timing is key; the longer it takes to come to closure on these arrangements, the less likely they are to work well. In fact, the longer it takes to come to closure in the first place, the higher the likelihood that the arrangement will never be made.

COMMUNICATION. No partnering relation can succeed without a concerted communication effort. Employees at every level should be given general information about the reasons for the arrangement as soon as a decision is made that it is going to take place. Progress reports must be issued on a regular basis until the start-up process is completed. It is the only way to avoid the paralysis that develops as a result of employees focusing on rumor and fear of the future.

LEADERSHIP. Strong leadership with clear mandates is essential to success. The faster the decisions about new responsibilities at the top are made, the more likely it is that leaders will lead and work to make the partnership a success and not play politics or job hunt instead. (In addition, there are specific leadership skills, discussed later in this chapter, needed for managing partnerships in the butterfly context.)

Partnering arrangements that take all of this into consideration have a far greater likelihood of being successful. But the signs of danger are worth noting. Power struggles between employees at every level can break out if the lines of authority are not established early. These struggles can result in an "us versus them" culture in which in-fighting occupies more time than productive work, causing everything from delays to outright sabotage. Another major problem that develops is a loss of commitment. Strong leadership and communications to build a new identity are critical to holding employees and creating the kind of loyalty and dedication that make partnerships work, especially when those involved in the project feel removed from their normal jobs.

KEY SKILLS FOR EXPANDING THE ORGANIZATION

When organizations enter into alliances of any kind, the actions of the CEO and top leadership will make the difference between success and failure. It is important that the leaders quickly explain the reason for an alliance, the impact it is likely to have on the workforce, and offer a timetable for making—and announcing—changes. The golden rule here is restraint: no matter how nervous everyone is, avoid making promises that may have to be broken. Until organizations evolve further and core workers feel secure and affinity workers are more comfortable with their choices (and organizations establish and adhere to the kind of provisions for worker protection that are the foundation for a new social contract), change will provoke adverse reactions.

Leaders must understand that, when combining forces with other organizations, the players will not be automatically playing by the same rules, nor will they necessarily have identical ethical standards. Explaining and clarifying the differences and ensuring that those involved in the alliance understand the ground rules are a time-consuming and often very difficult process. But understanding governance—and the differences created by different governance models—is critical, since the butterfly organization will be developing these relationships at all levels (manufacturing may create a joint venture for production of a part, while marketing may outsource the announcement of new products to a small firm, while the technology group may be having a new software program built to its specification with a clause that would allow the parties to the venture to jointly license the software to others).

The further along the path to butterfly organization, the easier these partnering relations will become. As this evolution takes place, however, three sets of skills—negotiation, boundary management, and network building—will be particularly valuable.

THE ART OF NEGOTIATING THE ARRANGEMENT

The ways in which leaders construct the arrangements that will be needed to grow the organization when the time is right will be critical to success. The skills that are used in labor negotiations or acquisitions and takeovers are somewhat different from the negotiating expertise needed for partnering. Traditional skills involve each side trying for the strongest win they can get, no matter what the cost to the other side. In partnering arrangements, negotiations should be aimed at creating trust through win-win scenarios, including the negotiation aimed at the eventual dissolution of the partnership. Both sides must focus on what is best for their own organization, but since the ability to find partners in the future is equally important, a reputation for fair dealing is part of the equation.

The arrangements that are meant to augment an organization's processes, technologies, and their ability to provide customer satisfaction, reach markets, lower prices, or develop, manufacture, or market new products or services all will have to be formally negotiated—often after an agreement in principle is reached. This less formal, preliminary approach is a part of the flexibility that marks the butterfly form. It means that many in the organization are empowered to decide upon and lay the groundwork for these agreements—within certain bounds. In most organizations, the bounds are financial—leaders at each level may enter into agreements that involve expenditures up to x dollars, with certain disclosure and other components to the agreement put on the table for evaluation. The formal contact is then drawn up and these conditions negotiated. In addition, the terms needed for ending the agreement, especially the timing of the notice of intent to terminate, must be negotiated and spelled out in the contract.

When it comes to large-scale arrangements or arrangements that will involve many different units and functional areas, the leader driving the negotiations is involved in more than negotiating across the table with the potential partner. In *The Manager as Negotiator*, David Lax and James Sebenius point out that, "within networks, the issues are linked, requiring negotiations that are at once 'upwards and downwards,' or 'side to side.'. . . Beyond specific transactions with 'outside' parties, managers negotiate about goals, authority, accountability, resources, and production."[14]

Clearly, those who are in a position to negotiate for the organization need to understand the big picture, to have a sense of other deals being constructed, of new directions that others might be planning to take. The leaders at all levels must communicate with one another and up and down; indeed, communication must be extremely up-to-date, particularly in periods of expansion, to avoid conflict. If a leader shakes hands with a potential partner and then has to back out, no matter how valid the reasons, the organization's reputation is affected. If this occurs frequently, the ability to partner quickly and effectively can be destroyed.

The steps for negotiating a partnering relationship include: information gathering to ensure a deep understanding of the reasons the potential partner wants the deal; recognition of what each side can gain that will ease the negotiating of the profits; recognition of the risks to each. It is important that the future of either company not depend heavily on continuation of the partnership, for that would make ending it difficult.

The analytic skills needed for negotiation include learning to ask oneself a set of questions that will prevent unwise agreements resulting from the anticipation of the advantages. Remember that the advantages depend on the terms—the idea of partnership is not enough. In *Negotiating Rationally*, Max Bazerman and Margaret Neale explain that good negotiators resist a common urge: holding on to an initial course of action because they are caught up in making the deal, never noticing that the value of the deal has fallen considerably because of concessions they are making. A "lose" scenario is likely if agreement alone becomes the goal, rather than the terms of the agreement. Good negotiators also take into consideration the decision processes of those with whom they are negotiating. Moreover, they learn from the negotiation itself, adding the information they can glean to the information they have—even if it is contradictory.[15]

MANAGING THE BOUNDARIES

The new organizational form will involve many groups drawn from various parts of the company working together. Some of these projects will be the result of strategic alliances that involve entire divisions; others may be the result of nothing more than a director of marketing working with a small company that is handling all its magazine advertisements; still others may consist of a pair of individuals working electronically to design a new component. These teams are formed to accomplish a specific goal or task and are given a time frame in which to do it. The amount of time devoted to the team will be determined by senior management, and the team members' compensation will reflect the time devoted to the team.

At the simplest level, the members of a part-time internal team each report to their own managers, and the team as a unit has a sponsor; that is, there is an individual who is responsible for the team and accountable for its success. In addition, the team itself has a leader who is responsible for, or puts someone in charge of, reporting the team's progress and problems to both the sponsor and to the managers to whom its members report—this leader is the boundary manager. To ensure a clear, consistent picture and to eliminate a lot of the politics that tend to arise, it is important that the team member chosen to be the boundary manager be a good communicator, have political savvy, and be well respected in the organization. In fact, the need for someone to manage the boundary should be taken into consideration in setting up the team.

The larger the project, the more critical the boundary manager becomes. In an article in the *Harvard Business Review*, Larry Hirschhorn and Thomas Gilmore argue that "managers in flexible organizations must focus on boundary management."[16] In massive projects, boundary managers are responsible for negotiating and resolving conflicts between different organizations, different sponsors, and different groups of management, and all without distracting the members of the team. There are times when boundary management involves dealing with differences of purpose and values. Boundary management requires an intuitive ability to raise issues that are about to create problems and resolve them before they become major impediments to progress.

On massive projects, it is not unusual to have more than one boundary manager, and they may even devote themselves to this endeavor full time. Most are chosen because they have influence within the organization and are politically astute, or they are trained facilitators and negotiators, or they have a long history of fair-dealing that has won them a great deal of respect within the industrial sector. Frequently, they are very senior current or former employees who are brought in to handle the boundaries on specific projects. When a current employee is assigned the role, the organization places someone temporarily in the manager's normal core position; for example, if someone has developed these skill sets in addition to her skills as an engineer, the organization may contract with another engineer to fill in for the period of the project plus a few months. The extra months are there as part of the social contract to allow the engineer who served as boundary manager to catch up and perhaps learn new skills while sharing the job with the departing contract engineer who is also given training as part of the exit clause in the contract. Another route would be for a partnering company to loan an engineer on a shared time basis to make up for half the time of the boundary manager. Developing flexibility without bureaucracy is essential.

For example, on a recent "proof-of-concept" project—a project aimed at intellectually proving the validity of a new way of organizing communications, both personal and electronic and for divisions within a large transportation conglomerate as well as with suppliers and customers—we recommended that there be three boundary managers. The objective of the project was to determine what it would take to construct the technological components needed, what rules of conduct and access would be needed, how the new way of communicating could be made acceptable, what implementation would involve in cost and time, and which were the best sites for a pilot project.

The first boundary manager was part of senior management, highly regarded not only by his peer group but by operational management as well; he had power and influence and was an excellent mediator. In addition, he was the individual who had the greatest chance of serving as a change agent if the project were to develop something that would enter the pilot project stage. The second boundary manager had significant operational experience and was also highly regarded within the company. His expertise would be useful in terms of being the "reality check" for the project. The third individual, who was selected to be the overall project manager, was chosen because of his analytical capabilities. He had the ability to absorb vast amounts of data and turn the data into meaningful information, but more important, meaningful insights that would help keep the project on track. In this example, three individuals and their competencies were necessary to make the project successful. At the time of this writing, the proof of concept has produced something that is likely to be moved into the pilot project stage. Moreover, the boundary managers have done an admirable job of keeping all those who will be needed to sponsor the project interested and involved—and likely to approve the project.

In the case of a project between teams from two organizations that involved a great deal of data sharing, the boundary manager role had much more to do with the electronic interface being constructed between the organizations. The role here was to ensure that proper "firewalls" were put in place to protect confidential information on both sides, while not offending sensibilities, given the trust between members of the organizations. In the future, depending on the nature of the specific partnering arrangements and the stage of evolution toward the butterfly form, boundary management is a job that is likely to evolve as well. Fortunately, it is a skill more and more core employees will be learning as part of their roles during times of expansion, when they serve as leaders of groups of affinity workers.

In *Managing the New Organization*, David Limerick and Bert Cunnington say that boundary roles make "collaboration easier to manage and also direct the attention of others in the organization to the importance of relationships and networks. The boundary function can be further strengthened by increasing the responsibility of all managers for focusing on boundary relationships. Such an expanded role should be built into job expectations, performance targets, and appraisal systems."[17]

BUILDING THE NETWORKS

Networking is one of the keys to the new organization. The dictionary offers two definitions of networking—"the exchange of information or services among individuals, groups, or institutions" and "the establishment or use of a computer network"[18]—both of which are applicable to the new organization. The dictionary, however, does not offer the additional definition that is one of the keys to tomorrow's organizations: "using computer networks both to exchange information in order to create usable knowledge and to tie organizations together." After all, the new organization is actually a network—of business and individuals joined together for a purpose.

Business networking in the most traditional sense involved outreach on a personal level to make contacts and eventually build relationships with individuals with whom you could share information that would benefit you professionally. Although usually developed on a face-to-face basis, these relationships were continued over the telephone and now are often maintained electronically, through e-mail and faxes, with only occasional meetings. Today, some of these relationships are beginning and developing electronically, with no personal contact.

Networking in the traditional sense began with a series of personal encounters and exchanges that over time built trust that led to deeper exchanges; electronic networking starts with contact with the idea of working together and continues on an assumption of trust. For many people, it is difficult to conceive of establishing a relationship without personal contact. But, those who enter relationships through technology tend to be comfortable with technology. They have had enough good experiences over time to be willing to accept the assumption of trust. Moreover, the more ethical the reputation of the organization with whom a person is connected, the greater the assumption of trust.

Personal networks, no matter how developed, will be critical to growing the organization. The chief operating officer, for example, will know which organization to turn to for process expertise through her networks and the human resources director will know where to go to acquire the personnel needed during a growth surge through his networks. The new chief information officer will have to be well connected to be able to select, according to Mark Dodgson, partners "with complementary technologies as well as technology and business strategies."[19]

These electronic networks will serve as the pathways between the various parts of the organization, the people who work for it at various times, and the organizations with which it develops relationships. Of course, since the people who use—or refuse to fully use—these networks are the keys to the organization's ability to perform, their understanding of and comfort with them are critical. Everyone must be helped to accept the fact that networks and networking are going to play an ever-larger role in the future, a role that will go far beyond business, affecting every aspect of life—economic, political, and social—in as yet unexplored ways.

FINDING THE GLUE

Constructing the butterfly is not the job of a single individual. Senior management teams—chief financial officers, counsel, chief operating officers, chief information officers, the head of personnel—will all have enormous responsibilities for the success of the new organization. They will at times be managers with few direct reports, with few of the trappings we have come to associate with power; instead, they will be the "brain" of a streamlined organism that moves around rapidly looking for opportunities for growth, with the ability to seize the right chance at the right time, working to make profits in the growth mode that will sustain the core organism when it is time to once again change direction. Bringing together individuals with these abilities is the key to being a good leader for this new organization.

11

THE GOOD LEADER

Most of us are like the characters in Ibsen's play Ghosts. *We're controlled by ideas and norms that have outlived their usefulness, that are only ghosts but have as much influence on our behavior as they would if they were alive. The ideas of men like Henry Ford, Frederick Taylor and Max Weber—these are the ghosts that haunt our halls of management.*

Robert H. Waterman, Jr.[1]

*N*ot every leader is the same. Leaders react to the problems facing their businesses in different ways depending on the industrial sector they are in, the kinds of businesses they lead, their own past experiences, and the picture they have of the future— their own as well as that of their organizations. Some leaders have worked their way up through command-and-control organizations and have all the right skills to lead in that environment. Although they realize that trying to run modern organizations by following the management precepts that have been a business tradition for most of this century is not working, the ingrained beliefs that color their behavior keep them from giving new ideas a real chance to succeed.

Other leaders, often driven by near desperation, try a parade of new things, hoping to solve the problems created by what *Fortune* describes as the "globalization of markets; the spread of information technology and computer networks; the dismantling of hierarchies; . . . and a new, information-age economy, whose fundamental sources of wealth are knowledge and communication rather than natural resources and physical labor."[2] As each new attempt fails to bring the promised rewards, they search for the next magic bullet. They hold on by downsizing yet again, managing to stem the bleeding temporarily and hold the bottom line for yet another quarter. Others have managed to make enough of the right changes to move their companies into a stronger position, but they are apprehensive about what the next wave of developments will bring. Moreover, many of the changes they have made are impacting their organizations in ways they do not understand. Their organizations seem to get harder to lead, not easier.

A few leaders have embraced new ways of working, restructuring their organizations (sometimes whole companies, other times strategic business units or divisions), fighting to make them more flexible and adaptable because they have accepted that change is now a way of life. They are engaging in carefully thought out, but rapid and continual modification processes. The changes they are making appear revolutionary because of the speed with which they happen, but since every aspect of life today moves more quickly, the only change that is revolutionary is the speed of change. And for organizations whose leaders have taken this path, there is forward movement.

This chapter will explore some of the characteristics of those leaders who have been successfully changing their organizations. It will focus on leaders who recognize that the old organizational forms and approaches will not work and who are struggling to provide the effective leadership necessary for steering their organizations in new ways. The leaders highlighted—and their companies—were selected through an analysis based on information gathered in four ways. The first is observation of leaders we have worked with on assignments involving business transformation. The second is discussions with fellow consultants and businesspeople at numerous levels to obtain their views of the kinds of leaders that are taking organizations down new roads. The third is interviews with leaders (some of whom asked not to be identified in order to protect the competitive advantage they believe they will gain by making certain changes) who we discovered were thinking about these issues and implementing changes or trying to grow their organizations in new and different ways; the criteria for pursuing these interviews was that the people interviewed not be the "usual suspects," those whose views are widely reported in the press. The fourth is research in the press and leadership literature that focused on well-known leaders who are heading organizations that have moved along the evolutionary road.

THE IMPACT OF THE NEW LEADERSHIP

Some organizations, as noted in Chapter 1, have been moved toward the butterfly form by their leaders' efforts in the face of outside forces. For example, ABB Asea Brown Boveri, Unilever, Destec Energy, the Audubon Society, Motorola, Lyondell Petrochemical, Boeing (the division involved in the design and building of the 777), Transnet of the Republic of South Africa, Shell Oil Company, the companies of Silicon Valley (particularly Hewlett-Packard, Sun Microsystems, and Intel Corporation), and NUMMI (New United Motor Manufacturing, Inc., a joint venture by General Motors and Toyota that was created to exist for twelve years but with built-in worker protection) are close to the butterfly model. Numerous others—Nike, Canon, British Petroleum, Apple—are moving toward butterflies from forms similar to virtual organizations in some ways, outsourcing many functions and depending on partnerships for manufacturing products while eliminating layers of management. And in two sectors, health care and multimedia entertainment/information, where alliances are being made and remade in order to deal with rapidly changing rules, regulations, and market realities, the new organizational structures are not yet in place, but the trend seems to lie in the direction of the butterfly form.

Many other leaders have begun to modify their organizations to make them more flexible and adaptable because they recognize that, for reasons beyond their control, old models no longer work— and their moves have made a difference. For example, many utilities, such as Central and South West (CSW), are changing in the face of deregulation (CSW, as discussed in Chapter 4, has addressed the issue of eliminating the concept of a permanent workforce in order to achieve more flexibility and is seeking new avenues of growth related to its core competencies).

Whatever the reason for these changes in relationships within or among companies, the changes being made in the direction of more flexible arrangements have additional impacts. Moreover, since complex adaptive systems move in new directions once they are impacted in any area, the evolution may have a momentum of its own. Of course, the leadership skills required to deal with these new entities, which are already exhibiting a number of characteristics of the butterfly form, will themselves be monumental—an evolutionary step in terms of what it takes to be a good leader.

DEALING WITH COMPLEX ADAPTIVE SYSTEMS

In a survey of some nine hundred executive leaders, Stuart L. Hart and Robert E. Quinn found that the "highest levels of performance were achieved by chief executive officers with high levels of 'behavioral complexity'—leaders who saw themselves as focusing on broad visions for the future while also providing critical evaluations of present plans. They also saw themselves tending to relational issues while simultaneously emphasizing the accomplishment of tasks."[3] In fact, leaders today deal with issues that are far more complex and far longer term than those of yesterday. Donald Hambrick, who has addressed these issues extensively, believes that strategic leadership—that is, top leadership—has to do with spheres external to the organization as well as internal, encompasses more complex and integrative issues, and that at heart it involves managing through others.[4] This last point is important: leaders must accept that there is no way they can be expert at everything; instead, they must know what they do not know and supplement the gaps in their knowledge by surrounding themselves with individuals who have that knowledge. What is perhaps most critical is that, because these new organizations are heavily based on the establishment of a culture of trust, leaders must also embody both aspects of the word *good*—a praiseworthy character as well as the capacity to advance the prosperity of the organization, often by breaking with traditional thinking.

PERSONAL CHARACTERISTICS

Those who will successfully lead the complex organizations of the future will have ethical standards that have given them a reputation that makes others trust them—and willing to partner with them.

They will have the kind of intelligence that allows lateral thinking and deep analysis of complex problems involving multiple dimensions. They will have extraordinary levels of energy. And they will study to find the gaps in their own skills and supplement them.

HONESTY, LOYALTY, AND INTEGRITY. These qualities together are the bedrock upon which trust is built. They arise out of, as noted in Chapter 4, those common beliefs that govern the actions of the majority of citizens, such as the Golden Rule, the Ten Commandments and other religious precepts, and the moral codes taught us by our parents and our schools. Trust is the key ingredient in the new organization because it is the basis on which the personal and electronic networks that enable the new organization are built. In *Managing With a Conscience*, Frank Sonnenberg calls trust the miracle ingredient, "the fabric that binds us together, creating an orderly, civilized society from chaos and anarchy. . . . If businesses are to thrive in the global marketplace, trust must be more than something that is talked about; it must be at the core of everything that is done."[5]

The leaders of organizations with the most impressive reputations for fair dealing, who always are mentioned when the subject comes up, turn to the concept whenever they discuss how they manage. James E. Burke, former chairman of the board of Johnson & Johnson, who brought the company through the infamous Tylenol incident with an enhanced reputation, says that "deep down, everybody has the yearning for trust, honesty and integrity. De Tocqueville once said [for example] that America is great because America is good. And when America ceases being good, it will cease being great."[6]

If trust becomes part of the aura of the organization, it enables the creation of multiorganizational networks, partnerships, and alliances, and serves as the foundation for long-term relationships with affinity workers. Internally, trust helps create loyalty to the organization and promotes followership. But keep in mind that a good leader, like a good general, earns the respect of the troops he or she commands—through actions as well as words.

INTELLECTUAL CAPACITY. Dealing with the complexity of the modern organization and the chaotic forces in the world requires more than accumulating information—it requires an ability to analyze, to think logically, to grasp and add to ideas and concepts, to examine everything from a holistic perspective. In short, it requires a keen intellect to lead organizations today; changing them requires an even more determined application of intelligence. Warren Bennis says that "leaders differ from others in their constant appetite for knowledge and experience, and as their worlds widen and become more complex, so too do their means of understanding. Dialectical thinking, a variant on the Socratic dialogue, is one such means. It presumes that reality is dynamic rather than static, and therefore seeks relationships between ideas, to aim at synthesis."[7]

ENERGY AND DRIVE. Leaders who attempt to transform organizations need incredible stamina to go through the rigors involved in selling their vision to their shareholders, boards, management teams, and employees, as well as myriad other stakeholders, and then to oversee the implementation of that vision. It often involves enormous changes that adversely impact current employees (every manager who has had to make these decisions lists them as the "hardest" task he or she has faced, the one that kept them up night after night). Jayme Rolls, a consultant and psychologist in Santa Monica, California, whose specialty is "helping leaders bear the trials of transformation," says that the result of these efforts is that "energy is sucked out of these people at an enormous rate—it's depleted from above and from below."[8]

Leaders are usually described as having stamina and drive and energy. In the case of the butterfly, the demands seem to be worse because so much of what is being done is groundbreaking, which requires an enormous belief in the rightness of ideas that are often untried, and the ability to sustain the push for those ideas over months and even years, especially when the transformations take place in organizations that are huge and global. Leaders at all levels are feeling the strain, working incredible hours and rarely getting a night's unbroken sleep as they deal with partners—and crises—around the globe in real time. The excitement of doing something new, their belief in their vision, and their fierce drive sustain them.

For example, Lawrence Bossidy, the acerbic, energetic CEO of AlliedSignal, works incredible hours, serving as a model for tireless devotion to a company. He is, however, admired rather than liked, admitting he is "too demanding," and explaining that placing "outsize demands" is necessary in today's competitive environment.

Bossidy, who believes that globalization and innovation are two of the most important roads to growth, has cut through the bureaucratic layers that once marked AlliedSignal to support new ideas. His philosophy of growth, in addition to globalization and innovation, can be summed up as: "Cut the fat, set killer goals, and claw your way to victory." He gives his managers challenges and expects them to meet them or face the consequences. His style of management is "blunt, unrelenting . . . willing [things] to happen."[9]

Arranging meetings with the appointments secretaries or public relations managers of these leaders provides insight into a life where "after a speech in Manila on Tuesday," there is a flight to the "Singapore plant for a Wednesday meeting, followed by a conference in San Francisco of the company's senior managers late on Thursday, and then a panel on national industrial issues over the weekend in Japan," and so forth. The personal costs are enormous, and at times so are the costs in terms of attention to the long-term future of the organization. Some leaders, aware of the problem, have carefully built time for uninterrupted thought about the future into their schedules.

KNOWING WHAT YOU DON'T KNOW. To start, those who plan to create a truly complex, adaptive organization must accept their own limitations, especially about issues that require decisionmaking at the highest level. The world has become far too complex, and it develops far too rapidly for an individual to know everything necessary to manage a large, multinational organization. Epictetus, a first-century Greek philosopher said, "It is impossible for a man to learn what he thinks he already knows."

From ABB's Percy Barnevik, the head of a huge global organization that is involved in transportation and electric power generation, who understands the need for leaders in local areas who can transform the operation to suit local cultures, to AlliedSignal's Lawrence Bossidy, who acts on suggestions for new products on the advice of his scientists without necessarily understanding the science behind those ideas (it is the business value of the ideas he uses for decisionmaking), top leaders whose companies are moving ahead are delegating enormous amounts of responsibility to their management teams. The expertise of hospital steering committees about technology needs; the advice of board members about foreign opportunities; the people skills of a day-to-day administrator who sees to it not only that things get done, but that the people in the organization care about the organization; the bridges built by chief financial officers to banks and investment houses; the process expertise of a chief operating officer who decides to replace an assembly line for widgets with a team structure—these are the knowledge banks that CEOs are tapping to supplement their own strengths.

Of course, for senior management delegation of work to succeed, it is critical that leaders choose the right people to work with, give them the authority they need to take action (along with the responsibility and accountability), and make certain that the culture of the organization is one that promotes the free exchange of opinions. Leaders must also create an atmosphere in which every individual's importance to the organization is clear and in which those below take the mandate to challenge superiors' decisions seriously.

GATHERER AND PURVEYOR OF INFORMATION

Leading a butterfly organization will mean leading a complex organization in a terribly complex world. Understanding that world, and the forces in it that can impact the organization, and conveying information about the organization and its goals to others—both internally and externally, but especially working with other leaders to determine possible new products and services through partnerships—are critical to maintaining a competitive edge.

GAINING A WORLD VIEW. Businesses do not exist in a vacuum. Economic, political, and social forces impact business, as do the decisions made by other businesses. Understanding what is happening in the world is a prerequisite for corporate decisionmaking. This is true for every business, no matter what form it takes, and it was as true yesterday as it will be tomorrow. The leaders of tomorrow's organizations will turn to the members of the board for information, seeking their knowledge and expertise in other areas, regions, industrial sectors (the shape and role of the board in the new organization is discussed in Chapter 5), as well as exploring and learning on their own.

Andrew Grove of Intel Corporation is typical of the leaders who are concerned with gathering as much information as they can. He sums up his philosophy as "Only the paranoid survive." This mindset is why he always looks over his shoulder. He picks other people's brains constantly out of his awareness that developments now take place at such speed that he must keep an eye on the thinking of others whom he considers just as paranoid. He "picks the brains of people like DreamWorks SKG's Steven Spielberg and Tele-Communications Inc.'s John Malone, trying to divine how to make PCs more entertaining and better at communicating. He consorts with the young propeller heads who run Intel Architecture Labs." Grove is so concerned with the changes taking place that could overtake his company that he has "dropped just about everything to pursue his dream . . . coming up with an improved consumer PC."[10]

In a world in which information of every kind is constantly being made available, where new developments take place daily, how can any leader keep up? There are numerous ways, ranging from participation in conferences and meetings to having white papers prepared by outside consultants to setting up internal groups to collect and distill such information. (In Chapter 4 of our first book, *Dynamic Planning*, we explore many of these approaches in detail, and explain that the added value of assigning the responsibility to an in-house task force is that it is a major step in the creation of a learning organization.)

COMMUNICATING EXTERNALLY. Leaders who are determined to move their organizations forward devote time to public relations, granting interviews and promoting their organizations. They also work to establish the image and reputation of their organizations with stakeholders and to make sure that their organizations are known for the good things they do for the communities in which they are based. They participate in conferences involving others in their major business sectors and give addresses at colleges and universities, to civic groups, and to industry specialists. They accept their roles as figureheads as graciously as they accept their direct roles as leaders of the organization. Herb Kelleher helps Southwest Airlines by reinforcing his reputation for energy, enthusiasm, and down-to-earth friendliness in the media—and seeing to it that his workforce reflects that image. It is also an image that then attracts the kind of people to the organization that have those qualities. Every trip on Southwest reinforces the Kelleher-Southwest image in some way; the image is so strong that a cheerful announcement by an attendant that a flight is in danger of taking off late "unless some of you can help get all the luggage stowed away quickly" is met by enthusiastic offers of aid and assistance by numerous passengers who have put down their newspapers and paperwork to jump up and help make a difference.

COMMUNICATING INTERNALLY. Every leader of an organization moving toward this new form is concerned with communications. The use of communications vehicles such as newsletters and e-mail and memos in these organizations is similar to, if somewhat more plentiful than, that in traditional organizations, but these leaders go further; they understand the importance of communicating personally as much as is humanly possible (and sometimes their goals in terms of personal communications seemed to put inhuman demands on them).

Bob Gower, president and CEO of Lyondell Petrochemical Company, a Fortune 500 company that was close to failure nine years ago but has since moved in the direction of a butterfly organization, has streamlined the company so that it "operates with minimum people." Among the changes he has made is a move toward "minimum management"; this involves granting people responsibility with accountability. He does this because he believes people will do their jobs well, providing "sustained high performance and sustained high quality . . . if you tell them what's going on." He adds, "As leaders, we have a responsibility to set the tone, to communicate the goals and to let employees know how things are going. That is basic, but it is often ignored when leaders forget what it means to lead. . . . I hold employee meetings every month at each of our locations. All employees need to know the same things I do in order to do their jobs well."[11]

The drive to communicate one on one with employees, to be a presence in the organization, was echoed by leader after leader. Some devote a considerable amount of time to this effort, because they believe it makes such a difference. For example, Charles Goff of Destec exchanges a few private words with every one of his almost 1,000 employees at least once a year; Percy Barnevik of ABB says that "real communication takes time and top managers must be willing to make the investment. . . . I personally interact with 5,000 people a year in big and small groups." Barnevik will often spend three hours with a group of some thirty managers gathered together from around the world to attend working sessions that last two to three days as part of the effort to bring everyone in the company together.[12]

HUMAN RELATIONS SKILLS

Good leaders tend to have an innate ability to make connections with other people. Not every leader is a true "people person" in the sense that they really enjoy interacting with large numbers of people, but leaders tend to either be that type or be so enthusiastic and intelligent about the core competency of the business that they attract a solid inner circle who can carry their image and beliefs into the organization, often by creating a myth out of admirable idiosyncrasies of the leader. Since many of these people are themselves good leaders, their perceptions are enough to inspire the all-important loyalty to the leader. Thus, in one way or another, these leaders create strong followers; they inspire hard work and dedication; they lead the charge to learning and experimentation through their own examples, attitudes, and the rewards they give to those who meet their expectations; and they communicate with their troops and the outside world, becoming a symbol of the organization.

"FOLLOWERSHIP." Larry Hirschhorn and Thomas Gilmore, advocates of what they call the "boundaryless company," believe that the emerging leadership role requires convincing subordinates to accept responsibility for "adequately informing their superiors and helping them to think clearly and rationally, even as they work to implement their superiors' requests. Paradoxically, being an effective follower often means that subordinates have to challenge their superiors."[13] This is a clarification for the business world of a philosophy of leadership that has been clear to leaders in other areas for centuries. Lao Tzu, a Chinese philosopher of the sixth century B.C., said, "To lead the people, walk behind them." Mahatma Gandhi, the turn-of-the-century Indian nationalist leader, explained: "I do not lead, I follow the people." Sociologist Amitai Etzioni summed it up in 1987: "The concept of leadership is 50% followership."[14]

This change takes more than telling followers that they should "challenge" what they are told. It requires building enough trust that subordinates believe that challenges will not have repercussions:

that being a "no" man or woman is a road to advancement. It takes building a record of responding positively to criticism, of reacting openly when struck by the truth, even when unpleasant, of comments from below. Hirschhorn and Gilmore put it very succinctly: "If subordinates need to challenge in order to follow, superiors must listen in order to lead."[15]

In the butterfly organization, leaders' belief in the importance of everyone in the core organization must cascade down the organization in order for followership to develop and move up the organization. (In its simplest form, it is a "top-down, bottom-up" process that makes the butterfly organization work effectively.) Not only must employees at every level believe in the organization and the leader at the top (a belief that does not necessary inspire measurable action), they must believe in their *immediate* leader and must perform for that individual who stands as a tangible representative of the leader, and who has the power to measure their performance and reward it. By creating followership in this way, top leaders make leadership easier at every level, driving the organization's beliefs deep into the culture.

INSPIRATION BY EXAMPLE. Thomas Gilmore believes that the time of the charismatic leader has passed. Although "organizations are increasingly dependent on effective leaders . . . leaders are increasingly dependent on their organizations to match them with their roles and enable them to work. Charisma breeds the sort of dependency that undermines an organization's ability to manage transitions effectively."[16] Today, it is not enough to make an occasional appearance to rally the troops. Leaders of the new organization must be more visible on a daily basis and keep in touch with their organizations because of geographic spread and the fact that so much of the organization is temporary. The stories that once made legends out of leaders do not work as well in organizations that no longer have a large, permanent workforce. Alliance partners need to have contact with leaders; affinity workers need to know that their immediate superiors have contact of some sort with leaders, even if it is only knowing that the leader of the work unit actually saw the organization's leader during a visit to the plant or attended a breakfast meeting at which her ideas were listened to.

The leader who is known to spend endless hours for the good of the organization, working to solve problems, getting the word about the organization out at conferences, has far more impact on the workforce—and the top management team he flies around the country with—than does the figure in the ivory tower consorting with fellow CEOs. Richard Brooks of CSW, Charles Goff of Destec, Percy Barnevik of ABB are all presences to those who work for them, and that promotes cohesion.

SUPPORT LEARNING. The leaders of butterfly organizations must understand the value of an educated workforce, for only then will the expenses of training and retraining make sense. The skills needed by employees change so rapidly that maintaining a core workforce that has the appropriate skills for each new development requires continuing education. Indeed, the value of education is clear: the National Center on the Educational Quality of the Workforce reports that, on average, "a 10% increase in work force education level led to a 8.6% gain in total factory productivity, while a 10% rise in the value of capital equipment increased productivity only 3.4%. The study was controlled for factors like age of equipment, industry, and establishment size."[17]

For example, Anton Moolman, chief executive officer and chairman of the board of Transnet in the Republic of South Africa, a company that has a number of divisions moving toward a butterfly form, promotes the practice of granting employees leaves for study and growth; many mangers use that time for study at universities throughout the world. The arrangement provides, in addition to salary, payment of tuition, airfare, and expenses. Some managers choose instead to use the time for reflection about the world, the company, their own lives—personal enrichment that enriches the company by providing a more motivated, enthusiastic workforce.[18]

ENTREPRENEURIAL SKILLS

Good leaders in butterfly organizations are always searching for new ways to do business and new business to do. They are individuals who accept responsibility and make decisions quickly, neither looking for consensus (but explaining why they make the decisions they do) nor always waiting to be sure the moment is exactly right (which often means being too late). More than anything, they trust their own vision and instincts and are willing to fail in order to learn.

PROMOTE INNOVATION. The butterfly organization searches constantly for new products and services to offer, reinventing the work it does—in keeping with its core competencies—in order to remain constantly competitive. Michael Perry, chairman of Unilever, an Anglo-Dutch international consumer products company that has established a culture based on the belief that the only way to succeed is to be flexible and innovate faster than anyone else, has driven that message into every corner of the organization. Unilever, he notes, is constantly "reinventing itself, trying to create new structures and new methods of working," all with the goal of creating more and more new products and markets for those products. One of the members of Perry's management team explains, "The priority for us is, number one innovation, number two innovation, and number three innovation. And just in case it is not quite clear, it is actually innovation."[19]

Leaders determined to promote innovation do not respond negatively when new ideas are suggested, though they will often ask for more information; they never condemn the failure of an innovation they supported; and they reward those whose ideas are successful. They provide the time, the environment, and the equipment for experimentation and brainstorming. At Unilever, they do this by bringing together groups from different areas, including outside suppliers and customers, in centers set up in different regions around the globe for the express purpose of innovation.

MAKING DECISIONS. Decisionmaking at the top often is a matter of intuition and experience—and today, speed. Building consensus about the wisdom of going with a new product and then doing detailed market research may cost a company the benefits of being first to market. For example, at Sun Microsystems, reacting quickly to an innovative idea as a means of achieving growth is a cultural norm. Scott McNealy, Sun's CEO, says, "We get all fired up. Our adrenaline gets going and we start knocking against walls. Our new microprocessor's success was 90% assumption and 10% fact."[20] The entrepreneurial decisionmaker accepts the risk of failure but trusts her own instincts—and the experience and knowledge accumulated over time—to be right often enough to ensure a pattern of success.

TAKING RISKS. When the future is unknowable, how do you determine the risks involved in any given action? Ralph Stacey, author of *Managing the Unknowable,* explains that the "old mentality encourages you to do nothing, or merely more of the same, until you know what will happen—until you can calculate the rate of return and specify the risk level." There is now, he argues, a need for a new mentality, one that allows the organization to "simultaneously handle both the knowable, closed changes involved in the day-to-day running of the existing business and the unknowable, open-ended changes involved in the innovative development of the business. The result is certainly organizational tension, paradox, and never-ending contradiction, but this provokes conflict and learning and thus is the source of creativity."[21]

Good leaders encourage risk taking by accepting that failure is a learning experience. The company best known for its innovativeness is 3M; it actively encourages risk taking. Art Fry, the developer of Post-Its, the product most closely associated with the idea of new product development, says, "People need the opportunity to make errors, to explore what look like blind alleys."[22]

Leaders who encourage risk taking are themselves risk takers. They accept the responsibility for failures by their people out of a belief that doing so is the only way to grow their organizations, to find new products, develop new processes, improve marketshare. Some, such as Percy Barnevik of ABB, have gone further, restructuring their organizations to find new ways to handle the chaos they see in the marketplace. Others, such as Jack O'Brien of Allmerica, have found new technologies that allow them to restructure the way they do their business. Still others, such as Scott McNealy of Sun Microsystems, have reinterpreted what a business is and how it operates. Leading a company through the evolutionary steps that will create the butterfly may be the ultimate in risk taking.

The "Ah-ha" Factor

In reading over this list, everyone who is in a leadership role of any sort will have seen him or her self very clearly in some of the descriptions. No one reaches leadership ranks unless they have some of these qualities. For this to be of real value, however, we suggest you go back to the beginning of the list and read it through again, trying to remember those points where you didn't immediately respond, "Ah-ha" or "Of course—so what's new?" The point is that leadership today is excruciatingly difficult and complex, making it is all too easy to be, say, a great visionary and good communicator, but such a poor manager that you have no followers, or to have an enormous drive to experiment but no talent to make the results of experimentation into a success in the marketplace.

GETTING THERE

The leaders who will help their organizations adapt to the rapid changes constantly buffeting their organizations with the least waste of time and effort are those who are most open to change and learning. They quickly recognize which issues are critical and attack them by logically analyzing huge amounts of information, abstracting knowledge almost by force of will. They understand complexity and are politically savvy. And they have a set of values that makes it natural for them to accept responsibility and accountability. They are decisive and do not fear sensible risk taking. These characteristics lead them to accept the difficult decisions and intense effort needed to create and run a butterfly organization.

MAKING A DIFFERENCE

In the course of conducting interviews and doing client assignments over the past several years, we have met with dozens of leaders and learned about many others who are confronting these issues in thoughtful and interesting ways. (Some of these leaders have been introduced in the preceding pages and will appear again below and in the next chapter.) A number of these leaders have insights of great value to those who would move their organizations in new directions. Very few, however, have consciously started from chaos and complexity theory. Among the exceptions is John Reed, who has introduced this school of thought to Citicorp, which is now "seeking to apply an understanding of complexity to its day-to-day operations." Colin Crook, chief technology officer of Citicorp says that "the use of complex adaptive systems analysis has so far produced 'very encouraging results.' The next stage," according to Crook, "is to look at the implications for corporate structure and corporate planning."[23]

This desire to find ways to "adapt" to the constant changes their organizations are facing was expressed over and over by leaders looking to grow their organizations without repeating the mistakes of past growth cycles. They realize that the challenges they are facing today cannot be overcome by traditional management techniques.

Aware that doing what they have always done is playing ostrich, they try to break the patterns that make rapid responses to constant change impossible. They try to address the impossibility of knowing what tomorrow and the next day will bring. They try to find ways to make their organizations more flexible. And they try to understand and employ—and anticipate—advances in both information and communications technology. Some have put in place a number of the principles necessary to create the butterfly organization and are moving their companies along the evolutionary path. Others are dealing with many of the issues and problems facing them in such a way that they are developing the mindset necessary for evolution.

DESTEC ENERGY, INC.

There is a tendency to centralize as companies get bigger, and to build in bureaucracy. We are constantly fighting that.

Charles F. Goff[24]

Charles F. Goff is CEO and chairman of the board of Destec Energy, Inc., a leading independent company based in Houston, Texas, that develops, builds, owns, and operates primarily gas-fired facilities for the generation of power. Founded in 1989 by The Dow Chemical Company, Destec went public in 1991. Goff, whose vision led to the formation of the company, has been head of Destec since it began and in August of 1995 was elected chairman of the board.

Goff, who considered himself a bit of a corporate "maverick" during his years at Dow, has built a company based on a number of management principles that shape a butterfly organization. For example, he was determined to make Destec "as flat an organization as possible," to "develop measures for softer things," "find ways to stay entrepreneurial," and "remain as flexible and agile as they grow as they were when they started." He believes in technology as an enabler of communications, as a "way to respond quickly when moving around fast." A strong believer in continually refining the organization and trying new things, he points to the benefits of innovations such as a quality program that, among other things, looked at meetings—the reasons for them and their outcomes—and ended up reducing the number of meetings held by two-thirds.

As Goff moves to grow the company, he takes time to read and reflect, reserving time on his schedule for thinking. A believer in teamwork and empowerment, he expends much effort on meeting each of his employees yearly, noting that with additional growth he would have to abandon his one-on-one meetings but would still strive to maintain a personal touch. That philosophy is reflected in his plans for moving the company into the global arena. As Destec moves into other countries, it begins by sending out a few individuals who get to know the area and then begins to hire from the local community to develop the operations. Goff says that "at the end of the day, I want the operation in the Netherlands, for example, to be thought of as a Dutch company."

As he looks to the future, one of Goff's main concerns has been maintaining the spectacular growth Destec managed in its early years. Unfortunately, over the past few years, the demand for power in Texas fell dramatically just as a number of Destec's contracts for energy ended. Goff, who had built Destec as a vertically integrated organization with "all the skills necessary to develop, design, engineer, construct, permit, finance, acquire, fuel, own, operate, and maintain power plants," has, in the face of the changes that have impacted the industry, rapidly reversed that decision, taking action to cut overhead and outsource some services. One of the things that makes it possible for him to move the company so rapidly and yet maintain quality control is the "knowledge book" that has been built up over the years; the book serves as an "expert system," containing historical and critical information about processes related to the core competencies of the organization provided by senior managers as soon as any project is completed. The book's contents, reviewed carefully whenever a decision about change is contemplated, serves as a guide to those changes.

Goff's focus on looking to the future and finding ways to respond quickly have put the company in a strong financial position, one that has allowed him to make these changes while continuing to look for new sources of growth, including reaching out to Latin America and Asia.

ABB ASEA BROWN BOVERI AND UNILEVER PLC

The only way to structure a complex, global organization is to make it as simple and local as possible. . . . All of our operations must function as closely as possible to stand-alone operations. Our [local] managers need well-defined sets of responsibilities, clear accountability, and maximum degrees of freedom to execute.

Percy Barnevik[25]

We are a business with a very strong culture of decentralization, and it stands us in good stead. The central linchpin of our creed is to put decisionmaking in the hands of the people who run our businesses at the periphery. . . . Those at the center provide strategic input, technological input, and the experience of what Unilever has learnt in other markets. The rest is left to those on the ground.

Michael Perry[26]

Barnevik and Perry are chairmen of two of the largest multinational organizations in the world—ABB and Unilever, respectively. ABB is a Swiss-Swedish company with core competencies in transportation, particularly locomotives, and power generation. Unilever is Anglo-Dutch company with core competencies in consumer products, marketing over 1,000, products from tea (Lipton) to soap (Lever 2000) to perfume (Obsession).

These organizations have moved very close to the butterfly form. They are organized as federations of national companies that maintain very lean cores, producing and selling their products through a combination of acquisitions to enhance their core competencies and processes and numerous alliances, as well as outsourcing arrangements in other areas, such as advertising, to augment those competencies (see Figure 11.1). The leadership of the organization

Figure 11.1.   The Butterfly Organization.

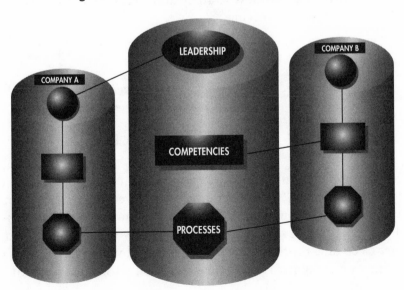

is managed through matrix structures that place leadership responsibilities on hundreds of managers each of whom is responsible for
a small local unit (they are expected to "think globally, act locally").

The core focuses on strategies and knowledge-gathering to
enhance innovation. Perry says that "in order to turn yourself into
a leader you have to be scouting ahead and creating markets." To
achieve this, Unilever has set up experimental innovation centers
where multidisciplinary teams are brought together to tear down the
walls between those in different functional areas in order to achieve
breakthroughs. ABB pursues research through joint ventures, cooperative agreements, collaboration with customers, and joint technical economic studies with government organizations abroad.

Both organizations have extensive training programs to build the
cadres of managers they need; in addition, they ensure that their people receive international experience and develop networks throughout
the organization. Both rely heavily on communications and information technology to provide information to everyone in their far-flung
organizations rapidly in order to avoid reinventing the wheel.

Floris Maljers, former chairman of Unilever, sums up the goals
of these types of organizations: to work, a massive transnational
company needs "a matrix of individual managers around the world
who nonetheless share a common vision and understanding of corporate strategy. . . . Everyone must share the values that lead to flexibility on every level. In a worldwide company incorporating both
unity and diversity, business strategy and structure are inextricably
linked—and always evolving."[27]

MOTOROLA

Since its inception, Motorola has been managing the concept of
renewal, a willingness to renew our technologies and to renew the
processes by which we run the institution.

                                              Christopher Galvin[28]

Christopher Galvin is president and chief operating officer of
Motorola, a huge ($17 billion a year in revenues) multinational
company that manufactures wireless communications devices—
cellular telephones, semiconductors, two-way radios, pagers—and
other electronic products.[29] A Baldrige award winner after years of
decline, the company is now known not only for the quality of its

products, but for its decentralized, flattened structure that allows rapid decisionmaking. It is a company that believes that getting to market first with the next generation of products is so important that the research it invests in is often in pursuit of products that will make its current products obsolete. (This is a trait common to the successful Silicon Valley companies mentioned below.) Gary Tooker, chairman and CEO—the other half of the two-man executive office—says that doing so is one of the ways in which the company maintains its competitive edge.

This focus on competitiveness thrives in Motorola's culture, which is dominated by teamwork and empowerment. Teams are set up with the responsibility for scheduling work, hiring (and, when it becomes necessary, firing) workers, and reducing overhead. The teaming concept has even been extended to suppliers and customers, who are treated as though they were partners in Motorola's operations. In fact, the company has developed such close relationships with some suppliers that it can count on almost real-time delivery from them.

When it comes to empowerment, Motorola is taking that concept to new levels as well. Henry Pujol, vice president and director of manufacturing operations at Motorola's Boynton Beach, Florida, plant, explains that Motorola has "very specific training plans, where we're getting the bulk of our manufacturing folks involved with learning to do multiple jobs. Almost daily, when our people come in they are assigned to different positions on the line. This is preparing them for the day when all of our people will be able to make decisions on the spot, doing debugging, identifying problems, and fixing the problems without a lot of other people having to be involved."[30]

As Motorola grows, acquiring new companies, it pushes its human resources departments to integrate those companies into the culture quickly. Melinda Watkins, an award-winning Motorola human resources manager, explains that to "be fast and flexible and to maintain the special Motorola culture of uncompromising respect for employees demands that the benefits department discover and develop vendors who understand Motorola's unique needs for employee satisfaction through quality programs, accessibility, and rapid response times."[31]

The culture at Motorola encourages the breaking down of boundaries between levels of workers. The result is management and labor cooperation that helps in reenginering, reduces the need for layers of management, and promotes innovation. And to ensure that its workers have the skills it needs when it needs them, Motorola is devoted to educating its employees. The company encourages the pursuit of multiple skills as an aid to flexibility and has developed compensation systems that provide rewards for acquiring additional skills.

The enthusiasm of Motorola workers helps promote a culture in which acrimonious confrontations end when meetings end—although they serve to truly assess the value of concepts put on the table. The focus on learning skills across functional areas and disciplines extends to service and managerial workers as well, resulting in an extremely deep management cadre. This makes expansion easy, yet ensures that the company has managers with usable, hands-on skills, which prove invaluable during periods of global expansion.

SILICON VALLEY: HEWLETT-PACKARD, INTEL, AND SUN MICROSYSTEMS

The underlying principle of HP's personnel policies became the concept of sharing—sharing the responsibilities for defining and meeting goals, sharing in company ownership through stock purchase plans, sharing in profits, sharing the opportunities for personal and professional development, and even sharing the burdens created by occasional downturns in business.

David Packard[32]

The Palo Alto garage that served as David Packard and Bill Hewlett's workshop in the late 1930s has been officially designated "the birthplace of Silicon Valley" by the state of California. There are a number of characteristics of this "high-tech" industry—cooperation, collegiality, and a focus on learning—that are similar to those found in the regions of Europe where cooperative networks and associations have been formed, creating, in essence, "regional butterflies." These butterflies are networks in which numbers of small- and mid-sized companies work together in loose associations, resulting in flexibility, well-trained workforces, high degrees of connectivity, and innovation (see Chapter 10).

Silicon Valley emerged from the entrepreneurial efforts of the many technical and engineering people drawn to the region by the educational establishments (Stanford and Berkeley) and research laboratories sited near those institutions. Their location means that there are always people with fine minds and new skills available to create the next wave of innovation. Because those who work in the area have ties that extend well beyond their current organizations, both through relationships formed during college and other positions they have held, and because of the spirit of academic collegiality that prevails, ideas are cross-fertilized and people tend to continue informal learning, thus maintaining skills. In addition, a more collegial management style, one that works against command and control and bureaucracy, also prevails. Of course, these companies also set up training programs because of the rapid changes in skills needed to keep up with technological developments.

In addition, as Homa Bahrami and Stuart Evans, writing in *The California Management Review*, point out, taking risks is part of the culture of the Valley and there is "no stigma attached to honest failure." They add that "swift action, mobility, and ephemerality are critical features of the Silicon Valley business dynamics. Organizational structures and business models undergo frequent strategic recalibrations and constant realignments." Moreover, the "Silicon Valley ecosystem achieves flexibility through 'diverse specialization,' [with] each firm focusing on what it does best and leveraging the capabilities of other entities for complementary activities."[33]

In addition to functioning in a butterfly-like way as a region, individual technology companies keep springing up (and some fade away) in the area, many following the Hewlett-Packard model of an extremely flexible, flattened, team-focused, innovative core with a focus on organization renewal through employee development.

This characteristic is noteworthy in the case of Intel Corporation, which changed in its early days from a company taking the usual approach of selling its equipment to information technology purchasers at major companies to a company with a marketing focus aimed at end users.[34] The structure of Intel is frequently changed, people are moved where they are needed, which allows the company to "operate as leanly as possible . . . [and] saves having to overhire in times of expansion. Reorganization is continual and evolving, a way of life; there is no such thing as a static job."[35] The company is always looking for new products, new approaches, and people are encouraged to upgrade their skills constantly.

This flexibility is reflected in Intel's office design: everybody's office is a cubicle, including that of the chairman of the company, and people constantly shift around depending on what area of the business is currently in need of their skills. The organization is flat (a half dozen layers), and everyone is encouraged to speak their minds. Andy Grove encourages his employees to practice "constructive confrontation," expressing opinions to anyone on any level.

Although the organization has grown enormously since it was started by a group out of Fairchild Semiconductor in 1963 and has built a global presence, it does so by taking the same kind of local approach that Unilever and ABB do. Intel also works hard to team its engineers with its customers by putting those engineers on one end of a customer "hot line." And Andy Grove spends time meeting with those outside the organization to make sure the company is prepared for every new challenge—and any competitor that is attempting to change the basis of competition.

Sun Microsystems, Inc.'s chairman and CEO, Scott McNealy, is a great believer in keeping his organization flexible and focused on core competencies. SunU, the training and development organization of Sun Microsystems, finds itself having to deal with constantly changing training needs because the parent organization's business "involves constantly changing technologies and products— many of them in new markets."[36]

These companies are representative of the "ecosystem" of Silicon Valley, an area that might one day be noted as a new stage in organizational evolution—a time when the development of a unique regional cooperative environment in pursuit of technology produced something akin to the Industrial Revolution.

TRANSNET

We have emerged from [the past five years] as a leaner, fitter and wiser organization. . . . However, as we look . . . at the road ahead, we see a different and even more awesome challenge, . . . namely:

* *the need to redesign our organization to accommodate current business and market realities and pressures . . .*

* *the need to preserve and grow the expertise and core skills which have made us successful in the past while opening up opportunities and avenues to those who have previously been denied these*

- *to arrive through mutual understanding and acceptance, and a sharing of opportunity and responsibility, at a Transnet family which is not only representative of our country's composition, but is even more dedicated and effective than what we have had in the past.*

We know that the road ahead will not be easy.

Anton Moolman[37]

Transnet of the Republic of South Africa is a fairly recently "commercialized" company (a term that means a movement to being a publicly held company during the first phase of which a majority of shares continue to be held by government) that hovers somewhere between an extreme federalist model and a holding company. At the moment, it is governed in terms of autonomous business units. For example, there are a small cluster of major units—Portnet, which runs the ports; South African Airlines; Spoornet, which runs the rail operations; Petronet, which runs the nation's gas and oil pipelines; Autonet, which runs the trucks and buses; and PX, the South African equivalent of Federal Express. In addition, there are dozens of smaller units that provide support for the major units, such as Datavia, which is the information services organization for the whole company (although any unit is free to obtain those services elsewhere); Esselen Park, a training center for employees at all levels that also offers its services to external parties; and Human Resources, which provides the usual services, with one important difference: its goal is to ensure a balance between the workforce (black and white, with adequate representation in the management ranks of females on each side) that reflects the demographic realities of the nation.

The head of this vast operation, almost 120,000 employees in 1995, down from 180,000 in the early 1990s when commercialization took place, is Anton Moolman, who was an officer of the company reporting to the minister of transportation before commercialization. Moolman has worked assiduously to change the company from a state-run, civil-service organization to a competitive enterprise that can handle the challenges likely to result from the lifting of sanctions and the deregulation of the nation's transport sector.

Moolman has pushed his senior managers to develop an entrepreneurial style, encouraging experimentation and risk taking. He
meets frequently with his senior managers to build consensus about
future directions, especially to obtain buy-in for his concept of
turning the company into a synergistic, value-added set of business units. He has promoted extensive investment in technology,
partly because of the vast area over which the companies operate
physically and partly because technology allows his managers to
interact with academics and business advisors in first-world nations,
and ultimately because technology is the critical enabler for a logistics company.

Moolman has now turned his attention to the issue of governance. He believes that the company has matured enough that it can
overlay a core-competency focus on its current business units. By
appointing selected individuals to coordinate the company's core
competencies for, say, land transportation, it could gain economies
of scale and speed for PX through the use both of Autonet and
Spoornet as appropriate, instead of having PX make arrangements
with only one unit, which might result in a more circuitous route.
The levels of complexity in the overlay of one layer of governance
over another are very difficult, and no one is yet certain that it will
work. But, as he has at every stage, Moolman is pushing for experimentation in the quest for growth.

DOING IT

These organizations and their leaders are putting in place many of
the principles that, as will be seen in the next chapter, taken together,
will create that most agile of organizational models—the butterfly.
Those principles emerge from the need to manage the impacts of
changes in the environment in which business operates on an organization's leaders, its governance, and its technology—and the
impacts caused by the changes in each of those on the others. The
movement of an organization in response to these impacts must be
dealt with rapidly and constructively, and in such a way that the
organization remains intact, but does not stagnate.

12

THE SEVEN PRINCIPLES OF BALANCE

Important principles . . . must be inflexible.

Abraham Lincoln

To maintain flexibility, tomorrow's successful organizations will constantly have to reposition themselves between stability (which can result in stagnation) and disorder (which may result in an inability to function). By staying poised somewhere between order and chaos, organizations can seize opportunities for growth in the ever-changing conditions that mark the current environment. Learning to maintain that degree of balance is an art, and as with most art forms, it requires a mastery of certain basics before reaching out to create something new. The basics needed to achieve non-disruptive organizational growth are seven principles that must be accepted as commandments. They are an outgrowth of an understanding of the ways that governance, technology, and leadership impact one another and thereby push the organization in new directions.

The first objection to accepting these principles as commandments will be to the idea that inflexibility is needed to create something that is highly flexible. However, in order to keep the organization from veering off course when it is impacted by a change in governance, technology, or leadership, there must be a mechanism to make it swerve back toward the center. That mechanism is the rules that enforce adherence to the seven principles. It is important to understand that while the principles are, like commandments, not subject to change, the organization-specific rules developed to ensure that the intent of the principles is fulfilled should be revisited frequently and amended if necessary. They are not rigid, in order to prevent the kind of sharp rebound that would itself encourage chaos.

The second objection will be to the difficulty inherent in living by principles that sometimes sound more biblical than organizational. They often demand of us better behavior than we may believe necessary for success, requiring taking risks, making hard choices, and accepting responsibility for our own actions and inactions. There is no easy answer to this objection. The simple truth is that when organizations become ever more complex adaptive systems, everyone in them must stretch to a higher standard, behaving as though they too were evolving to a new level.

THE CHALLENGE

Keep in mind that learning the principles is not enough, even acting on one or two will not bring dramatic results. The principles must permeate the culture of an organization and be evident in its actions. To ensure that they are incorporated into the culture, each must be analyzed in terms of the specific organization—the industrial sector it is part of, the products and services it currently offers, its core competencies, the governance currently in place in different areas, the technologies it uses and those it plans to acquire, and the people who lead and the people who work for and with it. Only then can the rules based on those principles be formalized and put in place. For example, if an organization is multinational, it will have to address the issue of ethics in terms of national differences and expectations; if it has heavy manufacturing plants as well as service organizations, it will have to address the issue of mixing and matching many different strategic and operational governance models; if it has reached a new level in terms of size, constant checks will be needed to make sure that it is not becoming so bulky it loses flexibility.

The rules needed to ensure that the principles are acted upon will differ for each organization. Once derived, they must be communicated to everyone, and responsibility and accountability for ensuring compliance must be assigned to key people throughout the organization. Unless they are taken seriously, nothing will happen. Moreover, organizations must remember that reinforcement is critical in the workplace of the future, where people are not part of the same company for long periods of time or may even be working for more than one company at the same time.

This chapter will explore the seven principles that are meant to ensure that the organization maintains its balance, explaining why each is necessary as well as some of the issues that must be addressed by those who develop the rule bases for each of them. It will pose a variety of questions that will serve as a "starter kit" for discussion, and then present examples of the rules in action to give some indication of what it takes to achieve results.

THE SEVEN PRINCIPLES

Those organizations that are moving in the direction of the butterfly form already adhere to a significant number of the principles; in fact, most organizations will find that, as a result of their efforts to adapt to the economic problems of the past several years, they already have put a couple of them in place. Some of them may exist as widely shared assumptions. The "magic" now may lie in setting forth an explicit program of adopting and then implementing additional principles on a timetable. The more principles an organization adopts, the more flexible it becomes. Except for the first principle, it is not the order in which they are adopted that is important, but rather that they are adopted.

1. SET ETHICAL STANDARDS AND DO NOT ACCEPT DEVIATIONS FROM THEM.

This principle is aimed at building an organization based on trust, honesty, and integrity. Those qualities make it possible for an organization to develop the kind of reputation that leads to the establishment of healthy long-term relationships with equally reputable stakeholders, ranging from employees (core and affinity), to current and future alliance partners, to the communities in which they are based (which provide needed social and economic services), to suppliers, and to customers.

Since most of the relationships necessary for building and maintaining the butterfly form require close interaction between the organization and its partners, including close electronic connections, and since organizations will be involved in numerous concurrent relationships, managing these relationships without a solid basis in trust is a costly and time-consuming endeavor. For example, valuable time is lost when an organization has to wait for elaborate formal contracts to be in hand before any work can begin; if the organizations and people involved in setting up a partnership have a strong reputation for ethical behavior, work can often begin before formalities are concluded. In a world in which new products and services become commodities in weeks, saving this time can make a critical difference to gaining marketshare.

The value of ethics, of course, goes far beyond the deal. People work better, faster, and smarter when they are proud of the organization they work for. It prevents game playing; it avoids time spent questioning values; it builds loyalty. On a personal level, employees who see their company denounced in the media for dumping toxic wastes or for cheating the local school board in a construction project or for hiring discrimination, fear that their own reputations will be damaged. Affinity workers with skills and experience enough to receive many offers will not select such organizations as the place to work. Potential alliance partners turn away from relationships with these organizations out of fear for their own reputations.

Organizations that set out to instill an ethical culture incorporate a statement about those beliefs in their credos and mission statements; their leaders speak publicly about the issue; and some put in place formal codes that employees, particularly those at the senior level, must sign. For example, the list of questions Dick Brooks of Central and South West (see Chapter 4) uses conveys the organization's values to his employees and the public: "Would I want what I am doing to be done to me?" "How would I feel if what I am doing appeared in the newspaper?" and "Would I want my spouse and my kids to know what I am doing? These questions set the ethical tone at CSW, but there is also a formal code governing internal and external behavior that includes a statement about seeing to it that the code is followed.

BUILDING THE RULE BASE. Corporations must decide what kind of public statements to make and what kind of codes to put in place. To do so, they must spend time discussing the issues. A starting point would be to address a set of basic questions, such as those below, which would then be augmented by follow-up questions tailored to the specific organization. These, therefore, should be treated as directional only:

• What is our responsibility to our stakeholders?

• How far do we have to go in explaining and communicating such concepts as conflict of interest and discrimination to our employees?

• How do we communicate the importance of reliability, honesty, integrity, fairness?

• How do we ensure that our organization's ethical standards are communicated and interpreted consistently in every choice we make?

• Do we reward ethical behavior?

• Do we deal with violators in a speedy, clear, and consistent fashion?

• How can we make clear our belief in the rights of individuals and our respect for their and other's property, material as well as proprietary, and intellectual?

In the course of constructing the rules, wide-ranging discussions should be held about the meaning of such terms as *ethics, values, honesty, integrity, beliefs, conviction, trust, "doing the right thing,"* and *openness*. These discussions, which must start with senior management, will help in formulating the rules that best fit the organization's culture.

MAKING IT SO. Once the rule base is developed, a number of things must take place to ensure implementation. Leadership must interpret those rules, put in place ongoing communications programs, provide training and education programs, and set up compensation procedures that reward adherence to ethical standards and mete out punishment for violators.

Because conflicting realities often are involved in ethical decisionmaking, management must set up mechanisms to ensure that everyone in the organization understands what the organization's ethical standards are. It helps to have a senior official in charge of ethics, to serve as an ombudsman. For example, Texas Instruments, which has a strong ethics program, put in place an ethics director who displayed posters of himself looking friendly and approachable; the caption beneath the photo said, "TI has a long-standing tradition of excellence in the ethical conduct of our business. TI has established the Ethics Office to help TIers understand what is needed to continue this tradition. I'm available to discuss any questions or concerns you have relating to business policies or practices at TI." The poster also contained information on how to reach him directly, promising "confidentiality or anonymity at your request."[1]

Such an officer is one possible road to driving ethics through the organization. Another is to see that the ethical values are driven down into the organization by making managers at every level formally responsible for communicating them, and making clear that employees who feel pressured to violate them have someone to turn to. Another way is to set up discussion groups that examine what are known as "grey areas," those ethical questions people confront that require more than a simple yes or no answer (remember the complications in the Levi Strauss case in Chapter 4). Another part of the process of instilling an ethical culture is setting up mechanisms to ensure that ethical issues are reflected in compensation. Performance reviews should include rewards for attention to ethical issues. For example, if one of a company's plants is located in an area with more stringent emission standards than its other plants, is the cost of meeting those requirements taken into account in evaluating profitability for compensation purposes?

The most difficult aspect of the problem is dealing with violations. If an organization uncovers clear and intentional violations of legal rules of conduct, immediate dismissal should result. If crossing the line is not as clear—say, the use of the company car for a pleasure trip at the end of a business trip—penalties must be imposed and rules issued to ensure that such behavior will not be repeated. In the case of problems that are the result of changes in what is considered acceptable behavior, such as sexism that never crosses the line into sexual harassment, training programs are necessary to ensure that "a hostile atmosphere," which is a violation, is not allowed to develop.

Unless issues are dealt with immediately and fairly, the ethical climate of the organization can quickly deteriorate, and it can find itself on a slippery slope. The issue is complicated for global businesses by a lack of understanding of the ethical standards prevailing in other nations. The organization determined to pursue ethical governance will have to address this issue.

2. ESTABLISH A SOCIAL CONTRACT.

This principle requires organizations to spell out conditions of employment with both core and affinity employees and make clear both what an employer believes is owed employees and the obligations of employees to the organization. The contract should address issues such as notice and severance, availability of education and training, and expectations about maintaining skills. Issues such as medical insurance, life insurance, and pension benefits, flex-time, and opportunities for growth and advancement need clarification, as well as expectations of loyalty and agreements about proprietary information, confidentiality, noncompetition, and accountability.

The reasons why organizations should develop such contracts in spite of the fact that at the moment there is no labor shortage will be explored further in the next chapter. Here, however, we will look briefly at the problems created by the destruction of the old social contract and the problems that will continue to emerge as technology changes and advances.

The effects of the downsizings of recent years have been made worse by the promises of "this is it, no more cuts are expected," followed by another 10 percent layoff, and so forth, every six-to-twelve months. These repeated bouts leave survivors feeling guilty because they still have jobs and fearful that they will be next. Among the other effects is a loss of loyalty to the organization, to which is added resentment as employees work longer and harder to do the work of those who have not been replaced. Yet these employees are afraid to protest because that might make them the first to go in the next, seemingly inevitable, round of layoffs. There is also a kind of discontent that arises from the flattening of organizations that results in fewer people driving to reach the top "by giving their all." When making it to the top seems impossible, people work to earn a living rather than to build a career.

BUILDING THE RULE BASE. The critical issue for those companies looking toward growth now, and in the future, is finding a way to ensure that they will have two things when it comes to employees: a loyal, trained group of core employees and sources of well-trained, skilled, eager affinity employees when they need them. Core employees will need up-to-date skills when the company is lean because that is when they will be called on to do the day-to-day work of the organization. They also will need the latest skills to be prepared for the next wave of growth, when they will have to integrate affinity workers into the organization and train them in the way the organization does things.

The following "starter kit" of questions can be used to begin the discussion of what kind of social contract an organization should have. But a warning is necessary: there are legal implications for the organization of putting such a code in place, some of which are federal, some state and local. It is therefore critical to consult with the corporation's legal counsel in developing and codifying the rule base for the social contract. The first level of questions are:

♦ What is our responsibility to our core employees?

♦ What kind of continual education and training programs do core employees need?

♦ How should termination of core employees be handled?

♦ What is our responsibility to our affinity workers?

♦ What kinds of arrangements do we have to make to ensure that there is an adequately skilled affinity workforce available when we need it?

♦ What benefit programs should be available to affinity workers?

The other half of the equation is what employees owe their employers. Employers have a right to ask employees to deal with them as fairly as the employees expect to be treated. The following questions will help in confronting this issue:

• What is the core employee's responsibility to the employer?

• What is a reasonable amount of notice for a core employee with critical skill sets to give an employer?

• How much responsibility do employees have for ensuring that the organization has captured the critical knowledge they have of the organization's key processes before leaving?

• How much responsibility does an affinity employee have in terms of protecting an employer's competitive information?

• How much loyalty does an affinity employee owe an employer?

• How much responsibility do affinity workers have for revealing ethical misconduct they have witnessed?

MAKING IT SO. Unless there are huge changes in American social policies, the way an organization deals with issues such as employee benefits will determine the employment decisions made by affinity workers. The trade-offs between an offer at a higher rate with no benefits, no retraining, and no guarantees of any type and a package at a lower rate that ensures continued employability will be carefully weighed, especially by the best workers. Companies that build solid reputations as good places to work will find it easiest to attract the best and brightest, something organizations must think about, since growth is likely to occur in similar industries simultaneously.

Jack Welch of General Electric sums up the situation facing business today this way: "With the general lack of security in today's business and economic environment, companies need to establish a new form of job security based on learning skills that ensure employability. One thing you can give people is employability, and that's the best security of all. Other companies like to hire GE management because they're so well trained. . . . The minute the leader withholds from people what's needed for their growth, we won't have a chance in this brutally competitive global environment."[2]

Even if a company decides it is wiser not to articulate these rules, the way they deal with employees will quickly become known within their industrial sector. In addition to reputation, leaders can articulate their belief in education and training and the kind of organization they are building in interviews with the media, at association meetings, and so forth. The kinds of benefits offered will also give employees a good picture of the organization. Whatever path taken, the need for a social contract cannot be ignored.

3. Maintain a strong, lean central organization based on core competencies.

Organizations must be careful not to become so enamored of downsizing and leanness that they end up losing the skills that are the source of their competitive advantage. *The Economist* argues that "much re-engineering has failed because companies are keener on slaking the stockmarket's thirst for quick fixes, usually by sacking workers, than on introducing structural changes. As well as destroying morale, this approach leads to 'corporate anorexia,' with firms too thin to take advantage of economic upturns."[3] Firms that downsize too far tend to lose their capacity for innovation, as employees find few opportunities to thrash out their ideas with others and too little time to even think about experimentation. There is also the danger that when the time comes to grow, the organization will not have enough core workers to lead the affinity workforce.

On the other hand, there is a temptation to permanently add people and positions (or divisions and organizations) during growth cycles, in part because in the past size was an indicator of success and in part because it seems as though keeping such people on staff will save time during the next growth cycle. If such decisions mean pursuing growth in a given area, be certain that you are not adding people and acquiring companies when acquisition through partnerships, alliances, and various temporary relationships might prove just as effective. For example, a company that has core competencies in miniaturization should not build a large marketing division when launching a new product. It should, however, add to its staff, say, a gifted designer discovered when the company added a few people on a temporary basis. Of course, if such an individual has been following an affinity work path, it is important to ascertain whether he or she is interested in moving to a more permanent position, given it requires putting on a leadership and teaching hat during growth periods. In the case of possible acquisitions, organizations must be certain that the relationship really adds to each organization's core competencies (which will sometimes be complementary) and that the product or service produced jointly will continue for a sufficient period of time to warrant an acquisition instead of an alliance.

BUILDING THE RULE BASE. All decisions about size must be made with an eye toward maintaining core competencies. Organizations must probe their assumptions about what it is they do best. Over time, corporations may have developed new core competencies that are hidden by legacies of the past. For example, utility companies often assume that the generation of power is a core competency; however, service or the management of information may have become a core competency, because it may have become cheaper to buy energy from elsewhere to resell. Thus, the questions that start the discussion must include:

+ What are our core competencies?

+ Are we expending our resources on competencies and processes that provide little added value to our customers?

+ Do we have the right number of people skilled in our core competencies and processes?

+ Do we have a way of capturing and transferring our process knowledge within the organization?

+ How can we leverage our competencies and processes?

+ Where should we focus in the future?

+ Can we form relationships with other companies whose competencies and processes complement ours?

MAKING IT SO. The leaders of organizations evolving to these new forms seem to have totally taken to heart the need to maintain a lean central organization. Percy Barnevik of ABB Asea Brown Boveri has found ways to run his enormous company in such a way that a corporate headquarters staff of 140 can coordinate the 200,000-plus ABB employees worldwide. Moreover, Barnevik uses the concepts of "thinking locally," and gaining core competencies through alliances and supplier and customer relationships in order to avoid building in areas that don't meet the organization's core competency requirements.

In addition, in order to maintain essential size, leaders of evolving organizations build workforce loyalty and create conditions that allow their employees to truly focus on the organization's strengths. Sam Walton of Wal-Mart expressed concerns that being "big might get in the way of doing a good job. Of course," he said, "being big has some real advantages, but being big also poses dangers. It has ruined many a fine company—including some giant retailers—who started out strong and got out of touch or were slow to react to the needs of their customers. Here's the point: the bigger Wal-Mart gets, the more essential it is that we think small."[4] Since Wal-Mart's core competencies are meeting customer demands for given products at the lowest possible price, losing that focus would be extremely costly.

4. DEVELOP LEADERSHIP SKILLS AT EVERY LEVEL OF THE ORGANIZATION.

The butterfly organization will flourish when it has leadership strengths at all levels of the core organization. Leadership at the top is simply not enough when the layers of bureaucracy aimed at conveying the demands of management and seeing to it that rules are followed have been eliminated. Employees must be given the training and have available the information they need to make appropriate decisions on their own. They must have an understanding of the goals and operations of the organization to be able to respond to situations of all kinds when they are on the front lines, with no one telling them exactly what to do. In addition, since today's customers expect immediate solutions to their problems from the people with whom they interact, employees at the front lines (such as customer service representatives who answer inquiries about account status, agents at the car rental counter, salespeople at a retail store) have to be given the education and training and then be empowered to make certain levels of decisions on their own. (Those who are uncomfortable with such responsibility have to be screened out and not placed in decisionmaking positions.)

Moreover, in the butterfly organization, leadership skills will be critical as affinity workers are added to the organization at every level and as alliances and other partnering arrangements become commonplace. Unless affinity workers are made to feel a part of the organization and trained in its ways, the full value of their skills will not be realized. And core employees also will have to have the skills and empowerment to manage relationships with peers from different divisions and organizations within the company and among alliance partners and outsourcers. Providing the core employees of the new organization with leadership qualities in the areas of decisionmaking, mentoring, responsibility, and accountability is the key to growth.

BUILDING THE RULE BASE. Although most people can be trained to some degree in leadership skills, it is important to remember that much learning in this area is a result of experience—and psychological comfort with leadership responsibility. Working for good leaders is critical to learning how to lead; of course, working for bad leaders teaches us what not to do, which may be just as helpful. The more opportunities people have to lead, and to make mistakes while doing so, the more they learn what works for them as leaders and what does not. In formulating rules for developing leaders, in addition to taking the need for observation and experience into account, it is important to open the discussion by asking:

- Does our organization have programs in place for developing leadership skills?

- How does our organization ensure that the individuals selected to fill core positions are those who will eagerly accept accountability and responsibility?

- How does our organization make clear that it will not accept playing politics as a substitute for performance?

* Does our organization make it possible for individuals with superior skills to play important roles and win recognition and rewards without becoming senior management?

* Do our top leaders have enough pride in themselves and the organization to take on any task, no matter how trivial?

* Does senior management accept risk taking, innovation, and failure if it results in a learning experience that is beneficial to both the individual and the organization?

* Does our organization develop individuals with negotiating and boundary management skills?

* Does our organization spend time and effort developing individuals with skill sets suitable for working in a collaborative environment?

* Is our organization growing leaders who also have expertise in specific areas?

MAKING IT SO. Organizations that understand the need for leadership at all levels will have to find ways to convince those at the top to cede some of their oversight and authority and become part of a new organization. This requires making sure core employees at every level receive enough training and have enough experience to meet the leadership roles they are assigned. Leaders at the top will not relinquish authority until they have some confidence that the result will be neither anarchy nor disaster.

Once everyone in the organization accepts the principle of leaders at different levels, it is critical that the demands of leadership do not result in a loss of skills. These core leadership employees must be able to resume day-to-day operational tasks during downsizings. A reluctance to remove someone who has performed well as a leader, someone who has provided a great deal of value during a period of growth and profitability, can lead to the vicious cycle of creating a bureaucracy that cuts profitability and again creates the need for downsizing. Preventing the loss of valuable operational skills is as important as building leadership, and as long as there are extra rewards for the superior performance, fairness can be maintained.

Mark Hazelwood, senior vice president of ARCO Transportation Company, believes strongly that "the world is too complex, too dynamic, too fast changing to expect one strong figure at the top to consistently make high quality decisions based solely on that person's knowledge and experience." He says that the time for command-and-control hierarchies has passed and that "to address the wide range of issues facing organizations today, many contributors are needed." Consistent with this belief, he maintains that everyone in the organization has the potential to add value through the exercise of leadership. There are, he also notes, debates about whether leadership is a result of training or whether people are born with leadership talent; the point is, "in the final analysis, leadership is a bank of experiences, thus people with experience placed in the right environment can develop leadership skills."

The role of top leaders, he says, is the most difficult because those in that position must meet the expectations of followers, who want "someone honest, who they can trust to be fair; they want someone forward looking, someone competent so they can respect them, and someone motivating and inspiring." At the same time, he adds, it is very important for leaders to "balance aspirational and inspirational leadership actions with a clear sense of reality." In discussing his own leadership style, he noted, "It is my sincere belief that people will not achieve their full potential, nor will they find their jobs fulfilling unless work can also be fun and enjoyable. Creating and maintaining an environment that encourages active participation and allows people to have fun is an important leadership responsibility."[5]

Hazelwood's ideas need to be applied to leaders at all levels in the new organization. Perhaps most important, however, is leadership pertaining to affinity workers. After all, if the corporate leaders of affinity workers can mange them in such a way that they have fun and enjoy the job, they will be creating workers who are eager to perform to their fullest and are likely to come back during the next business upturn.

5. BE OPEN TO LEARNING, ENCOURAGE EXPERIMENTATION, AND BE INNOVATIVE.

Organizations determined to react to changes in a timely fashion have to search constantly for information that is likely to trigger change. They must become Peter Senge's "learning organizations," gathering information from their boards, suppliers, customers, successes, failures, and experts in their own and other sectors, nations, and institutions. They must also learn to keep abreast of advances being made by those with whom they compete.

At the same time, organizations must constantly try new things, that is, to return to the quote that opened Chapter 1, "experiment . . . and learn from mistakes." Unless companies pursue new ideas and look for ways to replace products or services with new or vastly improved ones, they cannot grow. Although it is important to seek new ideas that leverage the organization's core competencies, some ideas may be so good that they warrant development through the establishment of alliances with organizations that have core competencies better suited to that product or service.

Once an organization is confronted with the result of experimentation, it must determine whether or not there is a business value inherent in the new idea. Unfortunately, the person or team who came up with the idea may not be the best person to determine a practical use for it. Companies striving to be innovative must assemble groups from areas such as marketing to determine which ideas to pursue—and they must pursue them, even if it means making current products obsolete.

BUILDING THE RULE BASE. This principle demands a great deal from everyone in the organization. It means devoting personal time to growth. It requires challenging assumptions and giving up preconceived ideas. It means taking risks and accepting that there is learning from failure. And it means caring for the success of the organization enough to stretch and demand the same of everyone else.

The discussions that lead to the building of the rule base should be ongoing. Only by testing itself frequently can an organization keep focused on finding new ways to succeed, experimenting even with the tried and true in order to grow. The following questions are a good place to start:

- Is our organization adverse to trying out new products or services?

- How does our organization learn from its mistakes?

- What mechanisms are in place to reward those who are innovative?

+ What does our organization know about its suppliers and customers?

+ What information does our organization collect about its competitors?

+ How do we collect information about trends that might impact us?

+ Is our organization a learning organization?

+ How often is the phrase "But we have always done it this way" heard in our organization?

+ How paranoid is our organization? (Remember Andrew Grove's belief that an organization always has to keep looking over its shoulder.)

+ Does our organization focus as much on the future as it does on today?

MAKING IT SO. Many organizations have taken steps in this area. Some add outside directors to their boards, set up teams to track technology developments, and bring in speakers noted for leading edge thinking to address their executives. They encourage their employees to join associations and attend conferences. Organizations with a focus on learning also provide educational opportunities to employees through tuition reimbursement plans, boot camps for specific new technologies, or corporate educational institutions. For example, Motorola has established Motorola University as a competitive tool. William Wiggenhorn, president of the university, states, "We figure if we can outlearn our competitors, we can beat them every time."[6]

When it comes to experimentation, companies take many different approaches. The company with one of the best records for successful experimentation is 3M. Its financial objective is to ensure that at least 30 percent of sales each year come from products introduced within the past four years. One of the ways it meets that goal is by selecting future employees for characteristics that indicate creativity.

Dr. Geoffrey Nicholson, staff vice president, 3M Corporate
Technical Planning and International Technical Operations, says
that the organization profiled twenty-five of its top innovators to
determine what characteristics to look for in new applicants.
Nicholson says that innovators tend to be "curious, creative, . . .
hands-on people. . . . The kind you need to solve problems in the
real world." But the most noteworthy characteristics, because they
were unexpected, were "broad interests outside the job, an attitude
of 'Do it first, explain it later,' and a tendency to swing between high
and low cycles of productivity."[7]

The issue of what is new is also important. Unless companies are
willing to search for products and services that will make the old
ones they offer obsolete, they are not being innovative. Far too
many companies fool themselves into thinking that innovation
means tweaking. Unfortunately, a company that depends for its
success on introducing with great fanfare, say, its "new electric
grill—the first available in a choice of colors"—will soon be overtaken by a competitor who provides a comparatively priced product that uses a different technology to overcome the failure of
electric grills to produces meals that really taste grilled.

According to Paul M. Cook, founder of Raychem Corporation,
which is known for its innovativeness, a company will be successful if it is willing to "obsolete itself as fast as it can" and understands
that "one of the biggest obstacles to successful innovation is success
itself." The problem, he says, is that "all too often a company will
develop an important new product and spend years asking itself the
same questions—how can we make it a little better, a little cheaper,
a little more sophisticated? . . . A truly innovative company never
stops asking more fundamental questions about its most successful
products. Are there whole new ways to solve the problem?" This
behavior, which as noted earlier, is typical of the technology companies of Silicon Valley, requires, according to Cook, gathering
together a group of people who enjoy trying new things and ensuring that they are in an environment that expects innovation and
rewards it. More important though is making certain that, once the
idea is generated, it is made practical. True success from innovation
requires mastering the "drudgery. The creative process usually
starts with a brilliant idea. Next you determine whether, if the new idea
worked, it would be worth doing from a business standpoint. . . .
Then comes the real work, reducing the idea to practice."[8]

6. AVOID RESTRUCTURING WHEN YOU SHOULD
BE REGOVERNING.

In practice, this principle is the least recognized, but it is critical to maintaining flexibility in a lean organization. Organizations must frequently reassess their governance models to determine whether they slow decisionmaking, prevent flexibility, inhibit creativity and learning, or create confusion in lines of authority in dealing with customers and suppliers. It is also important (as explained in Chapter 6) for organizations to frequently reassess their strategic and operational governance models to be sure that changes made in the way people work, in the way work is divided, and in technology have not brought changes in governance that are not recognized by leadership or taken into account by those managing the organization's technology.

Responsibility, authority, and accountability must be clear for an organization to run smoothly. If top leadership thinks the organization is hierarchical, but teams and alliances with shared responsibilities are the norm, numerous problems can result. For example, when a new product does not seem to be selling well, top leaders may decide to restructure the marketing group, unaware that the marketing of the product has been made the responsibility of the alliance partner of the division producing the product. Looking at partnering arrangements to be certain that the centralized functions are not delegated to others—or understanding that those who are internally responsible are in this case not involved—would prevent restructuring that might have no effect on the problem it is meant to solve.

Conflicting assignments, overlapping responsibility, and bypassing layers of management are all signs of governance mismatches. Organizations can have different governance models within different groups and divisions, but everyone must understand these differences and their implications and find ways to adjust to them if the organization is to run smoothly. Moreover, the technology providers must find ways to accommodate these differences in governance styles when constructing the networks that tie the organization together (as explained in Chapter 7).

BUILDING THE RULE BASE. In all too many organizations, constant restructuring and reorganization are the price of a failure to understand the governance models in place. Frequently challenging assumptions about governance can prevent the wrong kinds of decisions:

* What is our existing governance model?

* Is it appropriate for the way we compete today?

* Do we accommodate multiple governance models within our organization?

* Do the people in each part of our organization understand the governance model they are supposed to follow?

* Do our employees use our communications and information technology (IT) infrastructure to override our existing governance model?

* Can our IT function accommodate multiple business governance models?

* Do we assess the potential impact of differing governance models when forming relationships with external organizations?

* Does our board of directors scrutinize the effectiveness of the chief executive officer's governance model over time?

* What governance model should we prepare to move to in the future?

MAKING IT SO. Although many organizations fail to understand the implications of governance, Shell Oil learned to understand them in order to ensure that the technology that enables the sharing of information and facilitates communications accommodates the various governance models in the company's business units. The other major company with a focus on governance, as examined in the last chapter, is Transnet of South Africa. In both cases, the first step was gaining an understanding of governance and the various models that could be put in place. The second was helping leaders to understand how they could manage interactions between units and divisions with different governance models. The third was ensuring that those at different levels of the organization understood the limitations—and lack thereof—that accompanied each of the models so that they would understand how to deal with people who had less or more freedom of action than they did. This understanding made it easier for those in empowered, federalist groups to put up with some of the delays involved in seeking approval, and for those in centralist groups to understand the impatience, often barely contained, of those allowed to make on-the-spot decisions. Experience has taught us that dealing with governance issues requires learning and the patience that comes from understanding on the part of everyone involved.

7. ENSURE CONNECTIVITY.

Connectivity involves people as well as technology. For people and organizations to work together effectively, there must be trust on both sides. Establishing trusting relationships is harder in a wired world, where people are often connected without ever having an opportunity to meet and develop the trust that is so critical to long-term relationships. And yet organizations cannot ignore the advantages provided by electronic communications and information networks that tie together people and offices, enabling rapid responses to events and collaborative work regardless of time and location.

Realizing the benefits of connectivity thus requires establishing a reputation for trust and providing the electronic networks to facilitate interaction. In the new organization, workers—whether permanent employees who are asked to work at home a day or two a week as part of the effort to meet government clean air requirements or affinity workers who do their part-time jobs from home or executives who oversee operations at a foreign plant but also must take part in meetings at headquarters—all need to be connected to one another and to the information collected by the organization. The various units and divisions must share information about matters such as finances, staffing and resources available, and product availability. The organization's alliance partners, outsourcers, and other partners must be able to work together while far apart if the new organization is to profit from connectivity.

At the same time, organizations must be aware that connectivity can change them in subtle—and sometimes not so subtle—ways.

For example, connectivity can be used by employees to avoid hierarchical structures, thereby changing governance. Connectivity can also impact leadership as people with expertise in various areas access information and use it to draw different conclusions. Knowing that these changes are possible, organizations should watch for them and deal with them in a timely fashion.

BUILDING THE RULE BASE. The importance of connectivity to the new organization requires proactive efforts to make the use of electronic communications an intrinsic part of the culture. These efforts should involve periodic reassessment by senior management during which questions such as the following are raised:

+ Does our culture provide the right atmosphere for the open communications necessary for human connectivity?

+ Does the organization promote individual business networking?

+ How comfortable are our employees with electronic communications?

+ How comfortable are our leaders with electronic communications?

+ Does everyone in our organization understand the impact of connectivity on business governance?

+ Has everyone in the organization accepted the value of electronic communications of all types?

+ Have we made our decision about electronic connectivity on the basis of enhancing the current and future value we provide to our customers?

+ Have we extended the use of electronic communications to our dealings with our board, shareholders, and stakeholders?

+ Are we prepared to expand our electronic connectivity to external organization for the exchange of data, information, processes, and collaborative work?

◆ Do we have the proper security measures in place to ensure that only the appropriate information is shared?

MAKING IT SO. The first step in making this principle work takes us right back to the first principle: set ethical standards and do not accept deviations from them. Ethical standards are, after all, the basis for building the trust necessary for connectivity. Charles Handy believes strongly in the coming of organizations that are elements connected through technology, but warns that "high tech has to be balanced by high touch to build high trust organizations."[9]

The next step to ensuring connectivity is to be sure your technology is user friendly, provides the information and access needed easily, and is compatible—or can be made compatible—with the technologies of all players. For companies such as Wal-Mart, investigating and investing in new technologies is a business decision. In fact, it tends to be at the "bleeding edge" (a step past the "leading edge") of technology, adopting technologies well before they are generally available in the technology marketplace. Part of its business philosophy is to try different technologies to constantly enhance customer service, reduce costs, better understand the dynamics of customer buying behaviors, or experiment with different retail channels such as virtual retailing. The point is that it is not researching new technologies for the sake of technology, but rather as a mechanism for adding value to the customer.

In every conceivable way, connectivity is the cornerstone of the butterfly organization. Among the first organizations to adopt the butterfly form were environmental and special interest organizations. Much of the development and expansion of those organizations was aided by technology, especially computers that could facilitate the collection and use of mailing lists for fund-raising. As time has gone on, however, these organizations also use technology to collect data and contact legislatures.

Peter Berle, when president of the Audubon Society, explained the complex role that electronic networks play in the organizational structure of Audubon. The organization is really a web of some five hundred local chapters that are loosely tied to the national headquarters in New York, one hundred totally through electronic communications. The local chapters thus can spend a great deal of time focusing on community issues, but are available when national matters arise. For example, a major use of electronic communications for groups like his, he noted, is to send out calls about environmental issues over facsimile and e-mail, asking members, many of whom have personal access to faxes and e-mail, to contact their local representatives with information aimed at persuading them to vote for or against bills, or at times to solicit resources to deal with environmental emergencies.[10] (At times, groups of these organizations have joined together on an issue, thus managing to tie up all the communications systems of members of Congress that were involved in an important vote.)

Indeed, the history of organizations such as Audubon, Sierra, and Greenpeace over the past ten years offers businesses many lessons about the flexible, growing and contracting organizations of the future.

CONCLUSION

The seven principles are the key to migrating to a new organizational form. They are not, however, magic. None is easy to put in place, and most involve learning to challenge assumptions.

The danger facing organizations that strive to become more flexible is that after a few of the principles are in place, enough improvement may have occurred that the impetus to keep on changing is lost. Unfortunately, the world will continue to change, and without all the principles in place, soon the organization will not be able to change quickly enough, thus losing what it gained.

Some will object to the difficulties involved in adhering to some of these principles. Why should we do this? they will ask. The answer to that question is the subject of the Epilogue.

EPILOGUE

A CONTRACT FOR THE FUTURE

Let chaos reign, then rein in chaos. Does that mean you shouldn't plan? Not at all. You need to plan the way a fire department plans. It cannot anticipate fires, so it has to shape a flexible organization that is capable of responding to unpredictable events.

Andrew Grove[1]

*T*he seven principles for maintaining balance spelled out in the previous chapter are the tools for walking the tightrope between order and chaos in today's new business environment. They prevent businesses from becoming huge, unmoving masses comprised of unneeded layers of bureaucracy, antiquated processes, old products and services that are merely tweaked and polished to attract yet one more buyer. The organizational mindset that develops when these principles are in put place makes it possible for businesses to respond quickly as new technologies lead to the development of yet newer technologies, as competitors find new ways of doing business faster and better, and as new competitors emerge with products and services that make old ones obsolete. They make growth possible while ensuring that the organization acts in the best interests of all stakeholders.

The organizations we have been looking at provide examples of the success that comes from using these tools. When Intel ran into problems with a product line because of Japanese competition, it rapidly abandoned the line and focused on another, achieving even greater success in succeeding years. When Transnet of the Republic of South Africa took on an enormous pension fund debt as a condition of commercialization, many thought the debt would inhibit profitability for many years. Instead, in only four years, the company realized a net profit, while meeting that pension obligation. After showing remarkable profits for its first four years and becoming the first power producer to achieve $100 million in earnings, Destec was hit by a change in the market for power in Texas, but within months changed shape, found worldwide market possibilities, and began to recover. When Central and South West downsized, the packages it put in place for its employees who were leaving and for retraining those who remained were enormously expensive, yet it managed not to break its unparalleled record of increased dividends for forty-three consecutive years.

Indeed, butterfly organizations can realize unprecedented success. Sun Microsystems grew from a $115 million to a $5.9 billion company between 1985 and 1995. Hewlett-Packard continues to bring new products to market, growing steadily (since 1980, it has more than doubled sales at about five-year intervals), but it also recognizes when it is time to close unprofitable plants. Intel, with new competitors in hot pursuit, is spending $2.9 billion to expand and update equipment and facilities and spends nearly 10 percent of revenues on R&D each year. ABB, with revenues of almost $30 billion each year between 1991 and 1994, decided in 1993 to close fifteen plants, cut some 7,000 jobs (about 3.5 percent of its workforce), and invest 8 percent ($2.3 billion) of that year's sales in R&D. The following year, all of its numbers were higher than they had been in 1992, but Percy Barnevik says that restructuring will continue.

Constant restructuring in response to events is one of the many traits of organizations evolving to this new form. Also typical of these companies is a constant questioning of assumptions, especially in the area of technology, where developments are particularly nonlinear. James Utterback of the Massachusetts Institute of Technology, who calls technology forecasting a "precarious science," says that, instead of trying to guess what technological development may appear next, "managers and policymakers should make sure that their organizations are agile enough to respond to technological changes as they occur."[2]

These organizations also make a concerted effort to avoid complacency; in fact, Andrew Grove's comment that "only the paranoid survive" could be considered their mantra. Perhaps most important, these organizations are typically suspicious of solutions that sound "easy." Their lack of belief in silver bullets and quick fixes as well as their eagerness to try new things may explain why they have put in place so many of the seven principles.

These organizations are always looking for ideas and strategies that will help them to reduce operating costs, improve quality and productivity, increase revenues and profitability, and meet and exceed customer satisfaction. They accept the wear and tear of long-term, holistic approaches that require patience and an expenditure of effort from the top down, that demand that everyone in the organization accept change.

If this sounds overwhelming, there is good news. Except for the first two principles—setting ethical standards and establishing a new social contract—each brings fairly immediate rewards. Moreover, since adopting the whole package at once would make change management an all-consuming task, the best method is for senior leadership to review the principles and focus on any they may already have adopted in some form and then work on those, formalizing some of the rules, then to move on, adding another, and so forth. But keep two things in mind: first, stopping short of full adoption of the principles because you are achieving some degree of success with just one or two is not going to provide the flexibility you need down the road, and, second, until the first two principles are firmly in place, your evolution has not even begun.

THE VALUE OF ETHICS, INTEGRITY, AND TRUST[3]

When people work for an organization that they believe to be fair, in which everyone is willing to give of themselves to get the job done, in which traditions of loyalty and caring are hallmarks, people work to a higher level. The values of the organization's culture are absorbed by employees, becoming a part of them. They begin to believe that the customer is someone to whom they owe the finest possible products and services. Because they believe in the mission of the organization, they do not distinguish between their own and their organization's reputations. They work harder to fulfill their promises, to exceed customer expectations, to ensure that products are flawless and produced on time and within budget. In other words, they take pride in their work. When that happens, an organization builds a reputation for quality, which attracts more customers and increases market share and profitability.

THE WORKER IN THE ETHICAL ORGANIZATION

Much of the value of creating an organization dominated by ethical values is the effect it has on the attitude of workers. You notice the difference when you walk down the halls of a company. You can quickly tell how things are going without reading the company's financials. People in these organizations don't watch the clock; compensation is more than a weekly paycheck. In a company with a strong code of ethics, everyone understands the importance of moving beyond strict obedience to the letter of the law. Employees are free to be creative because they do not expect to suffer for trying something that may fail; they are willing to spend time learning because they know that the company invests in its people, not just in its machinery. In this culture, every employee works a little harder, does more than what is required—and everybody wins.

It also has become clear that those companies that address social issues do remarkably well. Companies that develop mentoring programs, hire the handicapped, or give employees time off for community activities, such as school programs, win the affection—and the business—of the residents of their local communities. Many companies have recognized the worth of these efforts; for example, Citibank has a policy that good works are good business. Paul M. Ostergard, Citibank's director of corporate contributions and civic responsibility, "feels that the bank has a vital role as a corporate citizen. Community development is what we are about as a bank in many respects. . . . When you look at the businesses that we are in, it is critical for us that the communities we do business in are healthy, so we make intensive investments in housing, job creation, and education."[4] (In 1992, Citibank spent $20 million worldwide on local, national, and international projects in education, health, community development, and the environment.)

In the case of environmental issues, companies that move beyond compliance do not suffer as a result of those efforts. The costs of addressing environmental issues are more than met by the benefits of doing so. Part of the reason lies in reputation. As the world has become more concerned about these issues, customers who take such concerns seriously often choose which company to buy from based on the company's reputation for environmental concerns. Companies that are "green," such as the Body Shop, find that potential customers that are interested in these issues are more likely to try their products, giving them a chance to prove themselves. In *The Total Quality Corporation*, Francis McInerney and Sean White point out that corporations that focus on the environment can gain in three ways: they improve their bottom line by eliminating waste, they offer their products at lower cost, and they gain customers because "consumers around the world have become 'green.'"[5]

Organizations would do well to remember that customers prefer to deal with organizations that seem to care. People hesitate to deal with companies that are cited for discriminatory hiring practices or for exploitation of foreign workers in much the same way they hesitate to cross a picket line. People want to encourage what is right, and they do so every way they can. A company that has a reputation for trustworthiness is one that everyone—from supplier to employee to customer—prefers to do business with.

THE NEW SOCIAL CONTRACT

Another issue raising great concern today is the abandonment of the old, implicit social contract between employee and employer. As noted earlier, for most workers, "a day's pay for a day's work" was the only contract in place. But the myth of lifetime employment—begun by organizations that offered security in lieu of wages comparable to those in the private sector, such as regulated monopolies and the civil service, and perpetuated in the decades after World War II by paternalistic companies, such as IBM and Kodak— became the aspiration of every worker. The growth of this myth was abetted by an economy that provided an abundance of jobs and a constantly increasing standard of living, including the possibility of realizing the American dream of owning a home of one's own.

Set against the stability of the past four decades, the disquieting impact of the dramatic changes that began in the late 1980s is more easily understood. From a nation whose every product was in demand, we became competitors in a global marketplace in which others could produce the same product better or cheaper—and sometimes both. Companies began to fight for survival, the economy faltered, people found themselves unemployed and frightened. Nowhere was this change more sharply felt than in the ranks of middle management, the group traditionally least threatened by and the most unaccustomed to unemployment. Charles Heckscher explores the issue of disenfranchised middle managers in *White-Collar Blues,* noting that "while middle managers make up 8 percent of the workforce, they have accounted for 19 percent of the cuts."[6] The media attention to the woes of this group as a way of bringing human interest to the constant announcements of downsizings had an additional, adverse effect. By highlighting the economic problems our nation was encountering and raising fears among those still in middle-management positions (and often those with considerable discretionary income), this coverage raised doubts about the future, resulting in diminished consumer confidence, which only served to increase in the downward economic spiral.

But it was not just middle management that suffered—and is continuing to suffer. Although the lay-offs among middle managers receive so much attention, workers at every level have been affected. What is perhaps most devastating about this situation is the realization that, while in the past lay-offs tended to be cyclical, today they reflect the permanent loss of a need for particular skills. Even if the economy bounces back, there will be many types of jobs (for example, linotype or telephone operators) that have virtually disappeared because of technological advances. While new jobs are being created, the workers displaced are not trained in the needed skills, and the new jobs are often in new, start-up enterprises that pay less and offer fewer benefits, or the jobs are being sent abroad.

The problem was summed up in a special report in *Business Week* that explained that the "worldwide shift to market economies, steady improvements in education, and decades of overseas training by multinationals are all producing a global workforce in fields ranging from product development to finance and architecture that is capable of performing tasks once reserved for white-collar workers in the West. . . . What's more," the report noted, "dizzying advances in telecommunications are making these workers more accessible than ever."[7]

RECOGNIZING THE NEED FOR ACTION

Ethical organizations intrinsically understand the value of establishing a social contract with workers. Indeed, until the recent spate of downsizings, under the old social contract there were few workers who questioned the wisdom of devoting their lives to their organizations, often at the cost of family life. But once the contract began to fall apart and employers starting saying good-bye without warning time and time again—the loyalty, devotion, and career aspirations found at one time among so many in the corporate world was destroyed. People no longer felt moved to spend endless hours at work. Yet fear of that good-bye and the economic disaster that might follow motivated many, particularly middle managers, to accept becoming what Juliet Schor described as the "overworked American."[8] The result of this, and the fact that the jobs that have replaced those lost just do not offer the same financial and psychic rewards, is a change in the way people perceive work.

The breakdown in the relationship between employee and employer poses a major problem for those trying to develop the new organization. Because the butterfly organization must be flexible, workers will not be able to rely on lifetime employment. One way to overcome this problem is to focus on lifetime *employability* rather than lifetime employment with a single organization. Heckscher says that if companies "can no longer play the parental role, . . . then they must accept that employees have to develop motivations and connections that go outside. . . . Company policies should encourage employees to be mobile . . . to develop marketable skills. In place of fostering obedience, they should foster independence."[9] Peter Herriot, director of research, Sundridge Park Management Centre, says that in the future "big firms will have to offer the best professional workers regular opportunities to add to their marketable credentials in order to recruit or retain them."[10]

If the situation is ignored, if a new social contract based on the new set of relationships is not put in place, dissatisfaction may grow to the point where new government policies aimed at protecting the American worker are deemed a necessity. There is also the possibility of a reawakening of interest in labor unions. Since the new organization is built on speed and flexibility, both these solutions may prove detrimental to constant change (although there may be an important role for associations of people who work in the same industry). Therefore, it is in the self-interest of all business leaders to create fair and equitable contracts for the future, making such developments unnecessary.

THE TERMS OF THE CONTRACT

The new social contract should deal with the rights and obligations of both employers and employees. It also must take into account the differences between core employees, who take on managerial roles in companies, and affinity workers, occupying jobs connected to skills. At a minimum, the contract must include apprenticeship systems that teach new skills in return for a commitment to work for the organization for a specified period of time; it also must include training to customize a worker's skills to suit the needs of the organization; it must provide education and training opportunities at the tail end of contracts, which would serve to make it in every worker's interest to fulfill a contract rather than search for a new position before the term of the contract is over out of fear of future unemployment.

Some companies have also seen the value of allowing employees to move laterally across the organization, picking up new skills as they go. At Sun Microsystems, "employees attend regular 'brown bag lunches' on such issues as 'navigating Sun's internal job-selection system.' At Raychem . . . workers can tap into 'IIINsiders' (the internal-information interview network), to arrange interviews with other employees, from the chairman down, who are willing to talk about what they do, and how they got to do it."[11]

The need to educate those currently outside the workforce is also critical. By 1995, half of the available workforce in the European Union was unemployed, a fact Charles Handy argues poses a dire threat. If business doesn't help alleviate the problems facing these displaced workers, "by including [them] in their plans for their human assets, the workforce will become increasingly useless to them and to themselves."[12] Businesses must accept that workers who are not part of the regular workforce will be needed when organizations once again begin to grow. This includes former employees of large organizations who have settled for jobs that require less skills, that pay far less than they earned before, because the skills that once made them valuable are no longer needed. As they work at these jobs, their skills become increasingly obsolete. Some are younger—college graduates who, unable to find jobs that match their educational backgrounds, have taken jobs that provide no training and no opportunity to hone the skills they do have. Again, with the rapid changes in skills needed because of technological advances, they will require additional training before they can be considered potential assets by organizations that are trying to grow. And, of course, all these people taking jobs for which they are essentially overqualified have left those with few skills little hope of employment, creating social problems for which everyone pays.

Some companies have seen the light. *The Economist* says that "spending on corporate education has grown by 5% a year for the past decade. Companies now fork out $50 billion a year on education and training, and account for about half of America's total spending on higher education."[13] The article goes on to explain that the need for continuing and specialized education has grown so apparent that some companies, such as Motorola and Sun Microsystems, are turning their education centers into profit centers, offering their courses to those outside the organization. The only problem with this scenario is that current corporate educational efforts are overwhelmingly aimed and middle- and upper-level employees.

One of the most important areas of the new social contact is the creation of portable benefits. Today, some thirty-seven million Americans are without health benefits. Many more are facing uncertainty in retirement. The problem of health coverage for all citizens is one the government has debated but has yet to solve. Public policy discussions of the pension question, however, tend to revolve around Social Security, rather than private pensions. Companies and employees must begin to look toward portable pensions if current workers are going to achieve a reasonable retirement income. Models for such a system can be found in the world of higher education and in the entertainment industry. Teachers and others associated with institutions that are involved with higher education are all part of a plan, TIAA-CREF, that they remain in as they shift from institution to institution. The entertainment industry has unions, such as the Writers Guild of America West, that offer access to health and pension plans to its eight thousand members who rarely work for a single employer for any length of time.

What is the cost of being socially responsible, of good relations with employees through, in addition to adequate basic benefits, such things as on-site health care, environmental programs, and worker self-management programs? According to Jerome Dodson of the Parnassus Fund, "there is almost no difference in financial return between the socially responsible companies and the rest."[14] *The Economist* notes that "there is a clear link between employment stability and skill training. But which, causes which? Most likely, the two are mutually reinforcing: too high a rate of labour turnover discourages investment in workplace skills; and workers who get no training are likely to show less commitment to their current employer and so may change jobs more often. A vicious circle develops as higher labour turnover produces a less trained and hence less loyal workforce. And the moral from all this? If a country's companies switch to more flexible types of employment contracts, individual firms may well prosper. But if workers get less training as a consequence, the country's economy might become less competitive."[15]

Reaching a New Level

We have it in our power to begin the world all over again. A situation similar to the present hath not appeared since the days of Noah until now. The birthday of a new world is at hand.

Thomas Paine, 1775

Hyperbole? As applied to business today, probably. While we are not really at a the point where the world of business is beginning anew, we are at a point where business is changing rapidly—and must continue to do so—in response to the events buffeting it. The nature of the responses will help determine the future of the world's economy because business is the engine of economic growth. Remember the words of Edward Filene quoted in the first chapter: "Good business rests on prosperous customers." Without them, he went on to say, we will have "super-competition, a battle of price-cutting which will quickly lead to a campaign of wage-cutting." That, in turn, he warned, "will let us in for all sorts of political, social, and industrial conflict."

In the end, if business does not see to it that it has customers who can afford its products, no one can win. Therefore, creating a strong, educated workforce that can afford the goods produced by other workers is as much the way out of economic turmoil today as it was in the past. That does not mean a return to the organizational form of yesterday—the changes that have taken place in the world make that impossible. It means instead moving forward, building dynamic, profitable corporations that are caring and flexible.

‖ Notes

Chapter 1

1. Edward A. Filene, *The Way Out: A Forecast of Coming Changes in American Business and Industry* (New York: Doubleday, 1924), p. 21.

2. Simon Caulkin, "Chaos Inc.," *Across the Board*, July-August 1995, pp. 35–36.

3. Gail E. Schares and John Templeman, "Think Small: The Export Lessons to Be Learned from Germany's Mid-Sized Companies," *Business Week*, November 4, 1991, p. 60.

4. From Ralph S. Larsen, "The Challenge of Change: Building a New Competitive Spirit for the 21st Century" (speech delivered at the Executives' Club of Chicago, Chicago, Ill., October 23, 1992), in *Vital Speeches of the Day*, December 15, 1992, p. 156.

5. Alfred D. Chandler, Jr., *Strategy and Structure: Chapters in the History of the American Industrial Enterprise* (Cambridge, Mass.: MIT Press, 1962), p. 383.

6. Otis Port, "Swan Song for Laissez-Faire?" *Business Week* (special issue, "Innovation") 1989, p. 174.

7. Filene, *The Way Out*. All the quotes in this section appear in this volume, which is worth reading in its entirety. It is surprisingly applicable today; indeed, one can read whole sections that sound current. At the same time, it is a wonderful picture of the state of American business and the national economy in the world in the years before the Great Depression.

8. James Gleick, *Chaos: Making a New Science* (New York: Viking, 1987), p. 8.

9. There is a great deal of literature on this new science; most of it is complex and difficult to read. For those who want a deep understanding of

the subject, see the notes to the next chapter. Over the past few years, many of those exploring the science at the Sante Fe Institute in New Mexico have been searching for practical applications. At the heart of this movement is Stuart Kauffman, author of *At Home in the Universe* (New York: Oxford University Press, 1995), with whom we have discussed the applications of the science of complexity to business.

10. Filene, *The Way Out*, p. 31.

11. Edward N. Wolff, *Top Heavy: A Study of the Increasing Inequality of Wealth in America* (New York: Twentieth Century Fund Press, 1995), p. 7.

CHAPTER 2

This chapter owes a great deal to the work of those who have explored chaos theory. Among our principal sources are James Gleick and Margaret Wheatley, both cited below. In addition, we have gained a great deal from David Ruelle, *Chance and Chaos* (Princeton: Princeton University Press, 1991); Diana Phillips Mahoney, "Seeing Order in Chaos," *Computer Graphics World*, July 1993; Robert Pool, "Chaos Theory," *Science*, July 7, 1989; H. Richard Priesmeyer and Kibok Baik, "Discovering the Patterns of Chaos," *Planning Review*, November 1989; and Michael V. Berry, I. C. Percival, and N. O. Weiss, eds., *Dynamical Chaos* (Princeton: Princeton University Press, 1987).

1. Rushworth M. Kidder, *An Agenda for the 21st Century* (Cambridge, Mass.: MIT Press, 1989), p. 202.

2. Peter Drucker, "The Coming of the New Organization," *Harvard Business Review*, January-February 1988.

3. Charles Handy, *The Age of Unreason* (Boston: Harvard Business School Press, 1990), sets forth a series of ideas relating to possible forms of future business enterprises.

4. James Brian Quinn, *The Intelligent Enterprise: A Knowledge and Service Based Paradigm for Industry* (New York: Free Press, 1992), p. 120; this volume presents a thorough review of most of the new organizational forms that are currently being tried.

5. John Huey, "The New Post-Heroic Leadership," *Fortune*, February 21, 1994, p. 44.

6. Beverly Goldberg and John G. Sifonis, *Dynamic Planning: The Art of Managing Beyond Tomorrow* (New York: Oxford University Press, 1994).

7. James Gleick, *Chaos: Making a New Science* (New York: Viking, 1987), p. 30.

8. Ibid., p. 8.

9. Margaret Wheatley, *Leadership and the New Science: Learning about Organization from an Orderly Universe* (San Francisco: Berrett-Koehler, 1992), p. 91.

10. Hyman P. Minsky, *Stabilizing an Unstable Economy*, A Twentieth Century Fund Report (New Haven, Conn.: Yale University Press, 1986), p. 10.

11. Wheatley, *Leadership and the New Science*, p. 99.

12. Quinn, *The Intelligent Enterprise*, p. 173.

CHAPTER 3

1. Stuart A. Kauffman, *The Origins of Order* (New York: Oxford University Press, 1993), p. 29.

2. David Berreby, "The Man Who Knows Everything: Murray Gell-Mann," *New York Times Magazine*, May 8, 1994, p. 26.

3. M. Mitchell Waldrop, *Complexity: The Emerging Science at the Edge of Order and Chaos* (New York: Touchstone, 1993), pp. 145–46.

4. Taiichi Ohno, *Toyota Production System* (Productivity Press, 1978). Ohno (of Toyota Motors) says that in the 1940s his management model was the U.S. supermarket.

5. "Special Report" (Grocery Manufacturers of America, Inc., Washington, D.C., August 1993), p. 1.

6. Lynne Joy McFarland, Larry E. Senn, and John R. Childress, *21st Century Leadership* (Los Angeles: Leadership Press, 1994), pp. 117, 128.

7. Sissela Bok, "Grappling with Principles," in *An Agenda for the 21st Century*, ed. Rushworth M. Kidder (Cambridge, Mass.: MIT Press, 1989), p. 12.

8. *Merriam-Webster's Collegiate Dictionary* 10th ed. (Springfield, Mass.: Webster-Merriam, Incorporated, 1993), p. 780.

9. Leif Smith and Patricia Wagner, *The Networking Game* (Denver: Network Resources, 1981), p. 2.

10. K. Hugh Macdonald, "Business Strategy Development, Alignment, and Redesign," in *The Corporation of the 1990s: Information Technology and Organizational Transformation*, ed. Michael S. Scott Morton (New York: Oxford University Press, 1991), p. 172.

11. Walter Wriston, "The Decline of the Central Bankers," *New York Times*, September 20, 1992, p. F11.

12. Thomas A. Stewart, "Managing in a Wired Company," *Fortune*, July 11, 1994, p. 56.

13. Margaret Wheatley, "Comprehending Chaos," *Brigham Young Magazine*, February 1993, p. 25.

CHAPTER 4

There is a large literature on ethics, much of it dealing with social choice, political values, and belief systems. Our focus here is on ethics within organizations, particularly business organizations. The literature we read to update us on developments in this area includes articles in a number of journals and newsletters ranging from the *Harvard Business Review* to numerous issues of *Executive Excellence*, a magazine edited by Ken Shelton that devotes many issues to exploring "how to create, sustain, and rebuild cultures of trust and truth." In fact, some of the material on the changes in the social compact that appears in this chapter are drawn from Beverly Goldberg, "The New World of Work," *Executive Excellence*, July 1994.

There are today many valuable journals devoted exclusively to these issues, including the *Journal of Business Ethics, Business Ethics Quarterly, Business and Professional Ethics Journal, International Journal for Value-Based Management, Business and Society Review, Ethikos, Business Conduct Quarterly*, and *Employee Responsibility and Rights Journal*.

In addition, there are numerous recent books of great value, most notably Francis J. Aguilar, *Managing Corporate Ethics* (New York: Oxford University Press, 1994); Christopher McMahon, *Authority and Democracy: A General Theory of Government and Management* (Princeton: Princeton University Press, 1994); R. Edward Freeman, ed., *Business Ethics: The State of the Art* (New York: Oxford University Press, 1991); and Marvin T. Brown, *Working Ethics: Strategies for Decision Making and Organizational Responsibility* (San Francisco: Jossey-Bass, 1990).

1. Frank K. Sonnenberg, *Managing With a Conscience* (New York: McGraw-Hill, 1994), pp. 187, 192.

2. Sissela Bok, "Grappling with Principles," in *An Agenda for the 21st Century*, ed. Rushworth M. Kidder (Cambridge, Mass.: MIT Press, 1989), p. 12.

3. Ken Shelton, "Cultures of Trust and Truth," *Executive Excellence*, July 1994, p. 2.

4. Simcha B. Werner, "The Movement for Reforming American Business Ethics: A Twenty-Year Perspective," *Journal of Business Ethics*, January 1992, p. 61.

5. Dan Cordtz, "Ethicsplosion!" *Financial World*, August 16, 1994, p. 58.

6. Andrew Stark, "What's the Matter with Business Ethics?" *Harvard Business Review*, May-June 1993, p. 38.

7. Ronald R. Sims, "The Challenge of Ethical Behavior in Organizations," *Journal of Business Ethics*, July 1992, p. 506.

8. Richard C. Bartlett, "Take the High Ground," *Executive Excellence*, July 1994, p. 18.

9. Paul Miller, "Ethics: Morality Matters in Modern Markets," *The Independent*, May 20, 1990, p. 26.

10. Ian I. Mitroff, Richard O. Mason, and Christine M. Pearson, *Framebreak: The Radical Redesign of American Business* (San Francisco: Jossey-Bass, 1994), pp. 130–31.

11. Lynn Sharp Paine, "Managing for Organizational Integrity," *Harvard Business Review*, March-April 1994, p. 106.

12. Woodstock Theological Center, *Creating and Maintaining an Ethical Corporate Climate* (Washington, D.C.: Georgetown University Press, 1990), p. 12.

13. Elmer H. Burack, Marvin D. Burack, and Diane M. Miller, "The New Corporate Prototypes and Employment Security," *Employment Relations Today*, September 1992, p. 287.

14. Dick Brooks and CSW's chief financial officer, Glenn Rosilier, discussed many issues with us in the course of a long interview in Dallas on September 23, 1994.

15. Laura L. Nash, "Business Ethics, the Second Generation: Still Searching for a Cognitive Fit," in *The Relevance of a Decade*, ed. Paula Barker Duffy (Boston: Harvard Business School Press, 1994), p. 118.

16. Richard A. Barker, "An Evaluation of the Ethics Program at General Dynamics," *Journal of Business Ethics*, March 1993, pp. 171–74.

17. Robert W. Cooper and Garry L. Frank, "Professionals in Business: Where Do They Look for Help in Dealing with Ethical Issues?" *Business & Professional Ethics Journal*, Summer 1992, pp. 46–47.

18. Russell Mitchell, "Managing by Values," *Business Week*, August 1, 1994, p. 52.

19. Kenneth R. Andrews, *The Concept of Corporate Strategy*, 3d ed. (Homewood, Ill.: Irwin, 1987), p. 70.

20. Edward A. Filene, *The Way Out: A Forecast of Coming Changes in American Business and Industry* (New York: Doubleday, 1924), p. 31. Filene went on to found an organization, the Twentieth Century Fund, to make sure it would happen; today, there is some hope that his belief might actually become a reality.

CHAPTER 5

The material in this chapter is again a mix of personal experience, interviews, and long exposure to the issues. The Twentieth Century Fund has been involved in some of the distinguished literature in this field: longtime Fund chairman of the board Adolf A. Berle, Jr., and Gardiner C. Means, *The Modern Corporation and Private Property* (New York: Macmillan, 1933); Edward S. Herman, *Corporate Control, Corporate Power*, A Twentieth Century Fund Study (New York: Cambridge University Press, 1981); Edward Epstein, *Who Owns the Corporation? Management vs. Shareholders*, A Twentieth Century Fund Paper (New York: Priority Press, 1986); the work of a recent Fund Task Force for which Robert Shiller wrote the background paper, "Who's Minding the Store?" (the report, along with the background paper, was published as *The Report of the Twentieth Century Task Force on Market Speculation and Corporate Governance* [New York: Twentieth Century Fund Press, 1992]).

We have spent the past fifteen years participating in countless board meetings as senior staff, serving on boards, and working with boards of both domestic and international companies as consultants, helping them formulate their business strategies as well as providing counsel on a variety of issues.

Turning to the literature, to gain a better understanding of boards and how they function today, the reader would do well to explore the journal *Directors & Boards*. Indeed, some of the material in the chapter is drawn from Beverly Goldberg and John G. Sifonis, "Anticipatory Capability," *Directors & Boards*, Fall 1994. A more formal examination of the subject should include the work of Ronald H. Coase, especially his classic article "The Nature of the Firm," first published in 1937 and reprinted in *The Nature of the Firm: Origins, Evolution, and Development,* eds. Oliver E. Williamson and Sidney G. Winter (New York: Oxford University Press, 1993). (Williamson's work in this field is invaluable.) For a good comparison of corporate governance in various countries, Jonathan Charkham, *Keeping Good Company* (New York: Oxford University Press, 1994); Ada Demb and F.-Friedrich Neubauer, *The Corporate Board: Confronting the Paradoxes* (New York: Oxford University Press, 1992). For a solid introduction to the issues of accountability, we would recommend both Robert A. G. Monks and Nell Minow, *Power and Accountability* (New York: Harper, 1991), and Joseph McCarthy, Sol Picciotto, and Colin Scott, *Corporate Control and Accountability* (New York: Oxford University Press, 1993).

1. Margaret Blair, "Corporate 'Ownership,'" *Brookings Review*, Winter 1995, p. 12.

2. Adolf A. Berle, Jr., and Gardiner C. Means, *The Modern Corporation and Private Property* (New York: Macmillan, 1933), pp. 2–3.

3. Jonathan Charkham, *Keeping Good Company* (New York: Oxford University Press, 1994), p. 188.

4. Edward Jay Epstein, *Who Owns the Corporation? Management vs. Shareholders,* A Twentieth Century Fund Paper (New York: Priority Press, 1986), p. 6.

5. Edward S. Herman, *Corporate Control, Corporate Power*, A Twentieth Century Fund Study (New York: Cambridge University Press, 1981), p. 18.

6. Ambrose Bierce, *The Devil's Dictionary* (New York: Dover, 1958), p. 25.

7. Leo Herzl and Richard Shepro, *Bidders and Targets: Mergers and Acquisitions in the US* (Cambridge, Mass.: Basil Blackwell, 1990), p. 73.

8. Paul Ingrassia, "Memo to Board: Management Isn't Always Wrong," *Wall Street Journal*, November 23, 1994, p. A14.

9. Robert A. G. Monks, "Shareholders and Director Selection," *Directors & Boards*, Spring 1995, pp. 10–11.

10. Eugene Fama and Michael C. Jensen, "Separation of Ownership and Control," *Journal of Law and Economics*, June 1983, p. 315.

11. Robert A. G. Monks and Nell Minow, *Power and Accountability* (New York: Harper, 1991), p. 78.

12. Charkham, *Keeping Good Company*, p. 274.

13. Ibid., p. 4. The Appendix to the book contains the full report of the Cadbury Code, pp. 367ff.

14. Arthur L. Ruffing, Jr., "The Future Role of the Audit Committee," *Directors & Boards*, Spring 1994, pp. 51–56.

15. Ada Demb and F.-Friedrich Neubauer, *The Corporate Board: Confronting the Paradoxes* (New York: Oxford University Press, 1992), p. 153.

16. Charkham, *Keeping Good Company*, p. 193.

17. TIAA-CREF, "A Policy Statement on Governance," *Directors & Boards*, Spring 1994, pp. 15–19.

18. Murray Weidenbaum, *The Evolving Corporate Board*, Contemporary Issues Series 65 (St. Louis: Washington University Center for the Study of American Business, May 1994), p. 12.

19. General Motors Corp., "The GM Board Guidelines," *Directors & Boards*, Summer 1994, pp. 5–9.

20. John G. Smale, "A Formal Codification," remarks before the Council of Institutional Investors, in *Director & Boards*, Summer 1994, p. 7.

21. Kirk T. Stewart, "Communicating in Real Time," *Directors & Boards*, Summer 1994, p. 47.

22. Interview at the Twentieth Century Fund headquarters in New York on November 30, 1994.

23. Weidenbaum, *The Evolving Corporate Board*, p. 24.

CHAPTER 6

The governance models presented were developed during assignments with Shell Oil Company and with the recently commercialized transportation conglomerate of the Republic of South Africa—Transnet; the teams we worked with provided great value in terms of knowledge and background.

1. Peter Drucker, *The New Realities* (New York: Harper & Row, 1989), p. 261.

2. Alfred D. Chandler, Jr., *Strategy and Structure: Chapters in the History of the American Industrial Enterprise* (Cambridge, Mass.: MIT Press, 1962); this landmark study of corporations as they worked in the Industrial Age provides a sound basis for studying the evolution of this form through the Information Age.

3. William Taylor, "The Logic of Global Business: An Interview with ABB's Percy Barnevik," in *Leaders on Leadership*, ed. Warren Bennis (Boston: Harvard Business School Press, 1992), pp. 68, 72–73.

4. Royal Little, "Conglomerates Are Doing Better than You Think," *Fortune*, May 28, 1984, p. 51.

5. Phillip I. Blumberg, "The American Law of Corporate Groups," in *Corporate Control and Accountability*, eds., Joseph McCahery, Sol Picciotto, and Colin Scott (New York: Oxford University Press, 1993), p. 337.

6. Little, "Conglomerates Are Doing Better than You Think," p. 55.

7. *Merriam-Webster Collegiate Dictionary*, tenth edition (Springfield, Mass.: Merriam-Webster, Incorporated, 1993), p. 1097.

8. James K. Glassman, "Diversification Works Best in Small Doses," *Washington Post*, May 14, 1995, p. H1.

9. This illustration comes from conversations with Stuart Kauffman at the Santa Fe Institute, September 23, 1994, and January 25, 1995. Some of the ideas discussed are explored in Stuart A. Kauffman, *At Home in the Universe* (New York: Oxford University Press, 1995), especially pp. 252–57.

CHAPTER 7

1. Don Tapscott and Art Caston, *Paradigm Shift: The New Promise of Information Technology* (New York: McGraw-Hill, 1993), p. 13.

2. Harlan Cleveland, *Birth of a New World* (San Francisco: Jossey-Bass, 1993), p. 3.

3. Myron Magnet, "The Productivity Payoff Arrives," *Fortune*, June 17, 1994, p. 80.

4. John Cross, "IT Outsourcing: British Petroleum's Competitive Approach," *Harvard Business Review*, May-June 1995, p. 94.

5. Lee S. Sproull and Paul S. Goodman, "Technology and Organizations: Integration and Opportunities," in *Technology and Organizations*, eds. Paul S. Goodman, Lee S. Sproull, et al. (San Francisco: Jossey-Bass, 1990), p. 263.

6. "A Survey of the Computer Industry: The Third Age," *The Economist*, September 17, 1994, p. S3.

7. Vaughan Merlyn and John Parkinson, *Development Effectiveness: Strategies for IS Organizational Transition* (New York: Wiley, 1994), p. 176.

8. James G. March and Lee S. Sproull, "Technology, Management, and Competitive Advantage," in *Technology and Organizations*, pp. 163–64.

9. Steve Lohr, "From Calculator to Communications Tool," *New York Times*, June 6, 1995, p. D9.

10. Dennis Kneale, "Unleashing the Power," *Wall Street Journal*, June 27, 1994, p. R6.

11. Faith Noble and Michael Newman, "Integrated System, Autonomous Departments: Organizational Invalidity and System Change in a University," *Journal of Management Studies*, March 1993, p. 195.

CHAPTER 8

1. George Harrar, "Interview with Ron Ponder," *Forbes ASAP*, April 10, 1995, p. 60. Ponder spoke as AT&T's corporate CIO.

2. The group responsible for this function today is called the information systems (IS) or information technology (IT) division, the information services department or some variant. (In the past, it was the EDP—electronic data processing—department.) The head is usually called the director of management information systems, chief information officer, IS manager, or vice president for information services.

3. Jon D. Pepper, "Getting Along with the CEO," *InformationWeek*, May 6, 1991, p. 36.

4. Marianne Kilbasuk McGee, "Keeping Current," *InformationWeek*, March 20, 1995, p. 158.

5. Bruce Caldwell, "Two Heads Are Better Than One," *InformationWeek*, April 17, 1995, p. 93.

6. Roger Woolfe, "The Path to Strategic Alignment," *Information Strategy: The Executive's Journal*, Winter 1993, p. 13.

7. Strategic Alignment Modeling was developed in academia by Professors N. Venkatraman and John C. Henderson, now of Boston University, and carried into the field by John G. Sifonis. See Beverly Goldberg and John G. Sifonis, *Dynamic Planning: The Art of Managing Beyond Tomorrow* (New York: Oxford University Press, 1994), for a detailed account of the development of this model and examples of its impact.

8. Scott Leibs, "Special Report: The Rise of the DIO," *Information Week*, May 17, 1993, p. 42.

9. Jerry Mirelli, "Deploying Resources; Solving the CIO Dilemma," *InformationWeek*, March 20, 1995, p. 188.

10. George Harrar, "Outsource Tales," *Forbes ASAP*, June 7, 1993, p. 38.

11. Ibid., p. 37.

12. John Cross, "IT Outsourcing: British Petroleum's Competitive Approach," *Harvard Business Review*, May-June 1995, pp. 95, 101.

13. James McGee and Laurence Prusack, *Managing Information Strategically* (New York: Wiley, 1993), p. 169.

14. Interview on November 22, 1993, at Shell Oil Company in Houston, Texas.

15. Pierre Wack and Peter Schwartz, both noted for their work in this area, were instrumental in helping Shell develop its approach to scenario planning. See Peter Schwartz, *The Art of the Long View: Planning for the Future in an Uncertain World* (New York: Doubleday, 1991).

16. Laton McCartney, "Interview: A View From All Sides," *Information Week*, September 13, 1993, p. 44.

17. Don Tapscott and Art Caston, *Paradigm Shift: The New Promise of Information Technology* (New York: McGraw-Hill, 1993), p. 13.

18. Carol A. Beatty and Gloria L. Lee, "Leadership Among Middle Managers—An Exploration in the Context of Technological Change," *Human Relations*, September 1992, p. 972.

19. Thierry C. Pauchant, Ian I. Mitroff, and Gerald F. Ventolo, "The Dial Tone Does Not Come From God! How a Crisis Can Challenge Dangerous Strategic Assumptions Made About Technologies: The Case of the Hinsdale Telecommunications Outage," *Academy of Management Executive*, Fall 1992, p. 66.

20. John W. Verity, "Hacker Heaven: So Many Computers, So Few Safeguards," *Business Week*, June 26, 1995, p. 96.

21. "Tech Managers Who Can, Teach," *InformationWeek*, May 29, 1995, p. 80.

22. Tapscott and Caston, *Paradigm Shift*, p. 308.

23. Gary Hamel and C. K. Prahalad, *Competing for the Future* (Boston: Harvard Business School Press, 1994), p. 292.

CHAPTER 9

Leadership has been the subject of intense study, but never more so than now. Businesses have worked diligently to streamline but have not yet found the road to growth; the "reinvention of government is proclaimed but not yet accomplished; . . . our organizations of every kind face threats from the economic conditions all around us." (James Krantz, "Lessons from the Field: An Essay on the Crisis of Leadership in Contemporary Organizations," *Journal of Applied Behavioral Science*, January 1990, p. 62.)

From 1902 to 1967, some 3,000 studies of leadership were conducted; over the next seven years, 2,000 additional studies were reported. Moreover, the literature has moved from a heavily academic focus to accounts of corporate leaders who have become icons or demons. The attention devoted to leaders—to those who seem to understand what it takes to make things happen in the corporate world—is not surprising given the problems that have been buffeting that world.

Among those who have influenced our thinking the most are Max Weber, especially his *The Theory of Social and Economic Organization* (New York: Oxford University Press, 1947); Edgar Schein, *Organizational Culture and Leadership* (San Francisco: Jossey-Bass, 1984); Robert Heller, *The Decision Makers* (New York: Truman Talley/Plume, 1991), which was originally published in 1989; Robert L. Phillips and James G. Hunt, eds., *Strategic Leadership: A Multiorganizational-Level Perspective* (Westport, Conn.: Quorum, 1992); Harlan Cleveland, *The Knowledge Executive: Leadership in an Information Society* (New York: Truman Talley/Dutton, 1989); Warren Bennis, ed., *Leaders on Leadership* (Boston: Harvard Business School Press, 1992); and books and articles by Robert Waterman, Tom Peters, Burt Nanus, Peter Drucker, and the hundreds of academics and leaders who have written articles for or been interviewed by *Harvard Business Review, Fortune, Business Week.*

The discussion of quality is drawn from Beverly Goldberg's experiences on the Ernst & Young and American Quality Foundation team that prepared the broad survey of quality efforts in four industrial sectors across four nations in the early 1990s.

For information on teams, see Jon R. Katzenbach and Douglas K. Smith, *The Wisdom of Teams: Creating the High Performance Organization* (Boston: Harvard Business School Press, 1993); for the open, learning organization, see Peter M. Senge, *The Fifth Discipline: The Art and Practice of the Learning Organization* (New York: Doubleday/Currency, 1990). For exploring the formal issues involved in negotiating—also important to our thinking in the next chapter—we were most influenced by Max H. Bazerman and Margaret A. Neale, *Negotiating Rationally* (New York: Free Press, 1992); see also Karl Albrecht and Steve Albrecht, *Added Value Negotiating: The Breakthrough Method for Building Balanced Deals* (Burr Ridge, Ill.: Irwin Books, 1993); and Roger Fisher and William Ury, *Getting to Yes* (Boston: Houghton-Mifflin, 1981). For collaboration, see Michael Schrage, *Shared Minds: The Technology of Collaboration* (New York, Random House, 1990); for diversity, R. Roosevelt Thomas, Jr., *Beyond Race and Gender* (New York: AMACOM, 1991); and for perhaps the best book on building a workplace with a culture of trust, see Frank K. Sonnenberg, *Managing With a Conscience* (New York: McGraw-Hill, 1994).

In addition, journals such as *Training, HR Magazine, Training & Development Journal, Personnel Journal,* and *Organizational Dynamics* provide numerous articles addressing different aspects of all of these issues.

1. M. Mitchell Waldrop, *Complexity: The Emerging Science at the Edge of Chaos* (New York: Touchstone, 1992), pp. 145–46. Waldrop is paraphrasing the ideas of John Holland, one of the most influential thinkers connected with the Santa Fe Institute.

2. Abraham Zaleznik, "Managers and Leaders: Are They Different?" *Harvard Business Review*, March-April 1992, p. 131. This article was reprinted in the 1992 issue as an HBR Classic.

3. William L. Gardner III and John R. Schermerhorn, Jr., "Strategic Operational Leadership and the Management of Supportive Work Environments," in *Strategic Leadership: A Multiorganizational-Level Perspective*, eds. Robert L. Phillips and James G. Hunt (Westport, Conn.: Quorum, 1992), p. 100. The essays that comprise this volume are essential background for anyone studying leadership, systems management, and organization theories and behavior.

4. Ibid, p. 104.

5. Kenneth E. Clark and Miriam B. Clark, eds., *Measures of Leadership* (West Orange, N.J.: Leadership Library of America, 1990), particularly, Gary A. Yukl, S. Wall, and R. Lepsinger, "Preliminary Report on the Validation of the Management Practices Survey."

6. Management Focus, "The Changing Nature of Leadership," *The Economist*, June 10, 1995, p. 57.

7. J. E. Osborne, "Looking at Leadership Like a Manager," *Supervisory Management*, August 1992, p. 8.

8. Lynne Joy McFarland, Larry E. Senn, and John R. Childress, *21st Century Leadership* (New York: Leadership Press, 1994), pp. 59, 186–87.

9. Martha Slice and Alan Gilburg, "Leadership for Empowerment," *Public Manager*, Fall 1992, p. 29.

10. Lawrence R. Rothstein, "The Empowerment Effort That Came Undone," *Harvard Business Review*, January-February 1995, p. 28.

11. Charles H. House and Raymond L. Price, "The Return Map: Tracking Product Teams," *Harvard Business Review*, January-February 1991, pp. 92–93.

12. Jon R. Katzenbach and Douglas K. Smith, *The Wisdom of Teams: Creating the High Performance Organization* (Boston: Harvard Business School Press, 1993), p. 65.

13. See Thomas L. Quick, *Successful Team Building* (New York: AMA-COM, 1992).

14. Daniel E. Mode, "Every Employee a Leader," *Public Utilities Fortnightly*, June 1, 1992, p. 19.

15. Katzenbach and Smith, *The Wisdom of Teams*, p. 3.

16. Peter M. Senge, *The Fifth Discipline: The Art and Practice of the Learning Organization* (New York: Doubleday/Currency, 1990), p. 236.

17. Jaclyn Fierman, "The Contingency Work Force, *Fortune*, January 24, 1994, p. 36.

18. Much of the material in this section is drawn from Beverly Goldberg, "The New World of Work," *Executive Excellence*, July 1994.

19. The material in this section is drawn from Frank K. Sonnenberg and Beverly Goldberg, "It's a Great Idea, But. . .," *Training and Development*, March 1992.

20. Bob Filipczak, "Looking Past the Numbers," *Training*, October 1994, p. 67.

21. Krantz, "Lessons from the Field," *Journal of Applied Behavioral Science*, January 1990, p. 61.

22. Frank K. Sonnenberg, *Marketing to Win* (New York: Harper & Row, 1990), p. 185.

23. Jim Braham, "No, You Don't Manage Everyone the Same," *Industry Week*, February 6, 1989, p. 29.

24. Tracy E. Benson, "The New Leadership," *Industry Week*, June 1, 1992, p. 13.

CHAPTER 10

1. Korn/Ferry International and Columbia University Graduate School of Business, *A Journal on Critical Issues Affecting Senior Executives and the Board of Directors: Reinventing the CEO* (New York: Korn/Ferry International, 1989), p. 54.

2. Peter F. Drucker, "The Information Executives Really Need," *Harvard Business Review*, January-February 1995, p. 58.

3. The material presented on mergers and acquisitions was first developed by John Sifonis in the late 1980s for a number of his clients at Arthur Young (later Ernst & Young).

4. Terence P. Pare, "The New Merger Boom," *Fortune*, November 28, 1994, p. 104.

5. John A. Byrne, "The Futurists Who Fathered the Ideas," *Business Week*, February 8, 1993, p. 103. This is part of the issue's cover story by Byrne, "The Virtual Organization."

6. Rand V. Araskog, *The ITT Wars: A CEO Speaks Out on Takeovers* (New York: Holt, 1989), p. 211.

7. W. David Gibson, "Holy Alliances," *Sales & Marketing Management*, July 1993, p. 85.

8. Steve Bergsman, "Emphasis on Core Competency Redefines Corporate Outsourcing and Boosts Strategic Alliances," *National Real Estate Investor*, August 1993, p. 30.

9. Rob Murakami, "Competitive Networks: How to Start and the Benefits to Expect," *CMA—The Management Accounting Magazine*, April 1993, p. 36.

10. Stanford Sherman, "Are Strategic Alliances Working?" *Fortune*, September 21, 1992, p. 77.

11. Gene Slowinski, George F. Farris, and David Jones, "Strategic Partnering: Process Instead of Event," *Research/Technology Management*, May-June 1994, p. 23.

12. This case was the subject of Beverly Goldberg and John G. Sifonis, "An Alliance of Business and Technology," *Management Review*, February 1994, and some of the material is taken directly from that article.

13. Gary Hamel and C. K. Prahalad, *Competing for the Future* (Boston: Harvard University Press, 1994), p. 199.

14. David A. Lax and James K. Sebenius, *The Manager as Negotiator* (New York: Free Press, 1986), pp. 339, 361.

15. See Max H. Bazerman and Margaret A. Neale, *Negotiating Rationally* (New York: Free Press, 1992); this is an invaluable volume for leaders at all levels.

16. Larry Hirschhorn and Thomas Gilmore, "The New Boundaries of the 'Boundaryless' Company," *Harvard Business Review*, May-June 1992, p. 106.

17. David Limerick and Bert Cunnington, *Managing the New Organization* (San Francisco: Jossey-Bass, 1993), pp. 232–33.

18. *Merriam-Webster's New Collegiate Dictionary*, 10th ed. (Springfield, Mass.: Merriam-Webster, Incorporated, 1993), p. 780.

19. Mark Dodgson, "The Future for Technological Collaboration," *Futures*, June 1992, p. 467.

CHAPTER 11

1. Robert H. Waterman, Jr., *Adhocracy: The Power to Change* (New York: Norton, 1992), p. 22.

2. Thomas A. Stewart, "Welcome the Revolution," *Fortune*, December 13, 1993, p. 66.

3. Stuart L. Hart and Robert E. Quinn, "Roles Executives Play: CEOs, Behavioral Complexity, and Firm Performance," *Human Relations*, May 1993, p. 569.

4. Donald Hambrick, "Putting Top Managers Back in the Strategy Picture," *Strategic Management Journal,* special issue, 10, 1989, pp. 5–16. Hambrick was guest editor for this special edition of the journal, which contains a number of invaluable articles related to these issues. In addition, see Robert L. Phillips and James G. Hunt, eds., *Strategic Leadership: A Multiorganizational-Level Perspective* (Westport, Conn.: Quorum, 1992).

5. Frank K. Sonnenberg, *Managing With a Conscience* (New York: McGraw-Hill, 1994), pp. 187, 189.

6. Lynne Joy McFarland, Larry E. Senn, and John R. Childress, *21st Century Leadership* (New York: Leadership Press, 1994), p. 138.

7. Warren Bennis, *On Becoming a Leader* (Reading, Mass.: Addison-Wesley, 1989), p. 138.

8. Thomas A. Stewart, "How to Lead a Revolution," *Fortune*, November 28, 1994, p. 48.

9. Shawn Tully, "So, Mr. Bossidy, We Know You Can Cut. Now Show Us How to Grow," *Fortune*, August 21, 1995, pp. 70–80.

10. Brent Schlender, "Why Andy Grove Can't Stop," *Fortune*, July 10, 1995, p. 91.

11. Bob Gower, speech at the College of Business Administration, University of Houston, September 27, 1994.

12. Interview with Charles Goff at Destec headquarters in Houston, Texas, November 19, 1993; William Taylor, "The Logic of Global Business: An Interview with ABB's Percy Barnevik," *Harvard Business Review*, March-April 1991 (reprinted in *Leaders on Leadership* [Boston: Harvard Business School Press, 1992], p. 84).

13. Larry Hirschhorn and Thomas Gilmore, "The New Boundaries of the 'Boundaryless' Company," *Harvard Business Review*, May-June 1992, p. 107.

14. Rushworth M. Kidder, *Agenda for the 21st Century* (Cambridge, Mass.: MIT Press, 1989), p. 72.

15. Hirschhorn and Gilmore, "The New Boundaries of the Boundaryless Company," p. 107.

16. James Krantz, "Lessons from the Field: An Essay on the Crisis of Leadership in Contemporary Organizations," *Journal of Applied Behavioral Science*, January 1990, p. 57. This article surveys much of the important literature on leadership; the book by Gilmore that Krantz is summarizing is *Making a Leadership Change* (San Francisco: Jossey-Bass, 1989).

17. Thomas A. Stewart, "How a Little Company Won Big by Betting on Brainpower," *Fortune*, September 4, 1995, p. 122.

18. John Sifonis met with Anton Moolman on a number of occasions in January 1992 and October 1994.

19. Alan Mitchell, "The Driving Force Behind Unilever," *Marketing*, April 8, 1993, p. 21.

20. Robert Heller, *The Decision Makers* (New York: Truman Talley/Plume, 1991), p. 82.

21. Ralph D. Stacey, *Managing the Unknowable* (San Francisco: Jossey-Bass, 1992), pp. 18–19.

22. Art Fry, "The Post-It Note: An Intrapreneurial Success," *SAM Advanced Management Journal*, Summer 1987, p. 6.

23. "Applications of Chaos," *Management Today*, July 1995, p. 14.

24. Interview with Charles Goff at Destec headquarters on November 19, 1993, followed by literature searches, especially press releases and corporate communications.

25. Taylor, "The Logic of Global Business," p. 77.

26. Andrew Davidson, "Sir Michael Perry," *Management Today*, May 1995, p. 52.

27. Floris A. Maljers, "Inside Unilever: The Evolving Transnational Company," *Harvard Business Review*, September-October 1992, p. 46.

28. Ronald Henkoff, "Keeping Motorola on a Roll," *Fortune*, April 18, 1994, p. 70.

29. See Henkoff, "Keeping Motorola on a Roll"; Linda Thornburg, "Success Is Built on Relationships," *HR Magazine*, August 1994; D. Keith Denton, "The Power of Flexibility," *Business Horizons*, July 1994; and Wesley R. Iverson, "Assembly Strategies," *Assembly*, September 1994.

30. Iverson, "Assembly Strategies," p. 15.

31. Thornburg, "Success Is Built on Relationships," p. 55.

32. David Packard, *The HP Way: How Bill Hewlett and I Built Our Company* (New York: HarperBusiness, 1995), p. 132.

33. Homa Bahrami and Stuart Evans, "Flexible Re-Cycling and High-Technology Entrepreneurship," *California Management Review*, March 1995, pp. 62ff. This article investigates the region as ecosystem in detail; many of its insights were valuable in our examinations of ABB and Unilever as well as the regions of Europe mentioned.

34. The information about Intel and Andy Grove is drawn from Sumantra Goshel and Christopher A. Bartlett, "Changing the Role of Top Management: Beyond Structure to Processes," *Harvard Business Review*, January-February 1995; Robert D. Hof, "The Education of Andrew Grove," *Business Week*, January 16, 1995; Schlender, "Why Andy Grove Can't Stop"; and Sally Helgesen, *The Web of Inclusion* (New York: Doubleday/Currency, 1995), chap. 3. Helgesen's insightful book, which we encountered as our book was in its final stages, looks at a number of organizations that have characteristics similar to those of the butterfly form; its focus is on the way information flows ensure flexibility in the postindustrial, technologically driven organization, and what that means to organizational architecture. Her insights on Intel are reflected here.

35. Helegesen, *The Web of Inclusion*, p. 55.

36. Peter A. Smith, "Reinventing SunU," *Training & Development*, July 1994, p. 23. The information about Sun Microsystems is drawn from this

article; Ivy Schmerken and Karen Corcella, "Interview with Scott McNealy, *Wall Street & Technology*, June 1994; and Heller, *The Decision Makers*.

37. The information about Transnet is the result of five years of work with this Siberg client that involved helping it begin its evolution into a butterfly organization. The quote from Anton Moolman that follows is from an internal Transnet memo.

CHAPTER 12

1. Francis J. Aguilar, *Managing Corporate Ethics* (New York: Oxford University Press, 1994), p. 126.

2. Lynne Joy McFarland, Larry E. Senn, and John R. Childress, *21st Century Leadership* (New York: Leadership Press, 1994), pp. 284–85.

3. *The Economist*, September 9, 1995, p. 69.

4. Sam Walton (with John Huey), *Made in America: My Story* (New York: Doubleday, 1992), p. 217.

5. Interview with Mark Hazelwood, Dallas, November 19, 1993.

6. Douglas A. Ready, "Educating the Survivors," *Journal of Business Strategy*, March-April 1995, p. 35.

7. From 3M's Home Page on the Internet: http://www.mmm.com/profile/index.html.

8. William Taylor, "The Business of Innovation: An Interview with Paul Cook," in *Leaders on Leadership*, ed. Warren Bennis (Boston: Harvard Business School Press, 1992), pp. 202, 194.

9. Charles Handy, "Trust and the Virtual Organization," *Harvard Business Review*, May-June 1995, p. 42.

10. Interview with Peter Berle at Audubon headquarters in New York City, July 11, 1994.

EPILOGUE

1. Andrew S. Grove, "From the Front," *Fortune*, September 18, 1995, p. 229.

2. Herb Brody, "Great Expectations: Why Technology Predictions Go Awry," *Technology Review*, July 1991, p. 43.

3. Some of the material in this section is drawn from Frank K. Sonnenberg and Beverly Goldberg, "Business Integrity: An Oxymoron?" *Industry Week*, April 6, 1992.

4 . Ashali Varma, "Citibank Raises Corporate Consciousness in Grants Program," *Earth Times*, November 5, 1993, p. 1.

5. Francis McInerney and Sean White, *The Total Quality Corporation* (New York: Truman Talley/Dutton, 1995), p. 5.

6. Charles Heckscher, *White-Collar Blues* (New York: Basic Books, 1995), p. 3.

7. Peter Engardio, "High-Tech Jobs All Over the Map," *Business Week*, 21st Century Capitalism (special edition, 1994), pp. 112–13.

8. Juliet Schor, *The Overworked American* (New York: Basic Books, 1993).

9. Heckscher, *White-Collar Blues*, p. 179.

10. "The Death of Corporate Loyalty," *The Economist*, April 3, 1993, p. 63.

11. "Pass the Dictionary," *The Economist*, May 7, 1994, p. 78.

12. Charles Handy, "Trust and the Virtual Organization," *Harvard Business Review*, May-June 1995, p. 50.

13. "Those Who Can, Teach," *The Economist*, October 28, 1995, p. 79.

14. Thomas Wyatt, "A Fund that Does Well by Doing," *Fortune*, December 13, 1993, p. 40.

15. Economic Focus, "Musical Chairs," *The Economist*, July 17, 1993, p. 67.

‖ SELECTED BIBLIOGRAPHY

Aguilar, Francis J. *Managing Corporate Ethics*. New York: Oxford University Press, 1994.

Albrecht, Karl, and Albrecht, Steve. *Added Value Negotiating: The Breakthrough Method for Building Balanced Deals*. Burr Ridge, Ill.: Irwin, 1993.

Andrews, Kenneth R. *The Concept of Corporate Strategy* 3d edition. Homewood, Ill.: Irwin, 1987

Araskog, Rand V. *The ITT Wars: A CEO Speaks Out on Takeovers*. New York: Holt, 1989.

Bahrami, Homa, and Evans, Stuart. "Flexible Re-Cycling and High Technology Entrepreneurship." *California Management Review*, March 1995.

Bass, Bernard M. *Bass & Stogdill's Handbook of Leadership*, 3d ed. New York: Free Press, 1990.

Bazerman, Max H., and Neale, Margaret A. *Negotiating Rationally*. New York: The Free Press, 1992.

Beatty, Carol A., and Lee, Gloria L. "Leadership Among Middle Managers— An Exploration in the Context of Technological Change." *Human Relations*, September 1992.

Bennis, Warren. *On Becoming a Leader*. Reading, Mass.: Addison-Wesley, 1989.

____. ed. *Leaders on Leadership: Interviews with Top Executives*. Boston: Harvard Business School Press, 1992.

Bennis, Warren, and Nanus, Burt. *Leaders: Strategies for Taking Charge*. New York: Harper & Row, 1985.

Benson, Tracy E. "The New Leadership." *Industry Week*, June 1, 1992.

Bergsman, Steve. "Emphasis on Core Competency Redefines Corporate Outsourcing and Boosts Strategic Alliances." *National Real Estate Investor*, August 1993.

Berle, Adolf A., Jr., and Means, Gardiner C. *The Modern Corporation and Private Property*. New York: Macmillan, 1933.

Berreby, David. "The Man Who Knows Everything: Murray Gell-Mann." *New York Times Magazine*, May 8, 1994.

Berry, Michael V., Percival, I. C., and Weiss, N. O., eds. *Dynamical Chaos*. Princeton, N.J.: Princeton University Press, 1987.

Bleeke, Joel, and Ernst, David, eds. *Collaborating to Compete: Using Strategic Alliances and Acquisitions in the Global Marketplace*. New York: Wiley, 1993.

Braham, Jim. "No, You Don't Manage Everyone the Same." *Industry Week*, February 6, 1989.

Byrne, John A. "The Futurists Who Fathered the Ideas." *Business Week*, February 8, 1993.

Chandler, Alfred D., Jr. *Strategy and Structure: Chapters in the History of the American Industrial Enterprise*. Cambridge, Mass.: MIT Press, 1962.

Charkham, Jonathan. *Keeping Good Company*. New York: Oxford University Press, 1994.

Clark, Kenneth E. and Clark, Miriam B., eds. *Measures of Leadership*. West Orange, N.J.: Leadership Library of America, 1990.

Cleveland, Harlan. *Birth of a New World*. San Francisco: Jossey-Bass, 1993.

____. *The Knowledge Executive: Leadership in an Information Society*. New York: Truman Talley/Dutton, 1989.

Coase, Ronald H. "The Nature of the Firm," reprinted in *The Nature of the Firm: Origins, Evolution, and Development*, edited by Oliver E. Williamson and Sidney G. Winter. New York: Oxford University Press, 1993.

____. *The Firm, the Market, and the Law*. Chicago: University of Chicago Press, 1988.

Cordtz, Dan. "Ethicsplosion!" *Financial World*, August 16, 1994.

Copeland, Lennie. "Learning to Manage a Multicultural Workforce." *Training*, May 1988.

Cross, John. "IT Outsourcing: British Petroleum's Competitive Approach." *Harvard Business Review*, May-June 1995.

Diebold, John. *The Innovators*. New York: Dutton, 1990.

Demb, Ada, and Neubauer, F.-Friedrich. *The Corporate Board: Confronting the Paradoxes*. New York: Oxford University Press, 1992.

Dodgson, Mark. "The Future for Technological Collaboration." *Futures*, June 1992.

Drucker, Peter. "The Information Executives Really Need." *Harvard Business Review*, January-February 1995.

____. *The New Realities*. New York: Harper & Row, 1989.

____. "The Coming of the New Organization," *Harvard Business Review*, January-February 1988.

Duffy, Paula Baker, ed. *The Relevance of a Decade*. Boston: Harvard Business School Press, 1994.

Epstein, Edward. *Who Owns the Corporation: Management vs. Shareholders*. A Twentieth Century Fund Paper. New York: Priority Press, 1986.

Fierman, Jaclyn. "The Contingency Work Force. *Fortune*, January 24, 1994.

Filene, Edward A. *The Way Out: A Forecast of Coming Changes in American Business and Industry*. New York: Doubleday, 1924.

Filipczak, Bob. "Looking Past the Numbers." *Training*, October 1994.

Fisher, Roger, and Ury, William. *Getting to Yes: Negotiating Agreement Without Giving In*. Boston: Houghton-Mifflin, 1981.

Foster, Badi G., Jackson, Gerald, Cross, William, Jackson, Bailey, and Hardiman, Rita. "Workforce Diversity and Business." *Training and Development Journal*, April 1988.

Freeman, R. Edward, ed. *Business Ethics: The State of the Art*. New York: Oxford Univeristy Press, 1991.

Geber, Beverly. "Managing Diversity." *Training*, July 1990.

Gell-Mann, Murray. *The Quark and the Jaguar*. New York: Freeman, 1994.

Gibson, W. David. "Holy Alliances." *Sales & Marketing Management*, July 1993.

Gleick, James. *Chaos: Making a New Science*. New York: Viking, 1987.

Gilmore, Thomas. *Making a Leadership Change*. San Francisco: Jossey-Bass, 1989.

Goldberg, Beverly. "The New World of Work." *Executive Excellence*, July 1994.

Goldberg, Beverly, and Sifonis, John G. *Dynamic Planning: The Art of Managing Beyond Tomorrow*. New York: Oxford University Press, 1994.

____."An Alliance of Business and Technology." *Management Review*, February 1994.

____."Anticipatory Capability." *Directors & Boards*, Fall 1994.

Goodman, Paul S., Sproull, Lee S., et al., eds. *Technology and Organizations*. San Francisco: Jossey-Bass, 1990.

Gordon, Jack. "Rethinking Diversity." *Training*, January 1992.

Goshel, Sumantra, and Bartlett, Christopher A. "Changing the Role of Top Management: Beyond Structure to Processes." *Harvard Business Review*, January-February 1995.

Hambrick, Donald. "Putting Top Managers Back in the Strategy Picture." *Strategic Management Journal*, special issue, 10 (1989).

Hamel, Gary, and Prahalad, C. K. *Competing for the Future*. Boston: Harvard Business School Press, 1994.

Handy, Charles. "Trust and the Virtual Organization." *Harvard Business Review*, May-June 1995.

____. *The Age of Unreason*. Boston: Harvard University Press, 1990.

Harrar, George. "Interview with Ron Ponder." *Forbes ASAP*, April 10, 1995.

____. "Outsource Tales." *Forbes ASAP*, June 7, 1993.

Hart, Stuart L., and Quinn, Robert E. "Roles Executives Play: CEOs, Behavioral Complexity, and Firm Performance." *Human Relations*, May 1993.

Heckscher, Charles. *White-Collar Blues: Management Loyalties in an Age of Corporate Restructuring*. New York: Basic Books, 1995.

____. *The New Unionism: Employee Involvement in the Changing Corporation*. New York: Basic Books, 1988.

Helgesen, Sally. *The Web of Inclusion*. New York: Doubleday/Currency, 1995.

Heller, Robert. *The Decision Makers*. New York: Truman Talley, 1991.

Herman, Edward S. *Corporate Contol, Corporate Power*. A Twentieth Century Fund Study. New York: Cambridge University Press, 1981.

Hirschhorn, Larry, and Gilmore, Thomas. "The New Boundaries of the 'Boundaryless' Company." *Harvard Business Review*, May-June 1992.

House, Charles H., and Price, Raymond L. "The Return Map: Tracking Product Teams." *Harvard Business Review*, January-February 1991.

Huey, John. "The New Post-Heroic Leadership." *Fortune*, February 21, 1994.

Jaikumar, Jay. "The Boundaries of Business: The Impact of Technology." *Harvard Business Review*, September-October 1991.

Katzenbach, Jon R., and Smith, Douglas K. *The Wisdom of Teams: Creating the High Performance Organization*. Boston: Harvard Business School Press, 1993.

Kauffman, Stuart A. *At Home in the Universe*. New York: Oxford University Press, 1995.

____. *The Origins of Order*. New York: Oxford University Press, 1993.

Kidder, Rushworth M. *An Agenda for the 21st Century*. Cambridge, Mass.: MIT Press, 1989.

Korn/Ferry International and Columbia University Graduate School of Business. *A Journal on Critical Issues Affecting Senior Executives and the Board of Directors: Reinventing the CEO*. New York: Korn/Ferry International, 1989.

Kotter, John P. *A Force for Change: How Leadership Differs From Management*. New York: Free Press, 1990.

____. *The Leadership Factor*. New York: Free Press, 1988.

Kotter, John P., and Heskett, James L. *Corporate Culture and Performance*. New York: Free Press, 1992.

Krantz, James. "Lessons from the Field: An Essay on the Crisis of Leadership in Contemporary Organizations." *Journal of Applied Behavioral Science*, 26, January 1990.

Lax, David A. and Sebenius, James K. *The Manager as Negotiator*. New York: Free Press, 1986.

Limerick, David, and Cunnington, Bert. *Managing the New Organization*. San Francisco: Jossey-Bass, 1993.

Little, Royal. "Conglomerates Are Doing Better than You Think." *Fortune*, May 28, 1984.

Lozano, B. *The Invisible Workforce: Transforming American Business with Outside and Home-Based Workers*. New York: Free Press, 1989.

McCahery, Joseph, Picciotto, Sol, and Scott, Colin. *Corporate Control and Accountability*. New York: Oxford University Press, 1993.

McFarland, Lynne Joy, Senn, Larry E., and Childress, John R. *21st Century Leadership*. Los Angeles: Leadership Press, 1994.

McGee, James, and Prusack, Laurence. *Managing Information Strategically*. New York: Wiley, 1993.

McInerney, Francis, and White, Sean. *The Total Quality Corporation*. New York: Truman Talley/Dutton, 1995.

McMahon, Christopher. *Authority and Democracy: A General Theory of Government and Management*. Princeton, N.J.: Princeton University Press, 1994.

Magnet, Myron. "The Productivity Payoff Arrives." *Fortune*, June 17, 1994.

Mahoney, Diana Phillips. "Seeing Order in Chaos." *Computer Graphics World*, July 1993.

Merlyn, Vaughan, and Parkinson, John. *Development Effectiveness: Strategies for IS Organizational Transition*. New York: Wiley, 1994.

Mills, D. Q. *Rebirth of the Corporation*. New York: Wiley, 1991.

Minsky, Hyman P. *Stabilizing an Unstable Economy*. A Twentieth Century Fund Report. New Haven, Conn.: Yale University Press, 1986.

Mitroff, Ian I., Mason, Richard O., and Pearson, Christine M. *Framebreak: The Radical Redesign of American Business*. San Francisco: Jossey-Bass, 1994.

Mode, Daniel E. "Every Employee a Leader." *Public Utilities Fortnightly*, June 1, 1992.

Monks, Robert A. G. and Minow, Nell. *Power and Accountability*. New York: Harper, 1991.

Morrison, Ann M. *The New Leaders: Guidelines on Leadership Diversity in America*. San Francisco: Jossey-Bass, 1992.

Morton, Michael S. Scott, ed. *The Corporation of the 1990s: Information Technology and Organizational Transformation*. New York: Oxford University Press, 1991.

Noble, Faith, and Newman, Michael. "Integrated System, Autonomous Departments: Organizational Invalidity and System Change in a University." *Journal of Management Studies*, March 1993.

Osborne, J. E. "Looking at Leadership Like a Manager." *Supervisory Management*, August 1992.

Packard, David. *The HP Way: How Bill Hewlett and I Built Our Company*. New York: HarperBusiness, 1995.

Paine, Lynn Sharp. "Managing for Organizational Integrity." *Harvard Business Review*, March-April 1994.

Pare, Terence P. "The New Merger Boom." *Fortune*, November 28, 1994.

Pasmore, William A. *Creating Strategic Change: Designing the Flexible, High-Performing Organization*. New York: Wiley, 1994.

Pauchant, Thierry C., Mitroff, Ian I., and Ventolo, Gerald F. "The Dial Tone Does Not Come From God! How a Crisis Can Challenge Dangerous Strategic Assumptions Made About Technologies: The Case of the

Hinsdale Telecommunications Outage." *Academy of Management Executive*, Fall 1992.

Peters, Thomas J., and Waterman, Robert H., Jr. *In Search of Excellence: Lessons from America's Best-Run Companies*. New York: Harper & Row, 1982.

Peters, Tom, and Austin, Nancy. *A Passion for Excellence: The Leadership Difference*. New York: Random House, 1985.

Phillips, Robert L., and Hunt, James G., eds. *Strategic Leadership: A Multiorganizational-Level Perspective*. Westport, Conn.: Quorum, 1992.

Pool, Robert. "Chaos Theory." *Science*, July 7, 1989.

Priesmeyer, H. Richard, and Baik, Kibok. "Discovering the Patterns of Chaos." *Planning Review*, November 1989.

Quick, Thomas L. *Successful Team Building*. New York: AMACOM, 1992.

Quinn, James Brian. *The Intelligent Enterprise: A Knowledge and Service Based Paradigm for Industry*. New York: Free Press, 1992.

Rothstein, Lawrence R. "The Empowerment Effort That Came Undone." *Harvard Business Review*, January-February 1995.

Ruelle, David. *Chance and Chaos*. Princeton: Princeton University Press, 1991.

Sayles, L. R. *Leadership: What Effective Managers Really Do and How They Do It*. New York: McGraw-Hill, 1976.

Schein, Edgar. *Organizational Culture and Leadership*. San Francisco: Jossey-Bass, 1984.

Schor, Juliet B. *The Overworked American: The Unexpected Decline of Leisure*. New York: Basic Books, 1993.

Schrage, Michael. *Shared Minds: The Technology of Collaboration*. New York: Random House, 1990.

Schwartz, Peter. *The Art of the Long View: Planning for the Future in an Uncertain World*. New York: Doubleday, 1991.

Senge, Peter M. *The Fifth Discipline: The Art and Practice of the Learning Organization*. New York: Doubleday/Currency, 1990.

Sherman, Stanford. "Are Strategic Alliances Working?" *Fortune*, September 21, 1992.

Shiller, Robert. "Who's Minding the Store?" Background paper for *The Report of the Twentieth Century Task Force on Market Speculation and Corporate Governance*. New York: Twentieth Century Fund Press, 1992.

Slice, Martha, and Gilburg, Alan. "Leadership for Empowerment." *Public Manager*, Fall 1992.

Slowinski, Gene, Farris, George F., and Jones, David. "Strategic Partnering: Process Instead of Event." *Research/Technology Management*, May-June 1994.

Smith, Leif, and Wagner, Patricia. *The Networking Game*. Denver: Network Resources, 1981.

Solomon, Charlene Marmer. "The Corporate Response to Workforce Diversity." *Personnel Journal*, August 1989.

Sonnenberg, Frank K. *Managing With a Conscience*. New York: McGraw-Hill, 1994.

____. *Marketing to Win*. New York: Harper & Row, 1990.

Sonnenberg, Frank K., and Goldberg, Beverly. "It's a Great Idea, But . . ." *Training and Development*, March 1992.

____. "Encouraging Employee-Led Change Through Constructive Learning Processes." *Journal of Business Strategy*, November-December 1992.

Sproull, Lee S., and Goodman, Paul S. "Technology and Organizations: Integration and Opportunities." In *Technology and Organizations*, edited by Paul S. Goodman, Lee S. Sproull, et al. San Francisco: Jossey-Bass, 1990.

Stacey, Ralph D. *Managing the Unknowable: Strategic Boundaries Between Order and Chaos in Organization*. San Francisco: Jossey-Bass, 1992.

Stark, Andrew. "What's the Matter with Business Ethics?" *Harvard Business Review*, May-June 1993.

Stewart, Thomas A. "Managing in a Wired Company." *Fortune*, July 11, 1994.

____. "Welcome the Revolution. *Fortune*, December 13, 1993.

Tapscott, Don, and Caston, Art. *Paradigm Shift: The New Promise of Information Technology*. New York: McGraw-Hill, 1993.

Thomas, R. Roosevelt, Jr. *Beyond Race and Gender*. New York: AMACOM, 1991.

Vaill, Peter B. *Managing as a Performing Art: New Ideas for a World of Chaotic Change*. San Francisco: Jossey-Bass, 1989.

Verity, John W. "Hacker Heaven: So Many Computers, So Few Safeguards." *Business Week*, June 26, 1995.

Waldrop, M. Mitchell. *Complexity: The Emerging Science at the Edge of Order and Chaos*. New York: Touchstone, 1993.

Walton, Sam, with John Huey. *Made in America: My Story*. New York: Doubleday, 1992.

Waterman, Robert H., Jr. *Adhocracy: The Power to Change*. New York: Norton, 1992.

Weber, Max. *The Theory of Social and Economic Organization*. New York: Oxford University Press, 1947.

Wheatley, Margaret J. *Leadership and the New Science: Learning about Organization from an Orderly Universe*. San Francisco: Berrett-Koehler, 1992.

Williamson, Oliver E., and Winter, Sidney G., eds. *The Nature of the Firm: Origins, Evolution, and Development*. New York: Oxford University Press, 1993.

Wolff, Edward N. *Top Heavy: A Study of the Increasing Inequality of Wealth in America*. New York: Twentieth Century Fund Press, 1995.

Woodstock Theological Center. *Creating and Maintaining an Ethical Corporate Climate*. Washington, D.C.: Georgetown University Press, 1990.

Wriston, Walter. "The Decline of the Central Bankers." *New York Times*, September 20, 1992.

Zaleznik, Abraham. "Managers and Leaders: Are They Different?" *Harvard Business Review*, March-April 1992.

Zimmerman, Joseph. *Curbing Unethical Behavior in Government*. Westport, Conn.: Greenwood, 1994.

‖ INDEX